Biblical Themes in Religious Education

Biblical Themes in Religious Education

edited by
JOSEPH S. MARINO

Religious Education Press
Birmingham, Alabama

Library of Congress Cataloging in Publication Data
Main entry under title:

Biblical themes in religious education.

   Bibliography: p.
   Includes index.
   1. Bible—Study—Addresses, essays, lectures.
2. Christian education—Addresses, essays, lectures.
I. Marino, Joseph S.
BS600.2.B46   1983   207   83-16124
ISBN 0-89135-038-1

Religious Education Press, Inc.
1531 Wellington Road
Birmingham, Alabama 35209
10 9 8 7 6 5 4 3 2

Religious Education Press publishes books exclusively in religious education and in areas closely related to religious education. It is committed to enhancing and professionalizing religious education through the publication of serious, significant, and scholarly works.

PUBLISHER TO THE PROFESSION

Contents

Preface

Every religious educator employs the Sacred Scripture as a primary resource in any religious education setting. The purpose of this book is to provide religious education scholars as well as work-a-day religion teachers at all levels with important biblical insights which can be integrated smoothly into their educational ministry. The book attempts to make the findings of biblical studies a yeasting force in the religious education ministry of the church.

The titles that were chosen represent many basic themes in religious education. The first two chapters explore in general the use of the Bible in religious education, chapter one from a religious educationalist's view, and chapter two from a biblicist's view. The other seven chapters include themes that are important in religious education: The Discovery of God, Faith, Discipleship, Prayer, Justice, Sin, Reconciliation. The treatment of these themes is not the same treatment as one finds in a biblical dictionary. Rather each theme is discussed in such a way as to uncover its import in religious education.

Each author, of course, treats his or her theme somewhat differently. In fact, the style of each author has been totally respected with few alterations coming from the editor. The contributors are truly outstanding. Two of them (Ugo Vanni and Horacio Simian-Yofre) are professors at the Pontifical Biblical Institute in Rome. Dermot Cox is professor of Scripture at the Gregorian University in Rome. Five of the contributors teach in American universities or colleges: David Smith at the College of Saint Thomas in St. Paul, Minnesota; Carroll Stuhlmueller at Catholic Theological Union, Chicago, Illinois; Alice Laffey at the Holy Cross College, Worcester, Massachusetts; Robert

Barone at the University of Scranton, Scranton, Pennsylvania; and James Michael Lee at the University of Alabama in Birmingham. Joseph Marino is in parish ministry in Birmingham, Alabama.

In the opening chapter, James Michael Lee sets the stage for the book by delineating the immediate relevancy of the Bible for a truly authentic religious education. As Lee notes, the Bible is not so much a book of theology as it is a record of religious experience, a record which enables the person who encounters the Scripture to engage in personal and ecclesial religious experience today. In the second chapter, I encourage the religious educator to explore the Scripture from the viewpoint of story. In my view, the Bible contains the normative stories of faith which set forth the still-contemporary religious experiences of our ancestors in faith. The challenge facing religious educators is to organically connect those religious experiences with the religious experiences of today.

Dermot Cox develops the theme that the discovery of God originates with human experience. David Smith explores the biblical meaning of faith and concludes that faith is basically "a trusting self-surrender" to God. Faith then establishes a relationship between God and us. Discussing discipleship and commitment, Ugo Vanni demonstrates from an analysis of the New Testament that discipleship is a gradual process from simply knowing Jesus to existentially following him to Jerusalem. As a person moves to full discipleship, he or she moves to a total self-fulfillment. Carroll Stuhlmueller defines prayer as "the attitude of faith and the silent composure of one's spirit as we listen to God, personally speaking the words of the Bible to ourselves today." He then examines the various elements of this definition. He sees prayer as an essential element in the experience of religious education. Horacio Simian-Yofre's chapter provides deep reflection on the theme of justice. He examines several texts from Scripture and uncovers the complexity in determining their meaning. Therefore he concludes that we cannot learn about justice simply by quoting biblical passages and trying to apply these passages directly to contemporary issues. Rather, the Christian meaning of justice is taught as one learns to discover the profound elements that comprise a just or unjust relationship.

Alice Laffey presents the biblical notion of sin primarily in terms of idolatry and injustice. Finally, Robert Barone analyzes the reconciliation by examining the writings of Paul, Mark, Luke, Matthew, and

John. From his conclusions on his research, he proposes eight theses which give clear insight into the theme of reconciliation.

There are many people who have contributed to the outcome of this book. First and above all, I wish to sincerely thank the authors of the various chapters. Their articles are a great contribution to religious education. Also, I wish to thank Peter Sheehan, Frank Muscolino and James Michael Lee for their constant encouragement and support. I was fortunate to have two outstanding secretaries: Rosalind Sullivan and Phyllis Coates. To them I am very grateful. I also wish to give special thanks to John Gilsenan and Randy Glaze.

It is my firm hope that this book will help us all in making religious education more imbued with the biblical perspective and more inter-penetrated with biblical insights.

JOSEPH S. MARINO
January 25, 1983

PART I

Basic Perspectives

CHAPTER 1

Religious Education and the Bible: A Religious Educationist's View

James Michael Lee

One of the richest blessings of the Bible is its simultaneous universality and relevancy. The Bible can be fruitfully looked at and used in a host of different contexts by a host of different people having a host of different concerns and needs. The Bible also has the power to effectively touch each person where that person is developmentally in his own immediate concrete existential situation.

This essay will look at the Bible from the standpoint of religious education in general and of religious instruction specifically.

Religious education is the broad process whereby a person learns something. Therefore a person is in the process of being educated religiously in many moments of his life and in a panoply of situations. The degree to which a person is effectively educated religiously depends on a variety of factors including the potency of the situation and the degree to which the individual consciously or unconsciously ingests the religious dimension of his experiences in a given situation.

Various societal groups and individuals endeavor to make religious education more focused and more effective by deliberately introducing intentionality into the overall religious education process. Thus the ecclesia institutes worship services, sets up counseling opportunities of diverse kinds, establishes schools, administers a wide variety of religious education programs for youth and the elderly, and so forth. An inspection of the intentional religious education efforts of groups such as the ecclesia or the family reveal that these efforts can be helpfully categorized into three primary functions: religious instruction, religious counseling, and the administration of religious education activities.

1

Religious instruction is that kind of intentional educational process by and through which desired religious learning outcomes are actually facilated in some way. Put more simply, religious instruction is a term which is synonomous with religion teaching.[1]

A vitally important fact to remember about all instruction, including religious instruction, is that this process is setting-free.[2] Religious instruction takes place in church-related school classrooms. Religious instruction takes place in and through the liturgy.[3] Religious instruction takes place in youth groups, in the family, in hospital visitations to the sick, and so forth. Classrooms and liturgy and youth groups and family and hospital visitations are not identical to religious instruction. However, all these and other settings are milieux in which religion teaching ought to be done if these activities are to fulfill their educational potential. In this connection Sara Little perceptively remarks that religious educators and other kinds of ecclesial ministers ought not to be blind to the rich potential for religious instruction inherent in the many activities which the ecclesia undertakes.[4]

Because of the very great importance of the Bible in Christian life, one would naturally think that both religious educationists and biblicists singly or in tandem would develop or incorporate sophisticated pedagogical research, theories, and practices in order to mine the rich religious instruction potential of this sacred book.[5] Thus it is a surprise and indeed an embarrassment to find that both religious educationists and biblicists generally have been remiss with respect to either developing or incorporating those sophisticated pedagogical research studies, theories, and practices which show special promise for effective teaching of the Bible.

Evangelical Protestant religious educators, as would be expected, have devoted considerable attention to the area of Bible teaching. However, these efforts are often of a pedagogically unsophisticated and even at times of a primitive variety in terms of educational research, theory, and practice.[6] Mainline Protestant religious educationists have generally neglected to pay requisite attention to the Bible's intersection with religious education. John Westerhoff reviewed the articles written in the professional journal *Religious Education* on the topic of the Bible. These articles were written by and large by mainline Protestant religious educationists. Westerhoff's investigation concluded that the number of articles written on the Bible in that journal during its seventy-five years of existence were, in his words, "shockingly few" and "generally insignificant."[7] Catholic religious educationists, who until recently have seldom distinguished themselves either in sophisticated pedagogical theory or in highly advanced knowledge of biblics, have usually failed to develop top-drawer research, theory, or practice in the area of biblical pedagogy.

Biblicists, for their part, have generally neglected to think of the religious instruction import of their seminal scholarship, to make adequate efforts at directly placing the fruits of their scholarship at the disposal of religious educators in a relatively usable manner, or, most important of all, to integrate their research and theories and procedures with the religious instruction mission of the ecclesia.[8] Thus Mary Boys can rightly declare that biblical scholars have an educational problem—the educational problem of making the inexhaustible riches of the Bible readily available to religious instruction.[9] Contemporary biblical scholarship has made awesome advances in the past one hundred years. However, the firstfruits of this magnificent scholarship seem to be restricted to the biblical specialists in a manner not entirely unlike the way in which the whole Bible itself was restricted to the clergy in pre-Reformation Europe. As Eugene Trester remarks, "It becomes increasingly obvious that the wealth of knowledge currently available in the realm of biblical scholarship has somehow tragically failed to flow out into the lives and minds of adults"[10]—and of children and youth as well.

I am the lone religious educationist represented in this book. All of my fellow contributors are biblicists who are endeavoring in this volume to place the firstfruits of their scholarship at the disposal of religious instruction. My essay in this volume will be targeted toward looking at the Bible from the distinctive standpoint of religious instruction. This standpoint suggests certain basic principles of or about the Bible, principles which are directly and organically related to religious instruction activity.

Principle #1: The Bible is Essentially a Religious Instruction Book and Not Primarily a Theological Treatise

In its fundamental purpose and texture, the Bible is basically two things. First of all, the Bible is God teaching every person who encounters it. Second, the Bible is the history of when God taught, how he taught, and what he taught. In other words, the Bible is essentially a religious instruction book.

The authors of the Bible saw both the Scripture and themselves primarily in religious instruction terms. The apostle Paul put it this way: "All the ancient scriptures were written for our instruction" (Rom. 15:4). Even the most cursory examination of the New Testament epistles reveals that the authors regarded the primary purpose and content of their letters as that of religiously instructing those who in one way or another would encounter these letters.

The Bible, then, was written by men of religion who were engaged in religious writing primarily for the twin purpose of communicating the substance and structure of religion on the one hand, and of facilitating religious experience in persons on the other hand. The Bible starts with religion, proceeds through religion, and ends with religion—from religion to religion.

That the Bible is primarily a religious instruction book is a fact which has been recognized by outstanding Christian theologians and authors down through the centuries. For example, Augustine writes that the Spirit of God who spoke through the holy authors of the Bible was unwilling to teach human beings those things which could not somehow be profitable to their salvation.[11] Thomas Aquinas held the same view: "The Spirit did not wish to tell us through the authors whom he inspired any other truth than that which is profitable for our salvation."[12]

The overwhelming preponderance of the major figures depicted in the Bible were primarily religious educators and not principally theologians. The great prophets in the Old Testament by and large were religious educators who concerned themselves principally with helping persons and society know, love, and serve the true God.[13] The greatest of all the New Testament missionaries, Paul the apostle, was primarily a religious educator whose task was to enable persons to live the Gospel without compromise.[14] So central was religious instruction to Paul's apostolate that he did not even baptize persons, but rather devoted his efforts exclusively to religious instruction.[15]

Jesus the Christ was primarily a religious educator and redeemer.[16] His task on earth was not that of a theologian. Any theology which he might have propounded was typically done in a religious instruction context and with clear religious instruction goals.

In terms of the basic nature of the Bible as a whole and of the central

message taught by various major biblical personages, theology is definitely at the service of religious instruction. Even those portions of the
Scriptures which might seem at first glance to be devoted primarily to
theology, such as certain passages in the Pauline epistles, are not
theology for the sake of theology but rather theology for the sake of a
better defined and more potent religious instruction.

The Bible is essentially a religious instruction book. It is not essentially a theological document, a political document, an economic
document. To be sure, the Bible may have important implications for
theology, politics, economics, and so forth. Many different and often
conflicting theologies have been derived from Holy Writ. A host of
varying political ideologies and economic conclusions have been deduced from the Scriptures. But derivations helpful to the work of
theology or politics or economics are just simply that, namely derivations. A derivation ought not to be equated with the reality from which
it is derived. It is rank imperialism to claim that the Bible is essentially
theology because theological meanings can be derived from it, or to
assert that the Bible is essentially a political document because political
ideologies can be deduced from it.[17]

The Bible is, of course, God's specific and focused revelation to
humanity. Because the Bible is revelation, it naturally invites theological investigation and reflection. However, it must be underscored that
revelation is not theology. Revelation is a dimension of religion—or
more accurately, revelation is one of the most indispensable underpin-
nings and most pervasive groundings of religion. Theology simply
explores revelation from a cognitive and scientific perspective. Because
revelation is primarily religious rather than theological, and because
revelation is ultimately instructional in purpose and texture, one can
legitimately conclude that revelation enjoys a greater natural relationship to religious instruction than to theology.

Religion precedes and antedates theology. Faith-hope-love precede
and antedate theology. Theology is nothing more than an intellectual
reflection on what was, or more specifically a certain kind of cognitive
exploration of some past event. Theological formulations and clarifications produce verbal definitions and conceptualizations of religion
from a theological perspective. Thus Bernard Lonergan writes that
theology "makes thematic what is already part of Christian living."[18]
Karl Rahner puts it this way: "Theology is the critical and meth-
odological reflection on faith."[19] Raymond Brown rightly notes that

every propositional doctrine has been the product of previous theological formulation.[20] To be sure, intellectual formulations and clarifications constitute the role and task of theology. It is manifestly outside the role or competence of theology to produce religion, to give faith or hope or love.

There are profound ramifications for religious instruction which flow from the basic principle that the Bible is essentially a religious instruction book and not primarily a theological treatise. This principle clearly implies that if a religious educator wishes to teach the Bible in a manner truly in keeping with the biblical spirit, then this educator must target his pedagogy chiefly toward teaching learners to encounter the Bible in such a way that it will enrich their own personal religious lives. More than anything else, the Bible speaks of a religious lifestyle. Thus to be truly biblical, the religious educator should structure the learning situation in such a fashion that the Bible is learned and lived as a special lifestyle in the here-and-now. To teach the Bible biblically, the religious educator should strive to engage the learner in religious thinking, in religious affectivity, in religious lifestyle. In doing so, the religious educator would do well to keep in mind the pregnant words of Helmut Thielicke: "In view of its structure, theological thinking is in some ways an 'alien' medium into which statements of faith must be transposed."[21] There is a significant substantive and structural difference between religious thinking and theological thinking, between religious language and theological language,[22] between religious lifestyle and theological lifestyle.

The point I am making here is nicely illustrated by an observation made by Raymond Brown concerning a common Bible. As a biblical theologian, Brown welcomes the eventual development of a scientifically-accurate translation of the Bible which could be used by Protestant and Catholic theologians alike. On religious instruction grounds, however, Brown believes that it would not be desirable to have only one scientifically-accurate translation of the Bible common to Protestants and Catholics. As Brown rightly observes, there is a variety of religious uses for the Bible. One translation, for example, might be splendid for a youth group but not too suitable for adult learners. Another translation might be ideal for use in solemn religious ceremonies but not very effective for informal prayer groups.[23]

Because the Bible is essentially a religious instruction book, it stands to reason that religion in one way or another should always be present in the teaching-learning of the Bible. This religion need not always be of the explicit variety. To be sure, in certain circumstances and with certain learners the requisite religious essence and texture of the Bible might more fruitfully be present in less than an explicit or evident manner.

By virtue of the fact that the Bible is not primarily a theological treatise, it is unnecessary to the task of religious instruction that theology always be present when teaching the Bible. Theology, after all, is essentially the theory of God using divine revelation as the norm. Theology properly constitutes only one theory of religion.[24] In addition to theology, there are other theoretical ways of looking at religion, ways which are just as objectively and epistemologically valid. Thus there is not only a theological theory of the religion, but also a psychological theory of religion, a sociological theory of religion, a historical theory of religion, a literary theory of religion, and so forth. Consequently, theological considerations might well be absent both manifestly and latently in some or even in many religious instruction activities involving the Bible. In such pedagogical activities, primacy of intellectual consideration can be accorded to the psychology of a religious personage, the sociology of a biblical event, the literary character of a biblical story, and the like. These cognitive considerations are as intrinsically correlated with religion as are theological considerations. The more that a learner appreciates the religiosity of the Bible as refracted through the prisms of various sciences and theoretical fields, the more vibrant and more open will his biblical religion be likely to become.

Where do biblical theology and other forms of biblical scholarship fit in with the basic points which I have been making in the last few pages? Put somewhat differently, why do I strongly advocate that religious educators steep themselves as deeply as possible in biblics? The answer to these two questions is simple: biblical scholarship enables the religious educator to more fully understand and appreciate the Bible and its religious nature. Such an understanding can be of inestimable assistance to the religious educator in helping learners of all ages and situations gain a more well-rounded and more finely-tuned awareness of biblical reality. Since biblical reality is essentially religious reality, any kind of diverse scholarly examination of the Bible can assist both teachers and learners to become more biblical as they jointly encounter the Bible in a progressively greater awareness of the richness of its texts and contexts. To be sure, neither biblics as a whole nor biblical theology as a particular are religious instruction. However, scholarly investigations in biblical theology, such as the historical-critical method of form criticism, the hermeneutic of salvation history, the demythologization to the kerygma, and so forth, can all cognitively enrich the learner's awareness that the Bible may be fruitfully viewed and meaningfully appreciated in a host of ways—even if none of these ways eventually proves over the course of time to the *the* only way or even *the* chief way of exploring the Bible.[25] The field of biblics is neither identical to religious instruction nor opposed to it. Rather, the field of biblics is a priceless aid in enabling both teacher and learner to better understand the Bible and its religious core. The religious educator, then, does not study the field of biblics for its own sake, but in order to utilize the finds of this vital field to significantly enrich his own religious instruction activity.

John McKenzie's fertile words beautifully sum up the basic point which I have been making thus far concerning the Bible as essentially a religious instruction book rather than primarily a theological treatise: "We [today in contemporary culture] would find the world of the ancient Hebrews ignorant of much that we take for granted, crude almost to the point of barbarism, narrow and provincial, uncomfortable for both mind and body; but it was a world in which men felt they could reach out and touch God. If we could gain some of this sense of divine reality, we should have heard whatever spiritual message the Old Testament has for us. The Bible is a sacred book; it comes from God and brings God to us."[26]

Principle #2: The Bible is Essentially a Disclosure of Religious Experiences

The Bible contains both historical and nonhistorical material. The historical material typically deals with events in which God was attempting to teach religion to his people, or with events which in one way or another were connected with the growing unto God of the children of Israel and later the Gentiles. The nonhistorical material generally treats either of the way in which God through the inspired writers wishes human beings to engage in religion, or with religious issues and problems inserted into perennial human situations and conditions which tend to transcend time and culture.[27] Examples of historical material are the book of Genesis, 1 Samuel, much of the Gospels, and Acts. Illustrations of nonhistorical material include Psalms, Job, portions of the Gospels such as the parables, and the Pauline letters.

At bottom, both the historical and nonhistorical sections of the Bible fundamentally center on religious experience. Religious experience—how it occurred and how it can best occur—constitutes the basic warp and woof of the gorgeous divine-human tapestry we call the Bible.[28] One of the most unbiblical, and in fact one of the most antibiblical acts which a religious educator can perpetrate against the Bible is to teach it in a manner other than in and with religious experience.

The Bible is a series of words from God. The Bible is also a series of words about God and about God's workings in the world. Therefore the only way in which biblical words can be authentically viewed and used is to see and employ such words in a religious manner. This important fact holds especially true for religious instruction.[29]

It is erroneous to regard the Bible as *the* word of God. To claim that the Bible is *the* word of God is to restrict God's revelation both to the verbal dimension of reality and to the Bible itself. God is infinite in nature and activity; thus God cannot be imprisoned within the confines of either the verbal or of any one verbal font. God reveals himself in the nonverbal as well as in the verbal. God encounters the human person in everyday life as well as in the Bible. The Bible is *a* word of God, and an enormously privileged word at that. But the Bible is not *the* word of God. Often God encounters the human being more relevantly and more personalistically in the nonverbal and in everyday life than he does when a person reads the Bible.[30]

To effectively learn and live the Bible, the individual must be taught to concentrate on the religious experience which he receives while reading the Bible and on the religious experience which is linguistically symbolized by the biblical words. Preoccupation with the words of the Bible simply as words is generally of little fruitful use in the work of religious instruction, since such verbal enthrallment typically ends up in squeezing the living waters out of religious experience from the biblical fountainhead.

Error begets error. The ontic error of regarding the Bible as *the* word of God quite naturally gives birth to the pedagogical error of making a false and lifeless idol of biblical words qua words. This serious ped-agogical error inevitably results in several consequences which are noxious and debilitating to religious instruction activity.

One debilitating consequence concerns the all too frequent endow-ment of biblical words qua words with a halo effect in which all religious instruction is reduced to the verbal. In this egregious error, religious instruction is defined as "the ministry of the word."[31] Such a restrictive conceptualization of religious instruction is reductionist in the extreme because it excludes the vast domain of the nonverbal from the scope of religious instruction. To be sure, the nonverbal is in all probability far more potent and more pervasive in religious experience than the verbal. Furthermore, since the verbal is principally limited at the intrinsic level to cognition rather than to affect or to lifestyle, the conceptualization of religious instruction as the ministry of the word almost inevitably runs aground on the rocks of rationalism.[32] Religious instruction is far wider than the ministry of the word; it is the ministry of all teaching activities, verbal and nonverbal, product and process, cognitive and affective and lifestyle. Even a rudimentary knowledge of the art-science of teaching would quickly reveal that there is no legiti-mate existential way in which religious instruction can be reduced to the verbal, to the ministry of the word.[33]

Another debilitating pedagogical consequence of the ontic error of regarding the Bible as *the* word of God is that religious instruction in the Bible[34] thereby tends to become reduced primarily to linguistic content and prowess. This unfortunate form of reductionism quite naturally leads to the enthronement of the quantitative. Thus the learner is led to believe that the enrichment of his own religious experience is a direct function of the number of biblical quotations he can exhale, or is a consequence of his ability to identify the particular book or subsection of the Bible in which a given biblical passage appears.[35] There is a vast difference between religiously experiencing the Bible and linguistically experiencing it. There is also a vast dif-ference between immersing oneself in the biblicity of the Bible and inundating oneself in the location and verbal subtleties of biblical texts.

Yet another unfortunate religious instruction result of regarding the Bible as *the* word of God is that the Word (*Logos*) is made virtually tantamount to the word. The unexcelled richness and infinitude of the Word is debased to the one reality it surely is not, namely the word.

Religious educators who have dethroned the Word to the word commit the inevitable follow-up error, namely, supposing that they can effectively teach the Word by teaching words.

In the course of teaching, the religious educator must, naturally, use words. What I am suggesting in this section is that the educator ought never to confuse words with religious experience. When the religious educator uses words, he should attempt, as appropriate to the existential context of the entire learning experience, to encase words in the living domain of religious experience.

A fundamental pedagogical principle involved in using words in religious instruction is that of infusing verbal content with as much of the wholly experiential as possible. The use of story or story-like pedagogical devices constitutes one pedagogical practice which enfleshes this principle. Story and story-like pedagogical devices enable the religious educator to overcome to a certain extent some of the severe limitations inherent in words, limitations such as abstractness, linguistic symbolism, second-handedness, lack of immediacy, and so forth.[36] A story creates a kind of concrete (as opposed to abstract) situation (as opposed to a series of concepts) which is directed toward personally lived experiences (as opposed to a lack of immediacy). Words are not nor can ever be direct purposeful immediate experiences. The strength and power of a story is that it elevates words to the vestibule of the personal, a vestibule in which vicarious experiences are mediated through linguistic symbols. When a story is told rather than read, it becomes more personal since the storyteller uses a host of nonverbal communication behaviors including facial expressions, paralanguage, extralanguage, posture, proxemic procedures, variations in tempo, eye contact, and the like.[37] A story constitutes a fine example of the deliberate structuring of a verbal pedagogical situation in order to attain a desired learning outcome.[38] Thus it is no accident that storytelling for learners of all ages is a time-honored teaching technique not only in nonreligious settings but in religious milieux as well.[39]

Principle #3: The Bible is Living Because it Speaks to Us Today

In an insightful observation which integrates sound biblical theology with sound religious instruction, Didier-Jacques Piveteau states that in teaching the Bible, "perhaps religion teachers have insisted too much on the grammatical form: 'God *has spoken*' or 'God *has saved*' as if God's action, which is outside human temporal categories, is regarded as being in the past. Yet, it is exact to say 'God *now speaks*' and 'God *now saves!*' "[40]

The Bible is a living reality. Therefore the Bible not only represents the divinely-inspired record of selected religious experiences which occurred in the days of yore, but also represents God existentially meeting and greeting all those who encounter Scripture. As far as we can tell, the more a person encounters the Bible in a spirit of openness-to-being and in a grounding of religious experience, the more that person will be able to derive religious fruit from his encounter with the Scripture. A primary task of the religious educator is to assist the learner to gain maximum religious benefit from his experience with and in the Bible.

Until relatively recent times almost all Christians regarded the Bible as a completely objective document. In this view the Bible is an unshakable historical document which presents objective, absolute, and unconditioned data about divinely inspired religious experiences and about divinely inspired dogmas.

In the nineteenth century there began to develop a growing conviction among biblicists and various kinds of theologians that the Bible is not totally objective but in fact is necessarily shot through and through with subjectivity. Many sources contributed to this growing conviction, including the rise of Romanticism with its exaltation of personal feelings and personal subjectivity,[41] and the growing recognition of the great impact which history and culture inevitably exert on all persons (including the sacred writers).[42]

Today most biblical theologians hold that the Bible is not totally objective but is tinged with subjectivity as well.[43] To be sure, the wonderful humanity which is in the Bible and which so touches persons who encounter the Scriptures is due in no small measure to the subjective dimension of the sacred text itself.

The Bible, then, has a twin structure. Each inextricable part of this twin structure is deeply intertwined with the other and interacts with each other. This twin structure is, of course, the objective co-structure and the subjective co-structure.

The contemporary recognition of the necessary subjective co-structure of the Bible is a great gift to religion in general and to religious instruction in particular. Awareness of the Bible's subjective co-structure helps the religious educator and the learner understand how and why the Bible is truly living in personal experience. Awareness of the Bible's subjective co-structure also helps both the individual believer and the ecclesia gain a more rounded and more nuanced view of cognitive church doctrine. In the latter connection, Raymond Brown observes that biblical theology and biblical criticism have the advantage of showing, not that formal cognitive church doctrine is wrong, but that such doctrine is necessarily imperfect because it is historically and culturally conditioned.[44]

The subjective co-structure of the Bible is especially pertinent to religious instruction because it directly touches one of the deepest foundations upon which the learner's faith is built. Thus a pivotal question in the religious instruction use of the Bible becomes: "In what do I biblically root my religious life and experiences?"

In responding to this crucial religious instruction question, one answer is certain—a person cannot (and ought not) base his religion either upon a theology of the Bible or upon any other cognitive interpretation of Scripture. The theories and views of biblical theology change so rapidly that it is next to impossible to base one's religion on them for anything like the long term—or even for the intermediate term.[45] There is a necessary pluralism in the veritable galaxy of biblical theologies about faith and religion.[46] At bottom, the validity and usefulness of these theologies are determined both by their congruence with the total ecclesia's faith[47] and by their serviceability to an individual's own religious experience. Consequently, it is the essential faith/hope/charity of the Bible, a faith/hope/charity which resonates in the life of the entire ecclesia and in the life of each person who encounters the Scriptures, that forms a bedrock basis for one's own personal religious life.[48]

The point I am making here can be illustrated in the whole matter of the search for the historical Jesus pursued so brilliantly by many distinguished biblical theologians in this century. Put succinctly, and perhaps a bit simplistically, the search for the historical Jesus consists in the careful scholarly investigation of the Bible to find out just who was the real Jesus who walked the earth. The scholarly search for the historical Jesus endeavors to separate the real historical Jesus of the Scriptures from the more hagiographically-thrusted accounts of Jesus found in the Bible. Careful biblical scholarship has shown, for example, that not all the sayings and deeds which the Bible attributes to

Jesus were actually said by him or done by him. These sayings and deeds seem to have been added later on in the church, and incorporated by the evangelists or other authors.

There is a certain vital sense in which the factual historical Jesus might form a base for our Christian faith/hope/love, for our religious life. But the full and unshakable base for a person's Christian faith/hope/love is the degree to which God reveals Jesus first *as* one reads the Gospels, and second *as* that person lives in the world. To encounter the inspired revelations of God in the Bible means, above all else but not excluding all else, that the person be faithful to the Jesus of the Bible rather than to the factual historical Jesus.[49]

Paul Tillich makes somewhat the same point in commenting about biblical theologian Martin Kähler's important book on the historical Jesus. Tillich asserts that one major and vital emphasis in Kähler's investigation into the historical Jesus "is decisive for our present situation, namely the necessity to make the certainty of faith independent of the unavoidable incertitudes of historical research. Finding the way in which this can be done for our time is one of the main tasks of contemporary theology"[50]—and, I might add, of religious instruction.

The necessity of basing one's whole religious life, not on the factual historical Jesus, but rather on the essential message of the Bible as the Bible addresses the person in his concrete existential situation is a major emphasis in the demythologization movement pioneered by Rudolf Bultmann.[51] Bultmann saw that what is decisive in our religious life is not so much the nonhistorical myths which may be part of the Bible, but instead the actual kerygma or core message which these myths reveal to us in the process of our encountering the Scriptures. From the viewpoint of religious instruction, the critical issue in the thesis of demythologization is not whether a particular biblical passage is historically factual in the objective sense or is myth, but rather what this historical fact or this myth reveals to us in our own religious life.[52]

When a person reads the Gospels for the purpose of doing biblical theology, one of his main concerns might well be the search for the historical Jesus. But when a person encounters the Gospels in order to become religiously educated, his concern for the historical Jesus is decidedly secondary. When a person encounters the Gospels in order to grow in his own religious life, whatever awareness he might have of the historical Jesus always receives its worth from the degree to which such an awareness makes more real and more comprehensible the person's here-and-now encounter with that Jesus who existentially addresses him as he reads the Gospels. In religious instruction, then, the main focus is on the living of the Jesus of the Gospels and not just on finding out about him in the historical sense.[53]

Biblical theologians are frequently aware of the necessity for separating biblical-theology uses of the Bible from religious-instruction uses of Scripture. Ernst Käsemann, for example, contends that it is futile to root our faith in the objectivity of Scripture because careful biblical research suggests that many objective "facts" recorded in the sacred text are not so objective after all. The Bible, observes Käsemann, is a record of faith. Therefore our faith, and the security which our faith brings us, is essentially a subjectivity and not an objectivity. This subjectivity is not a subjectivity anchored to the objectivity of the Bible. In Käsemann's view, this subjectivity is a subjectivity anchored to the inspired subjectivity of the Bible, a subjectivity which is not antipodal to objectivity, but rather a subjectivity which swallows historical objectivity and transforms it in the process.[54]

From the religious instruction point of view, the key point to keep in mind with respect to the nonobjectivity and to the historical nonfacticity of certain portions of the Bible is that the Bible is inspired. The Bible not only was inspired but is inspired. Inspiration is the touchstone for one's religious encounter with the Scriptures. Inspiration is a religious affair and hence does not extend itself to nonreligious phenomena such as natural science or geography or mathematics—or history. With respect to inspiration as inspiration, it does not strictly matter whether parts of the Bible are nonobjective or nonhistorical.[55] What matters is that the Bible is God's inspired revelation to us, and insofar as it is inspired revelation, insofar as it is the personal outpouring of God to us, the Bible is a sure and solid foundation for our religious life. It is inspiration, and not objectivity or historicity, which is the saving event. Inspiration is *in-spirare*, the breath of God cascading into the person who encounters the Bible in open faith, hope, and love.

Does the subjective co-structure of the Bible reduce the sacred text to sheer relativism? Does the subjective co-structure of the Bible transpose church doctrines founded upon Scripture to wisps of wind blowing willy nilly? The answer to both questions is an emphatic "Not at all!" What the subjective co-structure of the Bible does is to affirm the

humanity of the sacred authors and the humanity of those who encounter the sacred text. In Hudson Baggett's words, "The Bible was
written by human beings for human beings."[56] The Bible is not the
frozen breath of God or man. The Bible is a group of persons addressing the being of the person encountering the sacred text. The fact that
each sacred writer is a subjectivity constitutes one of the major reasons
why his divinely inspired words possess the inbuilt power to mesh
differently with various readers depending on how the personality of
the reader interacts with the personality of the writer. In terms of
religious instruction, the co-subjective structure of the Scriptures inherently demands that the religious educator should personalize the
Bible as much as possible in order to remain faithful to the essential
spirit and the basic pedagogical thrust of the sacred text. Personalizing
Scripture so as to free it to existentially address the needs and concerns
of the learner is not watering down the Bible for instructional purposes. On the contrary, this kind of personalization is necessary both to
preserve the fundamental co-subjective structure of the Bible itself and
to preserve the essential pedagogical thrust of the Bible as a saving
learning event in the personal life of everyone who authentically encounters the sacred text.

The subjective co-structure of the Bible does not undermine church
doctrine founded on Scripture. First of all, it must be remembered that
the subjective co-structure of the Bible is only one-half of the picture.
The objective co-structure forms the other half of the shape of Scripture, a half which is indispensable to and interactive with the subjective co-structure. Second, the subjective co-structure of Scripture is
existentially congruent with the way in which persons learn. Psychologically speaking, both the Bible and church doctrine are learned
according to the mode of the learner. Scripturally based church doctrine is introjected by the learner according to the texture of his own
personality system. The efforts of modern biblicists to bring to salience
the subjective co-structure of the Bible can, if taken properly, make
church doctrine more existentially true and more scripturally sound
because these efforts by biblicists are in fact highlighting from a different but complementary perspective the way in which people actually
learn and the way in which Scripture actually is.

The subjective co-structure of the Bible combined with the psychological manner in which a person learns constitutes one of the prime
factors accounting for the development of cognitive church doctrine.[57]
As scholars and ordinary believers interact with Scripture according to

both the subjective-objective co-structure of the Bible and the existential exigencies of their own personalities, new interpretations and fresh insights emerge on the personal meaning and ecclesial import of the inexhaustibly rich sacred text. Without the subjective co-structure of the Bible and the subjective personality structure of the person simultaneously encountering the Bible, the sacred text would remain unchanged and unchanging, a dead fossil writ into dead manuscript pages instead of the living disclosure of the living God.

The Bible will always be at once absolute and relative because the Bible has both a co-objective structure and a co-subjective structure. This twin structure accounts for the Bible being a sure foundation for one's religious life because it shows how the Bible is simultaneously universal and personal.

The Bible is a living book not solely because it possesses both a universal co-structure and a personal co-structure, but also (and uniquely) because both inextricable co-structures form the *inspired* message of God. But the Bible is also living when a flesh-and-blood learner interacts with it. Encountering the Bible is quintessentially a learning affair because such an encounter is a dynamic synapse between the living inspiration of God and the living engagement by the learner.

One of the bases for authentically teaching the Bible is that the Scripture is God's experiential word both in authorship and in the way in which a person encounters it.[58] Thomas Groome puts this twin axis of the encounter nicely when he observes that "the relationship between the text and ourselves cannot be a one-way application (Bible to life). Rather, the text and its context must be held in a relationship of mutual illumination and reciprocity with our own life text and context."[59]

If the inspired revelation of Scripture is to encounter the learner as fully as possible, then the core of religious instruction in the Bible must be the unmediated engagement of the learner with the sacred text. Scripture should speak directly to the learner.[60] The language of the Bible is inspired, and thus must necessarily have primacy of place when teaching the Bible.

One of the most effective ways to use the Bible in religious instruction is to assist the learner to be alert to what God is telling him as he encounters the sacred text. Thus the immediate emphasis generally ought not to be on "correct" interpretation but rather on encountering the Bible in a holistic, existential manner.[61] More often than not, cognitive interpretation follows rather than precedes the learner's existential encounter with the sacred text.[62] Furthermore, cognitive interpretation ought to be heavily admixed with vital affective learnings of the Bible such as a love for the Bible, an attitude with the Bible, an emotional bonding in the Bible, a valuing of the Bible, and so forth. If the learner is to encounter Scripture existentially and holistically, then the religion teacher must empower him to have an open heart and an open mind both to the Bible and to all of life. Unless the religious educator pedagogically embarks on this kind of empowerment, he runs the great risk of reducing religious instruction in the Bible into a somewhat dead (and deadening) cognitive affair. As Sara Little contends, the Bible will be taught and learned effectively in religious instruction when both teacher and learner treat it as God addressing the learner (and the teacher) in Bible activity, rather than simply reading a text.[63]

When I stress the primacy of the unmediated engagement of the learner with the sacred text, I am in no way implying that all or even most of the time teaching the Bible should be spent simply in reading the text. To be sure, there are a host of valuable pedagogical devices through which the learner can encounter the Bible directly. Role-playing and certain kinds of gaming procedures represent examples of two forms of such pedagogical devices. Furthermore, it is not only helpful but indeed it is often crucial that religious instruction in the Bible include a wide range of cognitive, affective, and lifestyle pedagogical practices which are *about* and *in* the Bible as contrasted to those pedagogical practices which constitute a direct encounter with the sacred text itself.

The ransoming capability and vivifying power of the Bible can only be genuinely unleashed for both learner and educator[64] when it is treated as the living and holistically existential inspiration of God rather than a set of verbal formulations.[65]

Principle #4: Teaching the Bible as Religion Includes Not Only Cognitive Content, But Even More Importantly Affective Content and Lifestyle Content

Because the Bible is a living document written in a spatiotemporal context by human beings under the inspiration of God, it is necessarily an amalgam of three principal contents of human life, namely cognitive content, affective content, and lifestyle content. Consequently, any truly personal and religious encounter with the Bible must perforce include cognitive content, affective content, and lifestyle content. Since the Bible is primarily an instructional document which is targeted toward the enhancement of religious experience, it is evident that lifestyle is the most important of these contents, followed by affective content, with cognitive content in the place of least emphasis. This statement is not made to demean the importance of cognitive content in teaching the Bible as religion, but rather to properly situate cognitive content within the galaxy of the various contents available to both the religious educator and the learner.

Cognitive Content

Quite obviously, an adequate intellectual grasp of individual biblical passages and of the Bible as a whole is an indispensable feature of religious instruction in the Bible. In facilitating the acquisition of cognitive content about the Bible, the religious educator should not be content to limit his teaching simply to knowledge outcomes. After all, knowledge constitutes the lowest level of the six categories of cognitive behaviors listed in the highly influential and illuminative taxonomy of the cognitive domain of human existence.[66] In order to teach the entire range of cognitive content about the Bible, the religious educator must also include teaching the learners to adequately comprehend the Bible, to intellectually relate or apply to their own lives those abstractions (universals) gained from reading the Bible, to analyze the various elements and relationships and principles expressed in the Bible, to synthesize the biblical themes and emphases, and to evaluate their own lives in terms of biblical principles.[67] Religious educators who restrict their biblical pedagogy simply to the knowledge component of the taxonomy are depriving the learners of the richness and depth of cognitive content about the Bible.

As appropriate to learners of different ages and developmental levels, the basic principles and applications of both hermeneutics and exegesis should be taught in biblical religious instruction. Unless learners acquire the skill of interpreting biblical passages and of examining these passages from a variety of perspectives intrinsically related to the composition of the text, their cognitive grasp of the Bible will be regrettably stunted. One of the great gifts of renewal which Protestantism conferred on all Christianity was to emphasize once again that the Bible is not a book politically restricted to a clerical caste or gnostically confined to Scripture scholars, but rather a book available to every person regardless of age or station or intellectual capacity. If religious educators fail to teach learners the basic principles and applications of hermeneutics and exegesis, as appropriate, then surely the Bible will in effect be a closed book since the learners lack the necessary interpretative and critical skills to render the Bible meaningful in their own personal lives and in the life of the ecclesia.[68]

A cardinal principle in the proper use of hermeneutics and exegesis in religious instruction activity is that both of these cognitive devices should be used in a way consonant with religious instruction rather than in a manner pertinent to theological instruction. (The purpose of religious instruction is to know, love, and live religion. The purpose of theological instruction is to become skilled in theological science. These two forms of instruction are ontically different.) In religious instruction, the use of biblical hermeneutics and exegesis is for the purpose of knowing, loving, and living the Bible and the God of the Bible more fully in one's own religious life.[69] In theological instruction, on the other hand, the use of hermeneutics and exegesis[70] is for the goal of understanding the theological meaning and import of a given text or passage.

Affective Content

Affective content is the name given to that set of learning outcomes which include feeling and feelings, emotions, attitudes, values, and love.

There is a deep and intrinsic nexus between affect and religion. It is virtually impossible, for example, to be religious without having strong feelings toward God. If religion is anything, it is having attitudes and values which are grounded in and soaked with religion.[71] And surely love is absolutely central to authentic religion.[72] Because religion is a way of life, and because religion constitutes what Thomas Aquinas calls a total orientation and relationship with God, religion must perforce be basically a matter of love. After all, as John the Evangelist reminds us, God is love (1 Jn. 4:8).

There is significantly greater intrinsic relationship between affect and religion than between cognition and religion. This fact ought never to be forgotten by religious educators who teach the Bible for the purpose of facilitating religious outcomes in learners.

Whereas theological language is essentially a cognitive and a predicative language, religious language is basically an affective/lifestyle language and a normative language.[73] As I state elsewhere,[74] religious language is a special technical language expressing thoughts, affects, and actions with respect to human encounters with God. What makes religious language special is that it is drenched with affectivity. Indeed, the heavy affective tenor of religious language is precisely what has led logical positivists to dismiss the truth-value of this kind of symbolic expression. Logical positivists, who are cognitivists to the core, claim that religious language is nothing more than "emotive language" and consequently devoid of meaning.[75]

The Bible is a religious instruction book. Hence for the most part, the Bible is written primarily in religious language rather than in theological language. Therefore the religious educator who wishes to be biblical in the sense of teaching the Bible in a manner which truly resonates with the fundamental structure and intent of the Bible must teach it both *as* religious language and *in* religious language. To do otherwise is to teach about the Bible rather than to teach the Bible.

Since the Bible is written in religious language it is heavily affective on the one hand and cognitively imprecise on the other hand. This fact suggests that in teaching the Bible for religious (biblical) purposes, the religious educator ought to stress feelings in the Bible, emotions for the Bible, attitudes toward the Bible, values of the Bible, and love in and with and through the Bible. In the end, these affective contents are far more important religiously (biblically) than cognitive content alone—though cognitive content is indeed important and necessary.

The primary religious language of the Bible and the cognitively imprecise language of the Bible bring rich cognitive and affective dividends. The religious affectivity and cognitive imprecision of biblical language renders the sacred text ideal for a wide variety of personal and meaningful interpretations. Such interpretations might not always be far removed from the general intent of the sacred writer or of the God who inspired the sacred writer.

That kind of affect known as attitudes is extremely important for religious instruction in the Bible. The pertinent empirical research suggests that attitudes largely account for a person's approach and subsequent response not only to values but to most of reality.[76] Attitudes condition virtually all learning. This is a powerful assertion, but an empirically validated one. Gordon Allport observes that "attitudes will determine for each individual what he will see and hear, what he will think, and what he will do."[77] Consequently, teaching biblical attitudes toward life and reality constitutes one of the most important tasks of any religious educator who is teaching the Bible. A person will necessarily live a biblically oriented life if that individual has positive attitudes toward the Bible and if his attitudes are biblically oriented. However, a person will not necessarily live a biblically oriented life if that individual simply has a knowledge of the Bible or of biblical themes.

One of the most ennobling forms of affect is love. Religious instruction in the Bible must, in one important sense, be education in love and for love. The Bible is a book of love. Mark van Doren and Maurice Samuel characterize the Bible as "a book drenched in love." As these two authors indicate, the creation of the world was an act of God's love, the quarrels between God and his Chosen People were really lovers' quarrels, and the great prophets and persons of God like Jacob and David were basically lovers of God and of man. Books like the Song of Solomon are written in the lyrical language of love.[78] To teach the Bible in a biblical fashion, then, demands that one not only teach the Bible as a record of God's incessant love for human beings, but also demands that one teach learners to live their lives from within the context of biblical love. Failure to teach the Bible from within the context of biblical love is to betray the Bible and its saving message. Morton Trippe Kelsey writes that "the only betrayal of life is the refusal to love."[79] If learning the Bible does not center around love and the living of love, then surely the religious educator has betrayed the fundamental religious nature and thrust of Scripture. Whatever else biblical learning might be, it is learning to love more deeply, it is learning to acquire a love-filled lifestyle.

I must emphasize that affects such as attitudes, values, and love can and are indeed taught—and taught directly. It is a major pedagogical fallacy to claim that "attitudes are caught, not taught." If teaching is narrowly (and incorrectly) defined as verbal presentation or proclamation, then of course affects such as attitudes or love cannot be taught since verbal behavior is intrinsically cognitive in orientation. However, if teaching is properly regarded as deliberatively structuring the pedagogical situation, then affects such as attitudes and love can be successfully taught. Homes, classrooms, churches, camps, and other settings in which religious instruction is enacted do indeed teach affective content directly. Indeed, these settings are in fact principal milieux in which persons like ourselves did in fact acquire the attitudes and values and loves which presently characterize our lives.

In 1965 Ronald Goldman published an important book which rocked much of the religious education world.[80] This book consisted of empirical data and conclusions derived from a careful experimental investigation of children's religious thinking. Among other things, Goldman's careful experimental study found that children up to about twelve years of age tend to cognitively garble and intellectually confuse the meaning of a great deal of biblical material such as the burning bush, the parting of the Red Sea, and the temptations of Jesus.[81] Quite a few religious educationists and educators suggested that in light of Goldman's findings, the churches ought not to teach the Bible to children under twelve. (Other, more radical religious educationists and educators, went on to claim that Goldman's data clearly showed that the Bible was an adult book written solely by adults solely for adults. The adult religious education movement was born.) What both of these religious education groups failed to realize was that Goldman's research was unequivocally directed at only one segment of children's learning, namely the cognitive domain. His research did not deal with children's affective learning of the Bible. My point here is that the Bible can and should be taught to persons of all ages in a manner appropriate to the here-and-now developmental level of each individual learner. In the case of children under twelve years of age, the Bible should be taught primarily as affective content, and of course as lifestyle content. The Bible is suffused with an enormous amount of affective content, and it is this content which is necessary for children to learn, and learn well. If the child does not learn basic biblical attitudes, if the child does not learn basic biblical values, if the child does not learn biblical love and love for the Bible, then the child has a feeble personalistic foundation in which to integrate those cognitively accurate biblical concepts which he will learn in adolescence and in adulthood. Speaking now for myself and only for myself, I can assert that my own present warm feeling-tone for the Bible, my own present positive attitude toward the Bible, and my own present love for the Bible are in large measure a direct result of the affective way in which my parents and my other early religion teachers taught me to feel for the Bible, to gain positive attitudes toward the Bible, and to love the Bible and its affective messages. To be sure, the Bible is a book written by adults. However, the Bible is a book written *for* persons of all ages. In this connection, it is well to remember the results of three companion research investigations of enormous significance for religious instruction. In these well-conducted empirical research studies, David Elkind found that the child is most like the adult in affects and least like him in cognitions.[82] Thus the greatest point of synapse between the adult biblical writer and his readers is not cognition but affect, a synapse as readily available to a child who encounters the Bible as to an adult.

It is a fairly common complaint that Protestant Sunday Schools and Catholic CCD programs are not having the desired religious effect on the students enrolled in these programs. I suggest that one major reason for this relative lack of success is that both the Sunday School and the CCD tend to stress cognitive content and concomittantly tend to neglect affective content. Because of the severely limited time which both programs have per week and per year, and because of the fundamental nature of the Bible and of religion, it would seem that a switch of primary emphasis from cognitive content to affective content (and to lifestyle content) would contribute significantly toward making Sunday Schools and CCD a success. I am not suggesting that cognitive content be eliminated or watered down; rather, I am suggesting that in Sunday School and in CCD solid cognitive content be taught either confluently with solid affective content,[83] or that solid cognitive content be inserted into a wider affective envelope.

Lifestyle Content

Lifestyle is clearly the most important of all the molar contents in religious instruction, including religious instruction in the Bible. Lifestyle content deliciously integrates the three major domains of human functioning (cognitive, affective, and psychomotor), not in a way which somehow "outers" these domains, but rather in a way which inserts them into a new global content. This new global content is a content in its own right, and not simply a combination or synthesis of cognitive, affective, and psychomotor contents. Lifestyle, or conduct, is the way an individual lives his life, the way he conducts himself daily, the way he acts and interacts with reality.

Christian living constitutes the major overarching goal of religious instruction in general and of biblical religious instruction in particular.[84] The highest form of religious instruction consists of facilitating a desired change in the learner's entire behavioral pattern along religious lines. It is surely important to know the Bible. But most important of all, it is imperative that a person live the Bible in his own here-and-now lifestyle.

Throughout the Gospels Jesus was always insisting on the primacy of a religious lifestyle over other forms of content. He was constantly stressing religious lifestyle in concrete performance terms as contrasted to vague ethereal terms or even to notional terms. For example, Jesus strongly underscored the centrality and indispensability of lifestyle religion when he stated: "It is not those who say to me 'Lord, Lord' who will enter the kingdom of heaven, but the person who does the will of my Father in heaven" (Mt. 7:21). When the followers of John the Baptist asked Jesus who he was, the Savior did not describe himself and his mission in notional terms but in concrete observable lifestyle behaviors: "Go back and tell John what you have seen and heard: the blind see again, the lame walk, lepers are cleansed, the deaf hear, the dead are raised to life, the Good News is proclaimed to the poor" (Lk. 7:22).[85] At the Last Supper, Jesus, as usual, emphasized religious behavior of the lifestyle sort: "If anyone serves me, he must follow me" (Jn. 12:26).

The followers of Jesus in the early centuries of the church carried on the Savior's emphasis on lifestyle content. In the early church Christianity was often referred to as "The Way," namely the entire pattern of life, or lifestyle. In the catechumenate of the early church, stress was placed not simply on knowing the basic tenets of Christianity, but far more importantly on living an acceptable Christian lifestyle.[86]

If religious instruction in the Bible is to be authentically biblical, it must involve not only cognitively studying the Bible for religious enrichment, but even more importantly praying the Bible and living the Bible in one's own daily life and in one's ecclesial life.

Thomas Merton observes that while an awareness of biblical scholarship is essential for a genuine cognitive understanding of Scripture, nonetheless one must not allow scientific study to deaden one's sensitivity to the existential reality of biblical experience. Merton notes that often the most religious people, those who read the Bible as a matter of pious duty or delight, often manage to evade a radically involved existential dialogue with the sacred text they are reading. In other words, such persons are reading the Bible rather than encountering it. Only by encountering the Bible within the context of one's personal and ecclesial life, only by existentially merging the Bible with one's here-and-now lifestyle, can one enable the Bible to become the living saving word of God rather than a dead text.[87]

One of the most pervasive and profound occurrences throughout the Bible is that of mysticism. Mysticism is a form of especially enriched religious experience. From the perspective of human personality, Abraham Maslow states that a mystical experience can either be a "peak experience" or a "high plateau experience." He goes on to assert that mystical experience constitutes the essence and core of religion, something which elevates religion above moral philosophy or ethics. Furthermore, states Maslow, all founders of world religions and virtually all the saints produced by world religions have enjoyed mystical experiences of one kind or another.[88] Maslow's statements certainly hold true for the Bible and for Christianity. Consequently, all religious instruction, especially religious instruction in the Bible, ought not only to highly value mysticism, but also to have mysticism as one of its goals,[89] and as far as possible structure the pedagogical situation in such a way as to facilitate mystical experiences in learners.[90]

Lifestyle content can only be taught through substantive content which is lifestyle in character. Like generates like; like is unable to generate unlike. Lifestyle content cannot be taught through substantive content which is cognitive in character, for example. Research investigations illustrate this point. A classic and frequently cited experimental research study conducted by Pleasant Hightower found "no relationship of any consequence" between the amount of biblical information a person possesses and the degree to which that person will tell the truth or will cheat.[91] Martin Maehr's empirical investigation discovered that only a low correlation exists between the level of biblical information possessed by learners and statements by these same individuals of how they would act in hypothetical, concrete situations.[92] Various empirical research studies of juvenile delinquents and of adult criminals suggest that "the delinquent child as well as the criminal adult is usually only too well aware of the fact that his conduct is contrary to moral precept; his evil-doing is not by and large due to ignorance."[93] Religious educators who imagine that they can teach lifestyle content by teaching biblical knowledge are deceiving both themselves and the learners whom they teach.

Lifestyle content can only be taught through pedagogical procedures which are lifestyle in character. If the religious educator is to teach the Bible with the goal that the learner will live biblically, then his pedagogical procedures must revolve around a lifestyle axis. Pedagogical procedures which revolve around a cognitive axis such as memorizing a biblical text or analyzing a particular biblical theme are not structurally capable of yielding lifestyle learning outcomes. Nor is careful reflection on a biblical text sufficient to bring forth lifestyle outcomes. Reflection, after all, is a cognitive activity which, consequently, will produce only cognitive outcomes. Lawrence Richards puts this entire issue nicely when he states: "When we take Scripture as a revelation of reality, the issue in the teaching process is not communication of biblical material for understanding, but the design of learning experiences through which the realities of the Word provide perspective and enable those realities to be known [and I might add, to be felt and lived] in personal experience."[94] Educationists and educators in the field of so-called "secular education" have developed lifestyle-soaked pedagogical procedures which can be of significant assistance to religious educators who aim to teach the Bible as a lifestyle content.[95]

Principle #5: Teaching the Bible As Religion Begins with the Learner As the Learner Exists Developmentally in a Particular Concrete Existential Situation

The nature of all learning is such that it necessarily occurs according to the existential mode of the learner.[96] This foundational statement also holds true for the learning of religion. To be sure, I am not aware of any body of empirical research which asserts that religion is learned in a basically different manner than other areas of reality are learned. On the contrary, the available empirical research evidence clearly indicates that religion learning is a form of general learning and takes place according to the fundamental principles and structure of the overall learning process itself.[97]

Because all learning occurs according to the mode of the learner, it necessarily follows that all learning must begin with where the learner is developmentally in a particular concrete existential situation. This foundational statement holds true for learners of every age, culture, and milieu. This foundational statement holds true for the learning of all forms of content, such as, for example, cognitive content, affective content, and lifestyle content.

The nature and definition of all forms of teaching, including religion teaching, is that it constitutes the facilitation of learning. Because all learning necessarily occurs according to the mode of the
learner, and because all learning begins where the learner is developmentally and situationally, it follows that a global conceptualization of
all forms of teaching is simply this: Teaching is that purposeful activity
which is structured in such a fashion that the learner knows, feels,
and/or lives the desired subject matter in terms of that learner's own
here-and-now developmental and situational existence.[98]

The foundational principles briefly discussed in the preceding three
paragraphs distinctly suggest that teaching the Bible as religion must
necessarily begin with and proceed through the developmental level
and existential situation of the learner. In other words, teaching the
Bible must start with and work through the experiences of the learner.
Of more than passing interest in this connection is that the incidents of
effective religion teaching recorded in the Bible take place along the
lines which I am suggesting. Let me give three illustrative examples of
this last-mentioned point.[99]

The first of these three examples deals with the efforts of Jesus to
teach cognitive content. In the parable of the wicked winegrowers (Mt.
21:33–46), the desired learning outcome is that of assisting those persons who are hearing the parable (disciples, chief priests, Pharisees) to
intellectually understand that since the Jewish religious leaders of that
day are rejecting Jesus, then his invitation to salvation will be expanded to include the Gentiles. In this parable, Jesus weaves his teaching around the developmental levels and existential situations of the
heterogeneous group of learners he is teaching. He uses a concrete
example (wine growing) which is familiar to the learners in their own
personal experience; he uses a linchpin Old Testament reference since
his hearers, especially the chief priests and the Pharisees, are steeped in
Old Testament knowledge; he uses the story and allegorical form of
verbal teaching since this pedagogical procedure was widely accepted
and understood by the learners he was teaching. In this instructional
incident, Jesus did not start with an abstract religious or theological
explanation of the divine call to the Chosen People or the conditions
necessary to preserve this divine call; rather Jesus started and worked
through the developmental level and concrete existential situation of
the learners.

The second of these three examples deals with the efforts of Jesus to teach affective content. In the episode of the washing of the feet (Jn. 3:1–17), the desired learning outcome is that the apostle gain a deep attitude and lasting value for that kind of humble and other-oriented service which is an essential hallmark of a true disciple of the Lord. In this incident, Jesus weaves his teaching around the developmental levels and existential situations of the homogeneous group of learners whom he is teaching. He uses an act familiar to the learners, namely washing the feet of another person. The learners have experienced in their own lives that a master does not wash another's feet, especially the feet of servants. Washing the feet of another person constituted part of the overall duties of a servant in those days. The learners had also experienced in their own personal lives the actual cleansing effect of water, and in their Judaic religious lives the symbolism of ablutions. In this instructional incident, Jesus did not start with or work through an abstract religious or theological explanation of the necessity of humble service for the Christian apostolate; rather, Jesus performed an affect-filled act which was enacted in elegant congruence with the developmental levels and concrete existential situations of the learners.

The third of these three examples deals with the efforts of Jesus to teach lifestyle content. In the episode in which Jesus beckons Peter to walk with him on the water (Mt. 14:22–33) the desired learning outcome is that Peter and the other apostles learn the *act* of faith. In this incident Jesus incorporates his teaching into a conduct-event which is taking place here-and-now in the developmental and situational experience of the learners. The learners encounter a singularly startling phenomenon, namely Jesus walking on the water. This is an experience of such a nature as to grip the learners existentially. Peter asks Jesus to walk on the water as well. Jesus involves Peter more deeply in the learning situation by beckoning the prince of the apostles to come to him. Peter proceeds, then becomes afraid, starts to sink, and eventually is rescued by Jesus. Peter and the other apostles directly experience the positive aspects of faith (Peter walks on the water) and also the negative aspects of a defective faith (Peter sinks). As fishermen or at least as persons familiar with the sea, all the apostles are developmentally aware of the principles and effects of floatation. Furthermore, all the apostles had frequently experienced floatation in their own concrete existential situations. In this instructional incident, Jesus did not start with or work through an abstract religious or theological explanation of the act of faith; rather, Jesus structured a pedagogical incident in such a fashion that the learners (and Peter in particular) were required to make and sustain the desired learning outcome, an outcome highly congruent with the developmental level and concrete existential situation of the learners.

Grounding one's religion teaching in the developmental level and situational context of the learner in no way represents a watering down of subject-matter content. Quite the contrary. The only way that teaching can be truly effective is to structure pedagogical activity around reality. In the case of teaching, reality consists in the developmental level and situational context of the learner. Apparently Jesus as a teacher did not believe that developmentally and situationally rooted pedagogy constituted watered-down religious instruction. A wide variety of modern empirical research evidence supports Jesus in this respect. [100]

David Bickimer beautifully underscores the fact that an essential basis of all teaching, and especially of religion teaching, is that it satisfactorily addresses the needs of the learner. [101] In this connection, it is well worth noting that one of the major features of the pedagogy of Jesus was that he frequently oriented his instructional activity around the very human needs of those with whom he dealt. [102] Over and over again the Gospels recount how Jesus was heavily involved in meeting the needs of persons and building much of his pedagogy around the effective meeting of these needs. In the following chart I have selected a few representative pedagogical incidents from the life of Jesus to illustrate this important point.

This little chart shows that the meeting of people's needs was not just a vestibule or entry vehicle to Jesus' religious instruction practice. Rather the meeting of people's needs formed an integral and inseparable part of Jesus' pedagogical activity.

Since the end of World War II, there has been a serious dispute in religious instruction circles about the proper starting place for teaching the Bible. [103] One side in this dispute, the Bible-centered position, asserts that authentic teaching of the Bible must always start with and work through the Bible itself. The Bible-centered position tends to emphasize memorizing biblical texts, applying principles of hermeneutics and exegesis to a better understanding of the sacred text, and comparing one text with another. In some instances, a few minutes at the end of each lesson might be devoted to the implications of Bible study for one's own life. The second side of this dispute, the experience-centered position, maintains that the authentic teaching of

GOSPEL EVENT	PERSON'S NEED	DESIRED LEARNING OUTCOME
The healing of the centurion's slave (Mt. 8:5–13)	Centurion's need to have his slave physically cured	The necessity and power of faith
The calming of the tempest at sea (Mt. 8:23–27)	Apostles' need to avoid drowning	The importance of completely trusting Jesus at all times; the mastery of Jesus over nature
The plucking of grain on the Sabbath (Mt. 12:1–8)	Apostles' need to assuage their hunger	A proper set of priorities
The rich young man (Mt. 19:16–30)	A good man's need to follow his convictions completely and strive for perfection	The necessity of total sacrifice for wholehearted discipleship
The blessing of the children (Lk. 18:15–17)	Parents' need to get the best for their children	Necessity of humility and spiritual rebirth
Zacchaeus the Publican (Lk. 19:1–10)	A man's need for personal acceptance	Universality of salvation
The good thief (Lk. 23:39–43)	A man's need for salvation	Power of Jesus to effect salvation; never too late to be saved
Marriage feast of Cana (Jn. 2:1–12)	A mother's need to help others in an embarrassing situation	Preeminence of meeting human needs in one's religious mission
The raising of Lazarus from the dead (Jn. 11:1–44)	A family's need to help a sick relative	The Last Things, especially death and resurrection; the glory of God

the Bible must always begin with and proceed through the learner's own experience. The experience-centered position stresses pedagogical procedures which foster the essential and ongoing synapse between the life experiences of the learner and the Bible.

It should be rather clear by this time that I strongly believe that the experience-centered position is correct as far as teaching the Bible as religion is concerned. All learning occurs according to the mode of the learner. This indisputable psychological dictum holds just as true for Bible learning as for any other kind of learning. Even if the religious educator attempted to be Bible-centered rather than experience-centered, what really happens in the pedagogical event is that the learners are in fact learning experientially, that is to say basically filtering and essentially reworking the biblical material according to the exigencies of their own particular developmental state and concrete existential situation. By failing to teach experientially, the Bible-centered teacher is in fact relinquishing the pedagogical benefits which every carefully structured instructional practice possesses, and instead ends up with that kind of random hit-or-miss learning which his pedagogy is supposed to eliminate. It is illuminative to observe that the pedagogical activity recounted in the Bible was typically done in an experience-centered fashion.

At least three general principles ought to be operative when teaching the Bible as religion.[104] First, it is impossible to separate the Bible from life, even if it were desirable to do so. Second, Bible texts must be taught experientially since they are learned only experientially. Third, biblical pedagogics must endeavor to help the learner interpret, feel, and live out life experiences from within the particular and overall context of the Bible—a context which, though supple, is an authentic and authoritative context nonetheless.

Experience-centered biblical pedagogy does not constitute a watering down of Bible learning. Quite the contrary. By basing biblical learning upon experience, the religious educator is grounding his instructional practice in reality rather than in his own wishful thinking or even in his own fantasy. By starting from and working through the learner's experience, the religious educator is thereby heightening the probability that the learner will not only learn the Bible-as-Bible more effectively, but also that the learner will successfully integrate the Bible into his own daily living.[105]

It is erronious to regard experience either as antipodal to content or as the absence of content. Experience is a genuine content in its own right. There is no such thing as learned content apart from experience. Conversely, one cannot experience nothing. To be sure, the more that learned content is experiential, the more powerful and realistic will this content be personally and ecclesially.[106]

Because each person necessarily learns according to the twin exigencies of his own developmental state and his own concrete existential situation, it might well be that at certain times and in certain circumstances the most effective way to teach biblically is not to teach biblical texts or even to teach the Bible. To teach biblically, it should be remembered, is not so much to teach just the Bible or to teach only the Bible. Rather, to teach biblically is to teach in a manner congruent with the Bible and with objectives consonant with the Bible. Since Scripture is the word of God, then of course God addresses us in a more focused and a more considered way in the Bible than he does in other kinds of revelation. Notwithstanding, forms of revelation other than the Bible do exist and are operative in the life of every person. At certain times and in certain situations, Scripture might not be as valuable for an individual's Christian living as a religious novel or a secular motion picture. The Bible has a certain saving power, but this saving power is not of the magical sort or the kind which works automatically with every person in every situation.[107]

Principle #6: A Wide Variety of Teaching Procedures Is Required In Order to Facilitate a Wide Variety of Learning Outcomes

Pedagogical procedures are not simply ornaments or helpful addenda to the work of teaching the Bible as religion. Quite the opposite is true. Pedagogical procedures are of supreme importance in the act of biblical pedagogy.

Viewed from the formal perspective, all teaching, including the teaching of religion, has two essential molar contents.[108] These two essential molar contents are substantive content and structural content. Substantive content refers to the form in which the content appears. Substantive content is commonly called the subject matter of the lesson. Structural content refers to the way in which the content is brought into activity and sustained in its activity. Structural content is commonly called instructional practice used in the lesson.[109] Every kind of religion lesson is an amalgam of these two essential contents.

The foregoing analysis reveals three fundamental and extremely important points about the content of religious instruction. *First*, the religious instruction act itself is the proper content of religious instruction. The content of religious instruction, then, is coextensive with the act of religious instruction. When any portion of the act is deleted, to that extent is content automatically deleted as well. Thus the religion which is taught in the religion lesson is not religion in itself, but only religion as this religion occurs in the religious instruction act. *Second,* substantive content is not the "what" of teaching, and structural content is not the "how" of teaching. Because structural content is an authentic content in its own right, structural content is also something learned, is also a "what." *Third,* the duality of method-content so frequently posited in religious instruction circles is fallacious.[110] The method-content duality is erroneous because method is a content in its own right; method is structural content. It is patently absurd to have a content-content duality. In the religious instruction act itself, substantive content and structural content are existentially mediated so that both of these contents are reconciled and subsumed into a new ontic entity called the religious instruction act.[111]

Instructional practice, then, is not only the way in which learning is facilitated; but it is also something which is itself learned. The way in which a priest preaches in the Sunday sermon, the way in which a mother deals with her son when she finds him cheating, the way in which a Sunday School instructor teaches the Bible to her class—all these pedagogical practices not only teach a content but themselves are content. The priest who preaches in a boring voice tone to a congregation which sits passively in the pews is directly teaching the parishoners, among other things, that religion is a rather boring affair and that the parishioner's proper role in religion is a passive one. The mother who uses firm reproach mixed with kindness when she discovers her son cheating is directly teaching her son that sin is bad and that sin can be forgiven. The Sunday School teacher whose classes center almost exclusively around memorization of biblical texts, knowledge of biblical names and places, and correct interpretation of biblical passages, is directly teaching her students that the Bible is a cognitive document more to be intellectually studied than loved or lived.

The only proper way to teach the Bible is for the teacher to make sure that the substantive contents and the structural contents are as fully congruent with one another as possible. The religion teacher who uses cognitive instructional procedures almost exclusively is thereby suffocating the affective and lifestyle essence of the Bible's substantive content. The CCD teacher who says "Johnny, I want you to copy twenty times 'The Lord is My Shepherd'" is using a structural content which slaughters the substantive content of Psalm 23.[112]

Authentic and valid teaching of the Bible as religion demands that both substantive content and structural content be present. The religious instruction act is a working amalgam of substantive content and structural content. Consequently a religious instruction act is as rich as the degree to which both contents are present and operative. Because of the ontic nature of the religious instruction act, any attempt to overemphasize substantive content to the neglect of structural content results necessarily in a religious instruction act which is not only weak but is also probably miseducative in terms of the outcomes which the religious educator desires to facilitate.

In the religious instruction act, substantive content and structural content are coequal partners. Neither is less valuable than the other; neither is subservient to the other. Any attempt to make one of the molar contents inferior or ancillary to the other does violence to the integrity of the religious instruction act and therefore to the effectiveness of this act.[113]

The pedagogical process involved in teaching the Bible is not just a vehicle to get substantive biblical content across to the learner, as some individuals erroneously believe.[114] Rather, the process of teaching the Bible strongly determines how the Bible will be learned, and what features of the Bible will be learned.[115] For example, Léon Arthur Elchinger notes that the substantive content of the Christmas narrative will be learned quite differently if it is told at just any time of the year, if it is learned by leafing through the pages of a picture book, or if it is enacted at Christmas when the event is lived by the Christian within the ecclesia which is celebrating the feast.[116] Surely the substantive content of the Christmas narrative will be quite different if this biblical account is taught in a cognitive manner such as in the intellectual reflection method of shared praxis,[117] or in an affective manner such as in the affective technique called "one way feeling glasses,"[118] or in a lifestyle manner such as actively participating in a Christmas liturgy or paraliturgy.

Structural content is not simply an indeterminate amorphous process. On the contrary, the pedagogical process has discrete elements and levels. In an effort to discover the major discrete elements of structural content and to specify the relationships among these discrete elements, I carefully investigated the teaching act itself. As a result of my investigation, I devised a taxonomy of the teaching act.[119] The elements of this taxonomy, in decending order from the most general to the most particular, are pedagogical approach, style, strategy, method, technique, and step. Approach is the primary, fundamental orientation of the teaching-learning act. The two most widely used approaches are the theological approach and the social-science approach. Style is the basic overall pattern or mode which serves as the indicator of the specific direction which the activities of teaching-learning will take. Examples of pedagogical style are teacher-centered versus learner-centered. Strategy is the comprehensive, systematized, concrete scaffolding on, around, and through which are placed the more specific methods and techniques of the teaching-learning act. Examples of pedagogical strategy are the transmission strategy and the discovery strategy. Method is the internally ordered set of pedagogical procedures which are arranged in discrete generalized bodies or classes. Examples of pedagogical method include problem solving and affective teaching. Technique is the concrete, tangible, specific way in which a pedagogical event is structured in a given instructional situation. Examples of pedagogical technique are telling, role-playing, and discussion. Step is the highly specific behavior unit or behavior sequence through which the here-and-now instructional practice is enacted. Examples of step include giving praise and giving directions.

Of the numerous practical functions for religion teachers accruing from the taxonomy of structural content, two are especially germane to the teaching of the Bible as religion. First of all, the taxonomy helps religious educators come to an awareness that instructional practice is far more nuanced and far more complex than the hopelessly outdated Mr. Fix-It mentality or the cookbook recipe view of religion teaching. The taxonomy of structural content can enable the religious educator to shuck the simplistic Mr. Fix-It remedies and cookbook "tips for religion teachers" advanced by so many writers and journals in the field and move instead to that kind of mature view of the religious instruction act which will enable the religion teacher to fluidly devise a wide variety of effective pedagogical practices for successfully teaching the Bible. Second, by putting the discrete elements of the pedagogical process in an intrinsically ordered relationship to one another, the taxonomy greatly assists the religious educator to orchestrate his pedagogical practice in a harmonious, congruent manner. One of the major causes of ineffective religious instruction is operational disharmony or incongruity among elements of the taxonomy. For example, a religious educator who adopts a cognitive or didactic teaching style ought not to choose an affective pedagogical method. The style and method are out of harmony with each other. Or again, a religious educator who selects the pedagogical strategy of discovery ought not to select the lecture or telling technique. The strategy and the technique are not congruent.

Though the Bible is primarily a religious instruction book and not a scientific treatise on pedagogy, still it is highly profitable for a religion teacher to examine the Bible from the pedagogical perspective.[120] I am in no way suggesting that the Bible is a validator of pedagogical practice. Rather, I am asserting that a wide variety of pedagogical practices can be found in the Bible just as a wide variety of instructional principles can be deduced from the sacred text.[121]

Both the Old Testament and the New Testament feature a wide variety of pedagogical procedures. Two major reasons can be adduced for this fact. First, the Bible discloses an infinite substantive content, namely God. Because God is infinite, a far wider variety of pedagogical procedures is required to teach this substantive content. As Gerhard von Rad writes in a somewhat related connection: "The Old Testament is committed to speak about God in no particular method or manner. On the contrary, its possibilities of expression extend from most devout submission all the way to an almost blasphemous parody of everything that is considered holy (in Job and some of the prophets)."[122] Second, the religious educators depicted in the Bible desired to facilitate a wide variety of cognitive, affective, and lifestyle outcomes. Consequently, these religious educators employed a great many different kinds of pedagogical procedures. These biblical personages apparently were well aware that pedagogical procedures do indeed exert a profound and direct effect on the nature and success of religious instruction.

The greatest of all the religious educators portrayed in the Bible, Jesus of Nazareth, seems to have been acutely aware of the fact that the successful facilitation of any learning outcome necessarily requires the use of that kind of instructional practice specifically targeted toward the desired outcome. In view of what was known about pedagogical practice in the first century, Jesus used a truly impressive array of pedagogical practices to bring about the learning outcomes which he desired.[123]

By its very nature, teaching is the facilitation of learning. Where there is no learning there is no teaching; where there is little learning there is little teaching. Consequently, every person teaching the Bible as religion should assiduously study, feel, and practice what it is to teach and how it is to teach.[124] This cardinal principle holds true for every kind of religious educator, be that person a parent, a grandparent, a clergyman, a schoolteacher, a youth worker, or whoever. Sincere parents voraciously read books and journals, as well as attend action-oriented workshops on the pedagogical principles and procedures of effective parenting. Religious educators who teach the Bible should have a similar thirst for increasing their understanding, expanding their affectivity, and sharpening their practice of biblical pedagogics. Teaching the Bible is of such crucial importance that only the best will suffice. The substantive content of biblical pedagogics is magnificent. Therefore, should not the enactment of the structural content of biblical pedagogics be as congruent as is humanly possible with the substantive content to which it is inextricably conjoined?

Principle #7: To Teach the Bible Well Involves Following the Teaching Model Which Jesus Used Rather Than Modeling Jesus as Teacher

The basic question which the aforementioned principle addresses is this: "Should a religious educator model the master teacher or should the religious educator master the teaching model?" Specifically, should the religious educator who is teaching the Bible as religion attempt to model Jesus the master teacher or should she endeavor to master the teaching model which undergirded Jesus' teaching?

Generally speaking, it is often pedagogically unwise and often impossible for every religion teacher to model[125] a particular master religious educator. According to one school of psychology,[126] modeling is possible only when there is a considerable similarity between the personality structure and background of the modeling teacher on the one hand and the model master teacher on the other hand—to say nothing of the similarity between the galaxy of circumstances in which the modeling teacher teaches and the galaxy of circumstances in which the model master teacher teaches. While teaching surely is not determined primarily on the basis of the teacher's personality,[127] nonetheless human instruction is necessarily mediated to some extent in a given teacher's personality structure. Thus it is difficult if not impossible, for example, for a religious educator with a cool or laid-back personality structure to effectively model an educator whose personality structure is hot and out-front. Because of the differences in personality, backgrounds, and pedagogical circumstances, no one master religious educator can serve as an adequate model for all other religious educators. The impossibility of a master religion teacher serving as a model for every other religious educator is enormously compounded when the master religious educator to be modeled is Jesus. This already enormous compounding factor becomes exponentially magnified when one takes into account the dissimilarity between the sociocultural backgrounds and pedagogical circumstances of Jesus on one side and the sociocultural background and pedagogical circumstances of the modeling teacher on the other side.

While it is often pedagogically unwise and often impossible for every religious educator to model a master teacher (especially when this master teacher is Jesus), nonetheless it is very possible and even desirable for a religion teacher to attempt to incorporate or appropriate the master religious educator's pedagogical procedures into his own instructional activity. But even here considerable difficulties present themselves. Pedagogical practices do not exist in a vacuum. In other words, pedagogical practices are not unaffected by such powerful variables as the personality of the teacher, the developmental level of the learner, the situational context in which the practice is enacted, and so forth. Thus if any religion teacher wishes to fully utilize the successful pedagogical practices of a master educator, then such a teacher must necessarily place the different variables involved in the master educator's pedagogy into a wider framework. This wider framework must be such as to allow him and every other religion teacher wishing to follow the master educator's pedagogical practices to effectively utilize these practices regardless of those specific variables which will be present in the pedagogical situations in which these practices will be enacted. The religion teacher, then, must universalize the master educator's pedagogical practices by getting to the very foundation of the master educator's pedagogy. This foundation is the teaching model, or more

accurately the theory of teaching which undergirds the master educator's pedagogical practice.[128]

It should be underscored that Jesus was a master religious educator,
not because of any mysterious factor or set of factors attached to the
actuality of his being God as well as man, but because he based his
pedagogy on an adequate theory of teaching and enacted this theory
with consummate skill.[129] To assert otherwise would be to do violence
to the whole realistic fabric of Jesus' religious educational ministry,
and to transmogrify his pedagogy into a spooky affair.

From what has been written thus far in this section it is evident that
the religion teacher who wishes to use Jesus the master educator as a
basis for her own instructional practice must ground her pedagogy in
the general teaching theory which Jesus used. The general teaching
model which Jesus used was not some unique teaching theory somehow devised solely or exclusively for him. Rather, the general teaching
theory which Jesus used is the same basic fundamental teaching theory
which any effective educator employs.[130]

In order to better understand the most basic and most general theory
of teaching, it might be helpful to cast this theory into a representa-
tional model.

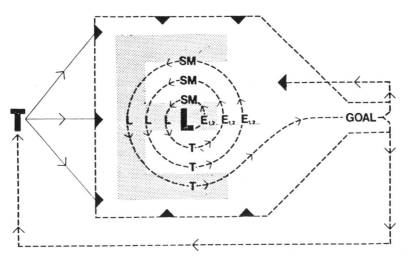

Before exploring the specific components in this general model of
teaching, let me point out two major features of this model. *First*, the
model highlights and accentuates the four major independent variables indispensable to every religious instruction act wherever and

whenever this act occurs. These four major variables are the teacher, the learner, the subject matter content, and the environment. *Second*, the model represents a system. For present purposes, a system is defined as any identifiable assemblage of complexly organized elements or subsystems which are interdependent, united by a common feedback network, and operates as an organized whole in order to attain some goal or produce some effect uniquely characteristic of the system functioning as a unit. Thus the teaching model which I am advancing embraces the countless advantages of any true system, most notably the way in which the system entails interactive relationships among the variables, relationships which themselves continually trigger that ongoing chain of correlative events which enable the system to fulfill itself.

In this model, T stands for the teacher, L for the learner, E for environment, and SM for subject matter content. The large square circumscribed by dotted lines represents the learning situation. Notice that the learning situation converges toward a tight, open-ended funnel, suggesting that the dynamics of the learning situation are targeted toward a desired outcome. Notice also that there is a large shaded-in E which covers the entire learning situation; this indicates that the learning situation is an environment, and therefore all four independent variables in the learning situation have their locus in an environment. Put another way, it indicates that everything contained within the large dotted-line funneled square comprises an aspect of the learning situation which is the instructional environment. Learning takes place within an environmental context and therefore is constantly being modified by all the relevant variables inside and outside it. The model indicates two functions of the teacher. The T outside the learning situation puts emphasis on the teacher as the initial and constant structurer of the learning situation. It is he who sets up the learning situation and continually adjusts it to promote the attainment of the desired learning outcomes. The T inside the dotted lines indicates that the teacher is also one aspect of the learning environment itself, a variable which dynamically interacts with the other variables in the ongoing instructional act. The environment is therefore one which is controlled by the teacher from both the outside and the inside, as it were. The model places the learner at the center of the pedagogical dynamic. This is where the cycle of learning (not teaching) begins. The cycle of teaching already began prior to this time when the teacher selected and structured a particular learning environment in which to situate the learner. This environment was selected and structured by the teacher on the basis of hypotheses he made on which kind of environment, subject matter content, and teacher variables are most predictive of success with this particular learner of group of learners.

In terms of learning, the model indicates that it is the learner—his maturational and developmental self, his perceptions, needs, and goals—that form the starting point. The circular lines indicate the path by which the learner learns; this is the path that the teaching act, therefore, will follow. First the learner acts as a stimulus to the teacher, setting in motion the actual teaching-learning process. The teacher responds to this stimulus by modifying his pedagogical behavior according to the nature and kind of learner stimuli he receives. The teacher, as an aspect of the instructional environment, modifies his own behavior so as to facilitate the attainment of the desired outcomes; as a variable outside the instructional environment, he modifies the entire environmental situation, as needed, to facilitate learning. Then the learner, as is indicated by the circular dotted lines, interacts with various aspects of this teacher-architected environment. $E_{1, 2}$; $E_{1, 2}$ . . . are symbols designating particularized aspects of the environment, for example, differentiated learning materials. (These particular environmental aspects differ from the large shaded-in E; the large E suggests that the teacher, the learners, the subject matter content, and particularized environmental factors also constitute larger, more global chunks of the environment with which the learner interacts.) Next, as suggested by the circular dotted line, the learner interacts with various kinds of subject matter content which the teacher has prepared or introduced; in our case this is biblical subject matter. Proceeding along the circular dotted lines, we see the overall process being continued until it terminates in the attainment of the desired objective. The circular dotted lines shooting into the funnel suggest that the instructional process is a task-oriented dynamic leading to the attainment of a desired objective or outcome. Each of the four independent variables acts and interacts with a structured learning situation to produce the outcome. It will be observed that the objective or outcome is open-ended as depicted in the model. This suggests that, once attained, the outcome acts as feedback both to increased or adjusted teacher behavior and to new learner activity; this feedback of the outcome to the teacher and the learner is shown by the dotted lines emanating from the outcome.

An absolutely necessary and extremely fruitful way for religious educators to significantly enhance the effectiveness of their Bible teaching is to consciously ground their pedagogical activity in a worthwhile theory of teaching such as that briefly outlined in this section. Regrettably there have been extremely few systematically constructed theories of instruction developed or utilized by religious educators. Those so-called "theories" of teaching advanced by religious education specialists generally have been speculative musings rather than genuine theory,[131] individualistic reports rather than scientific constructions,[132] and vague amorphous pronouncements about what religion teaching might be rather than carefully constructed systematic theory-building concerning that which teaching is and can be.[133]

The teaching theory advanced in this section brings to salience my longstanding thesis that the essence of all teaching consists in deliberatively structuring the pedagogical situation so that desired learning outcomes are thereby attained.[134]

To structure the pedagogical situation means that all four major variables necessarily present in every teaching act are so arranged that the intended learning objective is achieved. One reason why parents are generally more successful than school-based religious educators in teaching the Bible as religion to children and youth is that parents tend to be much more mindful than school-based religious educators of the paramount importance of structuring all four major pedagogical variables. School-based religious educators are frequently concerned with only one major variable (cognitive subject-matter content) to the relative neglect of the other three major instructional variables. This neglect seriously lessens the possibility that intended biblical learning outcomes will ever be attained by the students.

Since the Bible is basically a religious instruction book, and since the Bible deals among other things with the pedagogical activities of religious educators, it is hardly surprising that both the Old Testament and the New Testament are replete with examples of teaching incidents. Let us use the instructional activities of Jesus as an illustration of the importance of structuring the pedagogical situation in such a way that the four major variables are all accorded prominence.

Like all master religious educators of yesterday and today, Jesus had a few instructional failures as well as many instructional successes. Typically, Jesus' failures as a teacher occurred in large measure in those instances in which for one or another reason he did not accord active prominence to all four major variables in the pedagogical situation. The discourse on the Eucharist (Jn. 6:22–66) is a case in point. From an instructional point of view, Jesus failed to teach the learners that he is the Bread of Life, the Eucharist. "As a result of this discourse, many of his disciples went away and stopped accompanying him" (Jn. 6:66). When, however, Jesus deliberately and actively structured all four major pedagogical variables in the Last Supper, the learning outcome of the Bread of Life and the Eucharist attained by the learners present in that setting was decidedly different than what occurred in the earlier discourse on the Eucharist treated in the sixth chapter of John's Gospel.[135] Another example which illustrates the point made in this paragraph is that of the road to Emmaus (Lk. 24:13–35). When Jesus placed his primary instructional emphasis on only one of the four major pedagogical variables (subject-matter content of the cognitive verbal variety) as he was walking, the learners did not grasp the major point of the lesson Jesus was endeavoring to teach them. When, however, Jesus structured all four major instructional variables as the learners sat down with him at table, "their eyes were opened," and they understood as well as felt both the history of revelation and the consummation of revelation who was then in their very midst.

The concept of teaching as structuring the pedagogical situation in such a way that the four major instructional variables are operative reveals an essential difference between the teaching model and the preaching model of biblical pedagogics. Preaching places emphasis on only one of the four major variables, namely the subject-matter content. Furthermore, preaching unduly restricts the subject-matter content to just the verbal mode. The wide repertoire of instructional behaviors available to the religious educator is reduced in the preaching model to only one primary instructional behavior, namely that of lecturing. Small wonder that preaching, like all forms of lecturing, is one of the least successful instructional techniques for facilitating affective and lifestyle outcomes.[136] The theory of teaching and the strategy of structuring the pedagogical situation I am advocating surely show that teaching the Bible as religion is far more complex than standing in front of a group of learners at home or school or in a neighborhood group "presenting" or "imparting" the Good News. In short, the religious educator who wishes his Bible teaching to be successful should move away from the preaching model and the "presenting"-"imparting" strategy toward a teaching model and a structured pedagogical situation strategy.

Religious educators who teach the Bible as religion should open themselves to the many worthwhile pedagogical advances made during this century in the approaches, styles, strategies, methods, and techniques of teaching. Pedagogical approaches such as the social-science approach,[137] pedagogical styles like the psychological style or the life-experience style, pedagogical strategies like the discovery strategy[138] or the gaming strategy,[139] pedagogical methods such as the problem-solving method[140] or the affective method,[141] and pedagogical techniques like the role-playing technique[142] can significantly assist the religious educator to teach the Bible more effectively.

An educator teaching the Bible as religion should not close himself to the magnificent new advances made in scientifically-based pedagogy during this century just because one or another instructional strategy or technique is not specifically found in the Bible. Teaching biblically does not mean a slavish copying of biblical pedagogical practices or a narrow-minded stance which makes no allowances for instructional advances made after the first century of the Christian era. It must be remembered that the religious educators of the Old Testament and the New Testament were men and women of their times, persons who therefore were simply not able to avail themselves of the many fine pedagogical practices which were developed only centuries after these persons had died. Furthermore, contemporary teachers of the Bible who carefully examine the Scriptures from purely a scientific pedagogical point of view might be pleasantly surprised to discover a greater variety of instructional practices used by biblical personages than modern religious educators might typically imagine.[143]

Opening oneself to the great advances in scientifically based pedagogy developed during this century suggests that the religious educator vigorously eschew that kind of narrow mentality which suggests that so-called "secular" instructional practices may be unsuitable for religious instruction and that all teaching procedures must be evaluated on the basis of whether or not they are congruent with what is termed "God's method of teaching."[144] Unless one wishes to adhere to a radically dualistic view of religion and of nature, there is no such thing as a "secular" or "profane" teaching procedure as contrasted to a "sacred" or "holy" pedagogical practice. From the theological perspective, the doctrine of Creation, a doctrine existentially reinforced by the Incarnation, means that God is present and operative in every reality (including pedagogical practice) as that reality is in itself. From the educational point of view, there seems to be not the slightest sliver of justification for the claim that a particular pedagogical procedure is substantially or even accidentally secular in itself, and that some other instructional practice is substantially or accidentally sacred by nature. It is patently nonsensical to triumphantly assert that one or another general method of instruction is really "God's method." The silly and at bottom unbiblical attitudes of bifurcating instructional practice into the disparate realms of sacred and secular, and of asserting righteously that such-and-such a general pedagogical method is really "God's method of teaching," have wreaked considerable havoc on religious instruction all along the line, especially in blocking the infusion of invigorating modern scientifically based pedagogical practice into the lifeblood of religious instruction.

The Bible is not a treatise on the theory of teaching per se, or a synthesis of the findings of carefully conducted empirical research on pedagogical procedure. Consequently, the Bible is not a validator of instructional practice. One or another theological or literary interpretation of the Bible can validly assert what a particular pedagogical practice means to that theological or literary interpretation of the Bible. But this assertion is of a fundamentally different genre than the assertion that the Bible validates a particular pedagogical practice qua pedagogical practice.[145] Consequently, a religious educator who wishes to know whether a particular pedagogical practice in teaching the Bible will work or why it works will have to go to a theory of teaching to find the answers. On the other hand, a religious educator who wishes to learn a biblical-theological view of this pedagogical practice will have to go to biblical theology to learn the answer. Thus a religious educator who wishes to improve his instructional practice in teaching the Bible should immerse himself in the theory of teaching and in the skill of pedagogy rather than look to the Bible as the primary source for improving his teaching procedures.

If the religious educator is to be effective in teaching the Bible, he must perforce ground his pedagogy in social science. Bible teaching, after all, is essentially a matter of communication and facilitation of learning.[146] By definition, the processes of communication and the facilitation of learning fall under the purview of social science rather than theology.[147] To paraphrase Leon McKenzie, seeking solutions to instructional problems in theology or in the Bible is akin to seeking solutions to electrical problems in dentistry or in geometry.[148] Once the religious educator has become well-versed in both the theory of teaching and in the practical skill of the pedagogical process, he is then in a position to effectively incorporate religious/theological/historical/literary and other kinds of relevant content in such a fashion that the learners will understand the Bible, feel the Bible, and live the Bible in their personal and ecclesial lives.

Notes

1. For a further development of this point, see James Michael Lee, "The Authentic Source of Religious Instruction," in *Religious Education and Theology*, ed. Norma H. Thompson (Birmingham, Ala.: Religious Education Press, 1982), pp. 110–116.
2. Quite a few religious educationists and educators seem to forget this crucial fact. For two representative examples, see Jack L. Seymour, "Contemporary Approaches to Christian Education," in *Chicago Theological Seminary Register* LXIX (Spring, 1979), pp. 1–10; Jack L. Seymour, "Approaches to Christian Education," in *Contemporary Approaches to Christian Education*, ed. Jack L. Seymour and Donald E. Miller (Nashville, Tenn.: Abingdon, 1982), p. 32.
3. On this point, see John H. Westerhoff III, "Liturgy and Catechesis: A Christian Marriage," in Gwen Kennedy Neville and John H. Westerhoff III, *Learning Through Liturgy* (New York: Seabury, 1978), pp. 91–106.
4. Sara P. Little, "Religious Instruction," in *Contemporary Approaches to Christian Education*, ed. Seymour and Miller, p. 38.
5. It is the proper task of religious educationists to develop sophisticated pedagogical research, theories, and practices. While such development activity lies outside the province or competence of biblicists, nonetheless biblical scholars can be legitimately expected to incorporate pedagogical research, theories, and practices in that portion of their efforts devoted to teaching the Bible or helping others to teach the Bible.
6. Since the early or mid-70s a few vanguard scholars among Evangelical Protestants have begun to become thoroughly immersed in high-level empirical research, theory development, and practice generation in field of religious instruction.
7. John H. Westerhoff III, "Scripture and Education: Challenges Facing Religious Education," *Religious Education* LXXVII (September–October, 1982), pp. 472–473.
8. This statement should not be taken to imply that religious instruction constitutes *the* or even *a* primary task of the biblicist. Authentic religious instruction cannot and ought not be imperialistic. To be sure, biblics is its own autonomous field with its own separate and distinct ontic existence. My statement in the body of the text suggests that the biblicist can and as far as possible should help imbue the work of religious instruction with the biblical spirit and with the findings of his scholarship by placing the fruits of his

research at the disposal of religious educationists in a manner understandable and usable to a person who is a pedagogical rather than a biblical expert.

9. Mary C. Boys, "Religious Education and Contemporary Biblical Scholarship," *Religious Education* LXXIV (March–April, 1979), p. 183.

10. Eugene F. Trester, "Adult Biblical Learning in Community," *Religious Education* LXXVII (September–October, 1982), p. 540.

11. Aurelius Augustinus, *De Genesi ad Litteram Libri Duodecim*, 1, 9, 20.

12. Thomas Aquinas, *De Veritate*, q. 12, a. 2, *corpus*.

13. See Gerhard von Rad, *Old Testament Theology*, volume II, trans. D. M. G. Stalker (New York: Harper & Row, 1965), pp. 6–315.

14. See, for example, Rom. 1:13–15.

15. 1 Cor. 1:17.

16. Robert Alley views Jesus as a religious leader and a religious educator who, for instructional purposes, treats the Old Testament in three basic ways; (1) interpreting the whole of the Old Testament and also particular texts for the learners; (2) making innovations in the Old Testament text for the sake of wider human growth and growth in faith-hope-love; (3) making iconoclastic statements in which he challenged classic rabbinical doctrines and dogma— especially those of a legalistic variety—in favor of the law of love and the inner meaning of the Scriptures. Robert S. Alley, *Revolt Against the Faithful* (Philadelphia: Lippincott, 1970), pp. 22–39.

17. I believe that liberation theologians such as José Porfirio Miranda and some others are guilty of politico-economic imperialism when they attempt to transmogrify the Bible into an essentially political or economic document. It is well to remember that spirituality and religious experience have flourished in all kinds of political contexts and economic situations. See José Porfirio Miranda, *Marx and the Bible*, trans. John Eagleson (Maryknoll, N.Y.: Orbis, 1971).

18. Bernard J. F. Lonergan, *Method in Theology* (New York: Herder and Herder, 1972), p. 144.

19. Karl Rahner, "Theology," *Sacramentum Mundi* VI (New York: Herder and Herder, 1970), p. 235.

20. Raymond E. Brown, *Biblical Reflection on Crises Facing the Church* (New York: Paulist, 1975).

21. Helmut Thielicke, *The Evangelical Faith*, volume II, trans. and ed. Geoffrey W. Bromiley (Grand Rapids, Mich.: Eerdmans, 1977), p. 3.

22. On this important point, see Valerio Tonini, "Commentaire," dans Stanilas Breton, redacteur, "Langage Religieux, Langage Théologique," dans Enrico Castelli, redacteur, *Debats sur le Langage Théologique* (Paris: Aubier, 1969), pp. 127–128; also James Michael Lee, *The Content of Religious Instruction* (Birmingham, Ala.: Religious Education Press, in preparation).

23. Raymond E. Brown, *New Testament Essays* (Milwaukee: Bruce, 1965), pp. 30–33.

24. I give the term "religionology" to *the* theory of religion. On this point, see Lee, "The Authentic Source of Religious Instruction," p. 154.

25. For a fine scholarly intersection of biblical theology specifically with the field of religious instruction, see Mary C. Boys, *Biblical Interpretation in Religious Education* (Birmingham, Ala.: Religious Education Press, 1980).
26. John L. McKenzie, *The Two-Edged Sword: An Interpretation of the Old Testament* (Milwaukee: Bruce, 1956), pp. 20–21.
27. See C. Ellis Nelson, *Where Faith Begins* (Richmond, Va.: Knox, 1967), pp. 174–184.
28. John L. McKenzie, *A Theology of the New Testament* (Garden City, N.Y.: Doubleday, 1974), p. 31.
29. Even though various branches of theological science study and explore the words of the Bible from a scientific, cognitive, and therefore not in a directly religious fashion, still the theologian using the words of the Bible in his scientific inquiry recognizes and treats biblical words as essentially words of religious experience.
30. On this point, though from an admittedly different basic perspective, see Gabriel Moran, *The Present Revelation* (New York: Herder and Herder, 1972), pp. 74–148.
31. The National Catholic Directory defines catechetics as "a form of the ministry of the word which proclaims and teaches." (Catechetics is that branch of religious education whose foundations, goals, content, personnel, and legitimacy are authoritatively determined by and are politically controlled by the official Roman Catholic *ecclesiasticum*.) Inasmuch as the *ecclesiasticum* officially declares in several official documents that catechetics is a form of the ministry of the word, Berard Marthaler has no other choice than to adopt this position wholesale. Marianne Sawicki, a student of Marthaler's, also holds this view. Quite possibly the National Catholic Directory, and its unquestioning followers, are implicitly suggesting that one major difference between catechetics and religious instruction is that catechetics is exclusively a verbal affair while religious instruction is far wider in scope. National Conference of Catholic Bishops, *Sharing the Light of Faith* (Washington, D.C.: United States Catholic Conference, 1979), #32 (p. 18); Berard L. Marthaler, "Evangelization and Catechesis: Word, Memory, Witness," *Living Light* XVI (Spring, 1979), p. 35; Marianne Sawicki, "The Power and Ministry of the Word," *Living Light* XVII (Summer, 1980), p. 150.
32. Marianne Sawicki erroneously claims that cognition directly yields affect. The basic reason underlying her error in this regard appears to be her failure to adequately distinguish correlation and cause, namely that there is a fundamental difference between asserting that some affects accompany cognition and asserting that cognition causes affect. Berard Marthaler makes the similar error when he states that the ministry of the word is directed at nurturing a living, active, and conscious faith in persons and in communities. Philosophically and psychologically, cognition and affect are two distinct functional domains; hence one cannot yield the other, even though in everyday holistic human activity, both are intertwined. Sawicki, "The Power and Ministry of the Word," pp. 150–158; Marthaler, "Evangelization and Cate-

chesis: Word, Memory, Witness," p. 35. Of interest is that in claiming that words can nurture faith, Marthaler contradicts what he wrote a year earlier when he contended, just as gratuitiously, that no human activity can ever increase faith. Berard L. Marthaler, "Socialization as a Model for Catechesis," in *Foundations of Religious Education*, ed. Padraic O'Hare (New York: Paulist, 1978), p. 75.

33. Persons who equate religious instruction with the ministry of the word seem too prone to equate teaching with preaching or with proclaiming. Such individuals consciously or unconsciously operate out of a preaching model rather than out of a teaching model. On this point, see James Michael Lee, "The *Teaching* of Religion," in *Toward a Future for Religious Education*, ed. James Michael Lee and Patrick C. Rooney (Dayton, Ohio: Pflaum, 1970), pp. 56–59. For a position which advocates that teaching is preaching, see Domenico Grasso, *Proclaiming God's Message: A Study in the Theology of Preaching* (Notre Dame, Ind.: University of Notre Dame Press, 1965), p. 58. Lois LeBar properly contends that preaching and teaching are two separate functions having two separate sets of procedures. She laments the fact that while contemporary Christianity has given much scientific attention to preaching, it has given relatively little such attention to teaching. Lois LeBar, *Education that is Christian* (Old Tappan, N.J.: Revell, 1958), pp. 20–23.

34. I deliberately write "in the Bible" rather than "about the Bible" because I firmly believe that biblical religious instruction should be essentially in the Bible as contrasted to about the Bible.

35. Didier Piveteau, "Biblical Pedagogics," in *Toward a Future for Religious Education*, ed. Lee and Rooney, p. 95.

36. Edgar Dale's celebrated cone of experience is a model which illustrates in graphic form the relative lack of immediacy which words have with respect to all-powerful direct experience. Starting at the base of cone (the most potent and educable of our encounters with reality) and working toward the tip, the discrete elements comprising the cone of experience are: (1) direct purposeful experiences; (2) contrived experiences; (3) dramatized experiences; (4) demonstrations; (5) study trips; (6) exhibits; (7) educational television; (8) motion pictures; (9) recordings, radio, still pictures; (10) visual symbols; (11) verbal symbols. Though Dale's model is specifically targeted toward the anatomy of the instructional process, nonetheless it is applicable to other phases of intentional and nonintentional education. Edgar Dale, *Audiovisual Methods in Teaching*, 3rd edition (New York: Holt, Rinehart and Winston, 1969), pp. 107–135.

37. On this last point, see Joseph Anthony Wagner and Robert W. Smith, *Teacher's Guide to Storytelling* (Dubuque, Iowa: Brown, 1958), pp. 51–66; Anne Pellowsici, *The World of Storytelling* (New York: Bowker, 1977), pp. 99–175.

38. As I observe in *The Flow of Religious Instruction*, the essential nature and form of teaching consists in deliberatively structuring the learning situation. James Michael Lee, *The Flow of Religious Instruction* (Birmingham, Ala.:

Religious Education Press, 1973), pp. 200–201; 207–208; 234–237; 243–247. An effective story is one which is characterized by a carefully orchestrated and consciously goal-directed set of verbal procedures. See Marie L. Shedlock, *The Art of the Storyteller*, 3rd edition revised (New York: Dover, 1951).

39. For a fine treatment of the variety of storytelling in religious and non-religious cultures, see Pelowsici, *The World of Storytelling*.

40. Piveteau then continues: "(Of course, in the past God used men for the channels of his action, but this temporality was the temporality of those men and not a temporality of God.)" Didier Piveteau, "Biblical Pedagogics," in *Toward a Future for Religious Education*, ed. Lee and Rooney, p. 109.

41. There is a sense in which Friederich Schleiermacher comes out of this tradition. Schleiermacher tends to use personal religious feeling as the sole major touchstone of the Bible. See Friederich Schleiermacher, *The Christian Faith*, ed. H. R. Mackintosh and J. S. Stewart, trans. D. M. Baillie et al. (Edinburgh: Clark, 1928), especially pp. 3–78.

42. Georg Hegel and Wilhelm Dilthey were especially influential in this connection. Schleiermacher also came to grips with this issue. See G. W. F. Hegel, *Philosophy of History* trans. J. Sibree (New York: Collier, 1901), pp. 43–161; W. Dilthey, *Selected Writings*, ed. and trans. H. P. Rickman (Cambridge, England: Cambridge University Press, 1976), pp. 170–263; Friederich Schleiermacher, *The Life of Jesus*, ed. Jack C. Verheyden, trans. S. Maclean Gilmour (Philadelphia: Fortress, 1975), pp. 8–22.

43. Raymond Brown takes pains to note that the official Roman Catholic *ecclesiasticum* "teaches a *qualified* historical estimation of the Gospels." Brown cites a 1964 Biblical Commission Instruction to the effect that while the truths of the Gospels are indeed true, nonetheless these truths were developed historically through the end of the apostolic ministry and were filtered psychologically through the personalities of the individual evangelists. See Raymond E. Brown, *The Community of the Beloved Disciple* (New York: Paulist, 1979), p. 21.

44. Brown, *Biblical Reflections on Crises Facing the Church*, pp. 10–12.

45. A very bright young biblical theologian who received his graduate degree in biblics at Rome three years ago told me, in a dejected tone of voice, that much of what he had learned in biblical theology is already out of date.

46. The National Catholic Directory also affirms this point. See National Conference of Catholic Bishops, *Sharing the Light of Faith*, #16 (pp. 9–10).

47. Roman Catholics would add "as determined by the *magisterium*."

48. Karl Rahner notes that the ultimate unity of these theologies is "guaranteed by the Church's awareness of its faith." This statement seems a bit too cognitive and insufficiently experiential. I would say, rather, that the ultimate unity of these theologies is guaranteed by the ecclesia's lived experience of its faith/hope/charity. My reformulation also eases Rahner's apparent exclusivity of emphasis on the *magisterium*. I do agree with Rahner, however, in asserting that one of the major tasks of a biblical theologian is to strive to replace the

plurality of biblical theologies with the unity of a higher theoretical system. See Karl Rahner, "Bible: A: Theology," *Sacramentum Mundi*, volume 1 (New York: Herder and Herder, 1970), p. 176.

49. See Kurt Frör, *Biblische Hermeneutik: Zur Schriftauslegung in Predigt und Unterricht* (München: Kaiser, 1961), pp. 260–271.

50. Paul J. Tillich, "Foreword," in Martin Kähler, *The So-Called Historical Jesus and the Historic, Biblical Christ*, trans. and ed. Carl E. Braaten (Philadelphia: Fortress, 1964), p. xii.

51. See Rudolph Bultmann, "New Testament and Mythology," in *Kerygma and Myth: A Theological Debate*, ed. Hans Werner Bartsch, trans. Reginald H. Fuller(London: S.P.C.K., 1957), pp. 1–44.

52. My comments here are not intended as a confirmation—or a rejection—of Bultmann's hypothesis, but rather as one major implication which Bultmann's thesis has for the task of religious instruction.

53. On this point, see Paul Hoffmann, "Ich weiss was Ihr braucht," in *Ich will euer Gott werden*, ed. Helmut Merklin und Erich Zenger (Stuttgart: Katholisches Bibelwerk, 1981), pp. 153–155, 174–176.

54. Ernst Käsemann, *Essays on New Testament Themes*, trans. W. J. Montague (Naperville, Ill.: Allenson, 1964), pp. 48–62.

55. A central and sometimes overlooked issue in this connection is the epistemology of truth. One has severe difficulty in felicitously harmonizing the inerrancy of Scripture (inspiration) with occasional nonobjective and nonfactual passages in Scripture only when one holds a constricted and univocal epistemology of truth. Epistemologically speaking, truth is not simply the conformity of the mind to reality. Truth is also the validity of what one communicates according to what the communicator intends to communicate. Additionally, as the philosophical Existentialists affirm, truth is neither and both of the above statements; in such a view, truth simply *is*.

56. Interview with Hudson Baggett, November 3, 1982.

57. Two points are relevant here. First, most advances in cognitive church doctrine based on Scripture were in the beginning typically held in disfavor and often even condemned by the ruling ecclesiastical cadre of the time. Furthermore, most Christian religious bodies assert that when there is a conflict between personal conviction and official church doctrine, the person has the obligation to inform himself about official church doctrine as fully as possible and then to form his convictions along the line of official cognitive church doctrine. However, if these sincere and whole-hearted efforts fail, then the individual is obliged to follow his conscience.

58. This is also a foundational principle of biblical hermeneutic. See Rudolph Hermann, *Bibel und Hermeneutik*, Band III (Göttingen, Bundesrepublik Deutschland: Vandenhoeck und Ruprecht, 1971), pp. 100–215.

59. Thomas H. Groome, "Principles and Pedagogy in Bible Study," *Religious Education* LXXVII (September–October, 1982), p. 505. The text and context of Groome's own writings suggest strongly that he views the text and context of the learner as revolving around a cognitive axis. I differ sharply with him on this point. See, for example, Thomas H. Groome, *Christian Re-*

ligious Education (New York: Harper & Row, 1980), especially pp. 17 (footnote 5), 149, 185–201; Thomas H. Groome, "Christian Education for Freedom: A Shared Praxis Approach," in *Foundations of Religious Education*, ed. Padraic O'Hare (New York: Paulist, 1978), pp. 22–26; Thomas Groome "Shared Christian Praxis," in *Lumen Vitae XXXI* (April–June, 1976), pp. 186–208.

60. See Gerhard von Rad, *Biblical Interpretations in Preaching*, trans. John E. Steely (Nashville, Tenn.: Abingdon, 1977), pp. 16–17.

61. See Georgia Harkness, *Toward Understanding the Bible* (New York: Scribner's, 1954), pp. 21–23.

62. From a holistic standpoint, cognitive interpretation also accompanies the encounter with the text, or more accurately, is a necessary dimension of the encounter. In the body of the text, I am considering the formal cognitive interpretation of Scripture.

63. Sara Little, *The Role of the Bible in Contemporary Christian Education* (Richmond, Va.: Knox, 1961), pp. 166–168.

64. In every pedagogical situation, the religious educator is also a learner in the genuine sense of that word. The more that a pedagogical situation is authentic and relevant and alive, the more the religious educator can learn. On this point, see Iris V. Cully, *Imparting the Word: The Bible in Christian Education* (Philadelphia: Westminster, 1962), pp. 145–154. (On pedagogical grounds, I emphatically disagree both with Cully's conceptualization of the religious educator as a "proclaimer of the Good News" and with her view that the function of religious instruction is "imparting." To be sure, such a conceptualization almost guarantees that religious education will be the opposite of what Cully wishes it to be, namely authentic and relevant and alive.)

65. On this point, see Boys, *Biblical Interpretation in Religious Education*, pp. 294–296.

66. Benjamin S. Bloom et al., *Taxonomy of Educational Objectives: Handbook I: Cognitive Domain* (New York: McKay, 1956).

67. In delineating these desired learning outcomes, I am deliberately following the ascending order of divisions within the cognitive domain. These divisions, as set forth in the Bloom taxonomy, are knowledge, comprehension, application, analysis, synthesis, and evaluation. Within almost all of these broad categories are contained various divisions and subdivisions.

68. Rachel Henderlite, *Forgiveness and Hope: A Theological Basis for Christian Education* (Richmond, Va.: Knox, 1961), pp. 41–45.

69. On this point I strongly disagree with the rationalistic position espoused by some individuals with respect to the use of hermeneutics in past (and present) religious instruction. James Sanders, for example, claims that the Bible must be read originally and primarily from a theological vantage point. Only later and derivatively may a reader seek to gain religious implications from this basal theological interpretation. As I observed toward the outset of this chapter, the Bible is primarily a religious book written for religious instruction purposes. It is only secondarily, though very importantly, a theological book (as well as a book of literature, a book of culture, a book of

psychology, and so forth). Thus the primary reading and the anchor interpretation of the Bible ought always to be religious rather than theological,
literary, psychological, and so forth. The Bible contains theological implications, literary implications, psychological implications, and so forth. See
James A. Sanders, "Hermeneutics," in *Interpreter's Dictionary of the Bible*,
supplement (Nashville, Tenn.: Abingdon, 1976), p. 406.
70. Karl Rahner and Herbert Vorgrimler are guilty of theological imperialism when they erroneously assert that exegesis is a theological discipline.
Exegesis is a separate and distinct field, a field which integrates historical
principles, archeological data, philological material, anthropological findings, and so on, to critically examine any kind of text written in literary form,
theological or nontheological. Most specifically nonquantitative sciences,
fields, and disciplines all use exegesis and hermeneutics—exegesis and hermeneutics which are decidedly nontheological in nature. Theology, to be
sure, utilizes exegesis and hermeneutics. However, the use of these important
cognitive tools in theology no more makes exegesis and hermeneutics theological disciplines or fields than does the use of words in theological treatises
make linguistics a theological discipline. Karl Rahner and Herbert
Vorgrimler, *Theological Dictionary*, 1st edition, ed. Cornelius Ernst and
trans. Richard Strachan (New York: Herder and Herder, 1965), p. 159.
71. See Jeffrey Keefe, "The Learning of Attitudes and Values," in *Toward a
Future for Religious Education*, ed. Lee and Rooney (Dayton, Ohio: Pflaum,
1970), pp. 30–54.
72. Elsewhere I argue that love is even more fundamental and central to
religion than is faith. See Lee, "The Authentic Source of Religious Instruction," pp. 103–105.
73. In logic, a predicative is that which is affirmed or denied of the subject in
a proposition. For a brief but meaty discussion of theological language as
predicative and religious language as normative, see Valerio Tonini, "Commentaire," pp. 127–128.
74. Lee, *The Content of Religious Instruction*, chapter 6.
75. See, for example, Alfred Jules Ayer, *Language, Truth and Logic* (New
York: Dover, 1952), p. 58.
76. For a review of some pertinent empirical research on attitudes, with
particular attention to religious instruction, see Lee, *The Flow of Religious
Instruction*, pp. 106–119.
77. Gordon Allport, "Attitudes," in *A Handbook of Social Psychology*, ed.
Carl A. Murchison (Worcester, Mass.: Clark University Press, 1935), p. 806.
78. Mark van Doren and Maurice Samuel, *In the Beginning, Love: Dialogues on the Bible* (New York: Day, 1973).
79. Morton Kelsey, *Can Christians Be Educated?* (Birmingham, Ala.: Religious Education Press, 1977), p. 40.
80. Ronald Goldman, *Religious Thinking from Childhood to Adolescence*
(New York: Seabury, 1965).
81. Ibid., pp. 102–115.
82. For a summary of these three investigations, see David Elkind, "The

Child's Conception of His Religious Identity," *Lumen Vitae* XIX (December, 1964), pp. 635–646. Of interest is that Elkind is himself a psychologist specializing in the cognitive development of children.

83. For the standard treatment of confluent education, see George Isaac Brown, *Human Teaching For Human Learning* (New York: Viking, 1972).

84. For a development of this point, see James Michael Lee, *The Shape of Religious Instruction* (Birmingham, Ala.: Religious Education Press, 1971), pp. 55–65.

85. The point I am making here is reinforced rather than diminished by the fact that much of the material in this verse is an allusion to Is. 29:18–19; 35:5–6; 61:1 which refers to phenomena which Jews of that time expected of a Messiah.

86. Michel Dujarier, *A History of the Catechumenate: The First Six Centuries*, trans. Edward J. Haasl (New York: Sadlier, 1979).

87. Thomas Merton, *Opening the Bible* (London: Allen and Unwin, 1972), pp. 8–9, 24–25.

88. Abraham Maslow, *Religions, Values, and Peak-Experiences* (New York: Penguin, 1964), pp. vii, xvi, 26–27.

89. For a sophisticated advocacy of mysticism as a major goal of religious instruction, see David Arthur Bickimer, *Christ the Placenta: Letters to My Mentor on Religious Education* (Birmingham, Ala.: Religious Education Press, 1983).

90. Religious educators who hold a transcendist position usually deny the possibility of deliberatively structuring the pedagogical situation in such a way as to facilitate mystical experiences. Religious educators who hold an immanentist position usually affirm the possibility of deliberatively structuring the pedagogical situation in such a way as to facilitate mystical experiences. Experimental research such as that conducted by Ralph Hood tends to support the immanentist position. For a survey of transcendism and immanentism in religious education, see Ian P. Knox, *Above or Within?: The Supernatural in Religious Education* (Birmingham, Ala.: Religious Education Press, 1976). See also Ralph W. Hood, "Eliciting Mystical States of Consciousness with Semistructured Nature Experiences," *Journal for the Scientific Study of Religion* XVI (June, 1977), pp. 155–163.

91. Pleasant Roscoe Hightower, *Biblical Information in Relation to Character and Conduct* (Iowa City, Iowa: University of Iowa, 1930), p. 33.

92. Martin J. Maehr, "The Relationship of Bible Information to Certain Specific Beliefs and Practices," unpublished doctoral dissertation, University of Nebraska, 1955.

93. H. J. Eysenck, "Symposium: The Development of Moral Values in Children: VII—The Contribution of Learning Theory," *British Journal of Educational Psychology* XXX (February, 1960), italics deleted.

94. Lawrence Richards, "The Teacher as Interpreter of the Bible," in *Religious Education* LXXVII (September–October, 1982), p. 516.

95. For a taxonomy approach to teaching lifestyle content, see Norman W. Steinaker and M. Robert Bell, *The Experiential Taxonomy* (New York: Aca-

demic Press, 1979). For one kind of theoretical grounding for a pedagogy of lifestyle content, see James E. Walker and Thomas M. Shea, *Behavior Modification* (St. Louis: Mosby, 1980). For instructional approaches and procedures in teaching lifestyle content, see Sivasailam Thiagarajan, *Experiential Learning Packages* (Englewood Cliffs, N.J.: Educational Technology Publications, 1980); David Wolsk, *An Experience-Centered Curriculum* (Paris: UNESCO Press, 1975); Jo Ann Freiberg, "Experiential Moral Learning," unpublished master's thesis, University of Alabama in Birmingham, 1978).

96. This basic principle, affirmed centuries ago by Aristotle and Aquinas, has been repeatedly confirmed in the empirical research investigations of modern social scientists.

97. See, for example, the many empirical research studies cited in Merton P. Strommen, ed., *Research on Religious Development* (New York: Hawthorn, 1971).

98. For a fuller development of this point and its implications, see Lee, *The Flow of Religious Instruction*, pp. 206–229. See also Little, "Religious Instruction," in *Contemporary Approaches to Christian Education*, ed. Seymour and Miller, p. 39.

99. I must emphasize that my use of these illustrative examples is just simply that, namely my use of *incidents recorded in the Bible*. My use of these examples in no way implies or fails to imply that Jesus actually spoke, felt, or conducted himself precisely in the fashion recorded in the Scripture. My emphasis is on the recorded incident rather than on the actual objective historicity of the incident. Both for inspiration and for pedagogical structure, it is immaterial whether the event I am treating actually happened precisely as recorded, whether the original actual event was later embellished by the inspired writer for religious instruction purposes, or whether the event is totally a myth in the Bultmann sense.

100. For a review of this research with specific reference to religious instruction, see Lee, *The Flow of Religious Instruction*, pp. 58–148. For reviews of some of this research with specific reference to general instruction, see Brenda Munsey, ed., *Moral Development, Moral Education, and Kohlberg* (Birmingham, Ala.: Religious Education Press, 1980; Herbert L. Leff, *"Experience, Environment, and Human Potentials"* (New York: Oxford University Press, 1978); David Stea, "Space, Territory, and Human Movements," in *Environmental Psychology*, ed. Harold M. Proshansky, William H. Ittelson, and Leanne G. Rivlin (New York: Holt, Rinehart & Winston, 1970), pp. 37–42.

101. Bickimer, *Christ the Placenta: Letters to My Mentor on Religious Education*.

102. Melvin Worthington, "New Testament Educational Practices," in *Christian Education*, ed. Douglas J. Simpson (Nashville, Tenn.: Randall, 1978), p. 57.

103. For a nice simple summary of some of the major theses in this heated dispute, see Dorothy Jean Furnish, *Explaining the Bible to Children*

(Nashville, Tenn.: Abingdon, 1975), pp. 81–100. Though Furnish's book is addressed specifically to biblical pedagogics with children, nevertheless most of the points which she makes apply equally well to biblical pedagogics with youth and with adults. My only reservation about Furnish's treatment is that she views teaching the Bible as chiefly a verbal and a cognitive affair (e.g. "To teach the Bible is to talk about life" p. 81). Talking is a verbal activity.

104. These three principles represent a reworking, and in some sense a restructuring, of the three principles of teaching biblically offered by Dorothy Furnish. See ibid., p. 87.

105. In an easy-to-read book on experiential education for religious outcomes, see John Hendrix and Lela Hendrix, *Experiential Education: XED* (Nashville, Tenn.: Abingdon, 1975).

106. On the topic of experience as content, see Lee, *The Shape of Religious Instruction*, pp. 13–19.

107. For a fine development of this important point, see Luis Alonzo Schökel, *The Inspired Word*, trans. Francis Martin (New York: Herder and Herder, 1965), pp. 370–376.

108. For a further development of this point, see the first chapter in Lee, *The Content of Religious Instruction*, in preparation.

109. In using the term "lesson" here and in my other writings, I am not denoting an instructional event which takes place in a classroom or in any other kind of formal setting. Rather, I am denoting an instructional event which is structured in one way or another by the religion teacher regardless of setting.

110. Quite possibly a fundamental reason why religious educationists and educators have clung so tenaciously to the erroneous method-content duality is because they have generally never begun to probe deeply the dynamics of the teaching-learning act. Advocacy of the method-content duality (sometimes referred to as the process-content duality) recurs over and over again in religious instruction literature. See, for example, Jack L. Seymour and Carol A. Wehrheim, "Faith Seeking Understanding: Interpretation as a Task of Christian Education," in *Contemporary Approaches to Christian Education*, ed. Seymour and Miller, pp. 136–140. For critiques of the method-content duality, albeit from two very different perspectives, see Gabriel Moran, "The Future of Catechetics," *Living Light* V (Spring, 1968), pp. 9–10; Lee, *The Flow of Religious Instruction*, pp. 28–31.

111. Lee, "The Authentic Source of Religious Instruction," in *Religious Education and Theology*, ed. Thompson, p. 173. I should also note that the use of the term "method" here follows popular parlance. I prefer the term "procedure" in this case, since in my terminology a method is a level of procedure rather than procedure itself.

112. On this point, see Didier Piveteau, "Biblical Pedagogics," in *Toward a Future for Religious Education*, ed. Lee and Rooney, p. 111.

113. Both on theoretical and on empirical grounds, I contend that Josef Goldbrunner seriously errs when he claims that instructional practice is simply a "handmaid" to subject-matter content. See Josef Goldbrunner, "Cate-

chetical Method as Handmaid of Kerygma," in *Teaching All Nations*, ed. Johannes Hofinger, revised and partly translated by Clifford Howell (Freiburg im Bresgau, Bundesrepublik Deutschland: Herder, 1961), pp. 108–121.

114. See, for example, Elizabeth Achtemeier, *The Old Testament and the Proclamation of the Gospel* (Philadelphia: Westminster, 1973), p. 19. In Achtemeier's view, the pedagogical process "is only a tool for proclaiming the word." For another disvaluation of structural content though from a different perspective, see Malcolm L. Warford, *The Necessary Illusion* (Philadelphia: United Church Press, 1976), pp. 71–73.

115. See James Michael Lee, "Process Content in Religious Instruction," in *Process and Relationship*, ed. Iris V. Cully and Kendig Brubaker Cully (Birmingham, Ala.: Religious Education Press, 1978), pp. 22–30.

116. Léon Arthur Elchinger, "The Bible and Catechesis," in *Teaching All Nations*, ed. Hofinger, p. 147.

117. Groome, *Christian Religious Education*, pp. 184–232.

118. Harold C. Lyon Jr., *Learning to Feel—Feeling to Learn* (Columbus, Ohio: Merrill, 1971), pp. 145–147.

119. For a fuller treatment of this taxonomy, see Lee, *The Flow of Religious Instruction*, pp. 28–38.

120. One of the riches of the Bible is that it can be fruitfully examined from a wide variety of perspectives such as theology, literature, psychology, pedagogy, and so forth. For example, Maria Kassel endeavors to show that many of the findings which Carl Jung discovered in his years of psychotherapeutic practice can also be found in the Bible, such as archetypes, animus and anima, the dark brother, and so forth. Maria Kassel, *Biblische Urbilder: Tiefenpsychologie Auslesung nach C. G. Jung* (München: Pfeiffer, 1980).

121. Melvin Worthington, "New Testament Educational Practices," pp. 57–61.

122. Gerhard von Rad, *God at Work in Israel*, trans. John H. Marks (Nashville, Tenn.: Abingdon, 1974), p. 15.

123. For a fine scientific examination of the pedagogy of Jesus, see J. T. Dillon, "The Effectiveness of Jesus as a Teacher," *Lumen Vitae* XXXVI (April–June, 1981), pp. 135–162.

124. See Locke E. Bowman Jr., *Straight Talk About Teaching in Today's Church* (Philadelphia: Westminster, 1967).

125. In the sense that it is used in this section, modeling is a psychological construct which denotes imitation of the model's behavior or identification with one or another aspect of the model's personality functioning.

126. Albert Bandura, "Social Learning Theory of Identificatory Processes," in *Handbook of Socialization Theory and Research*, ed. David A. Goslin (Chicago: Rand McNally, 1969), pp. 244–247.

127. For a detailed critique of the personality pseudo-theory of religious instruction, see Lee, *The Flow of Religious Instruction*, pp. 151–160.

128. The term "model" here is used in the sense of a system of interrelated facts and laws subsumed in one theory which serves as a *functional description* of the reality being looked at. A model, then, is the style in which theory is

couched, a way of seeing from a new perspective the interaction among the elements of theory within the overall unity of theory. Theory and model have the same formal structure but different epistemological structures. See Lee, *The Shape of Religious Instruction*, pp. 128–158; Richard E. Snow, "Theory Construction for Research on Teaching," in *Second Handbook of Research on Teaching*, ed. Robert M. W. Travers (Chicago: Rand McNally, 1973), pp. 81–82.

129. It is immaterial and irrelevant to the point I am making to inquire whether Jesus was totally aware, partially aware, or unaware of the teaching theory he adopted. The fact of the matter is that a pedagogical examination of Jesus' instructional practices reveals that he grounded these practices in a theory of teaching.

130. In this section I am dealing with the most general or universal teaching theory rather than any specific theory or model of teaching. For a fine overall treatment of some of the most important specific models of teaching, see Bruce Joyce and Marsha Weil, *Models of Teaching*, 2d edition (Englewood Cliffs, N.J.: Prentice-Hall, 1980).

131. For the essential difference between speculation and theory, see Lee, "The Authentic Source of Religious Instruction," in *Religious Education and Theology*, ed. Munsey, pp. 117–121.

132. In this connection, Nathaniel Gage trenchantly observes that individualistic teaching theory is useless to other educators because it is based solely on one person's own intuition of the teaching process and hence leaves no genuine validated blueprint for other educators to follow. Gage goes on to state that since 1960 teachers "seem to have been more than ever at the mercy of powerful and passionate writers who shift educational thinking ever more erratically with their manifestos." N. L. Gage, *The Scientific Basis of the Art of Teaching* (New York: Teachers College Press, 1978), p. 11.

133. Thus, for example, Gloria Durka and Joanmarie Smith advocate "proposing" as their basic theory of teaching. Not only do these two writers fail to adequately define proposing (their definition of "proposing as growth" is so vague as to be useless except as ceremonial language), but they also fail to specify the major independent variables involved in the teaching act together with the way in which these variables interact. Needless to say, this so-called "theory" of proposing fails on virtually every test of the definition, composition, criteria, and outcomes of authentic theory. See Gloria Durka and Joanmarie Smith, *Modeling God* (New York: Paulist, 1976), pp. 83–90.

134. James Michael Lee, "The *Teaching* of Religion," in *Toward a Future for Religious Education*, ed. Lee and Rooney, pp. 59–64.

135. It is irrelevant to this example (or to the one which follows) to introduce theological considerations such as "God gave the grace of learning to the apostles at the Last Supper but withheld this grace to many persons in the discourse on the Eucharist." First of all, this kind of theological consideration is a gratuitous assumption and so can just as gratuitously be denied. Second, I believe that it is erroneous to posit grace-in-actuality as something wholly extrinsic or completely foreign to nature and to the cause-effect operations of

the world. I contend that nature works, and that teaching is effective, not because of a series of "zaps" emanating from a wholly extrinsic grace, but primarily because the relationships of cause-effect such as those which take place in instructional activity are graced when they occur in harmony with the graced nature of a God-impregnated world. Grace is a supernatural *habitus* of the human person and indeed of all creation according to the nature and exigencies of each distinct portion of creation. When a religious educator consciously or unconsciously rejects the grace-filled operations of God-soaked creation (as when this educator uses an incomplete or faulty instructional practice), then such an instructional practice is thereby inherently ungraced and graceless. See Lee, "The Authentic Source of Religious Instruction," in *Religious Education and Theology*, ed. Thompson, pp. 192–197; Matthew Fox, *On Becoming a Musical, Mystical Bear* (New York: Paulist Deus, 1976), pp. 147–151; Thomas Aquinas, *Summa Theologica*, I, qq. 110–114.

136. This fact has beem amply confirmed by empirical research studies. For one well-known research study of adult learners, see Jacob Levine and John Butler, "Lecture versus Group Discussion in Changing Behavior," *Journal of Applied Psychology* XXXVI (February, 1952), pp. 29–33.

137. For a meaty summary of the social-science approach to the teaching of religion, see Harold William Burgess, *An Invitation To Religious Education* (Birmingham, Ala.: Religious Education Press, 1975), pp. 127–165. For a helpful overview of these and some other important pedagogical styles in teaching the Bible as religion, see Robert Davidson, *The Bible in Religious Education* (Edinburgh: Hansdel, 1979), pp. 37–51.

138. Lee S. Shulman and Evan R. Keislar, ed., *Learning by Discovery* (Chicago: Rand McNally, 1966); Harold Morine and Greta Morine, *Discovery: A Challenge To Teachers* (Englewood Cliffs, N.J.: Prentice-Hall, 1973).

139. A fine book on the enactment of the gaming strategy to teach the Bible is that by Steven Brams. This book uses variations of sophisticated game theory to show the learner the network of interactive thoughts, feelings, and action-decisions involved in better understanding and appreciating and living out such interactive biblical incidents such as the temptation game, the birthright game, Rahab's game, and so on. Steven J. Brams, *Biblical Games: A Strategy Analysis of Stories in the Old Testament* (Cambridge, Mass.: MIT Press, 1980).

140. D. T. Tuma and F. Reif, eds., *Problem Solving and Education* (Hillsdale, N.J.: Erlbaum, 1980); Norman R. F. Maier, ed., *Problem Solving and Creativity in Individuals and Groups* (Belmont, Cal.: Brooks/Cole, 1970).

141. Thomas A. Ringness, *The Affective Domain in Education* (Boston: Little, Brown, 1975); William C. Shutz, *Here Comes Everybody* (New York: Harper & Row, 1971); Harold C. Lyon, Jr., *Learning to Feel—Feeling to Learn*.

142. Malcolm E. Shaw et al., *Role Playing* (San Diego, Cal.: University Associates, 1980); Wallace Wohlking and Patricia J. Gill, *Role Playing* (Englewood Cliffs, N.J.: Educational Technology Publications, 1980); Diane

Dormant, *Rolemaps* (Englewood Cliffs, N.J.: Educational Technology Publications, 1980).

143. In this connection Lois LeBar writes: "Although the Bible was not written as a textbook of educational philosophy or method, the believer who seeks 'buried educational treasure' will be richly rewarded. These treasures are not grouped by categories and openly displayed for the casual observer, but are 'hidden' for the earnest seeker who is willing to dig for them." Lois LeBar, *Education that is Christian* (Old Tappan, N.J.: Revell, 1958), p. 50.

144. For a representative example of this constricted mentality, see Johannes Hofinger, *The Art of Teaching Christian Doctrine*, 2d edition (Notre Dame, Ind.: University of Notre Dame Press, 1962), p. 62.

145. For a fuller and more nuanced treatment of this important issue, see Lee, "The Authentic Source of Religious Instruction," in *Religious Education and Theology*, ed. Thompson, pp. 144–146.

146. On this point, see Martin J. Buss, "Understanding Communication," in *Encounter with the Text: Form and History in the Hebrew Bible*, ed. Martin J. Buss (Philadelphia: Fortress, 1979), pp. 3–8.

147. For a contrast of the social-science approach to the theological approach in teaching religion, see Lee, *The Shape of Religious Instruction*, especially pp. 182–224. For an opposing view, see Joseph M. Gettys, *How to Teach the Bible* (Richmond, Va.: Knox, 1949), especially p. 13.

148. Leon McKenzie, *The Religious Education of Adults* (Birmingham, Ala.: Religious Education Press, 1982), p. vii.

CHAPTER 2

Religious Education and the Bible: A Biblicist's View

Joseph S. Marino

Introduction

Saint Jerome once wrote: "Ignorance of the Scriptures is ignorance of Christ."[1] In a more positive perspective his profound insight could be rephrased to read, "Knowledge of the Scriptures is knowledge of Christ." Since religious education has as its primary goal to deepen the Christian's life in Christ (which includes knowledge and love of Christ), then clearly the role of the Bible is paramount in religious education. The sacred author in 2 Timothy 3:16 reminds us: "All Scripture is inspired by God and can profitably be used for teaching, for refuting error, for guiding peoples' lives and teaching them to be holy."

Even though the necessity of the Sacred Scriptures in religious education is so obvious, the religious educator who may have little formal training in biblical studies may often be overwhelmed in determining the meaning of the Scriptures and communicating its message. To merely quote key passages of the Bible in the classroom is not enough in allowing the ultimate meaning and power of the message to penetrate into the heart of the student. The distance of time, culture, and language between the inspired word and the audience of today calls for a prayerful and careful examination of the text in order that the meaning of the text will come alive for the Christian of today.

Consequently, the purpose of this chapter is to give the religious educator a biblicist's perspective of the use of Scripture in the catechetical setting. First, the nature of the Bible will be discussed. Second, concrete suggestions for using Scripture in the teaching situation will be given.

The Bible as Story

Many definitions of the Bible have been proposed. Among these are the Word of God, the Inspired Word of God, the Holy Writ, the Sacred Scriptures. All of these definitions are of course true, but they give primary emphasis to the divine origin of the Bible.[2] The implication of these definitions is that the Bible is a divine piece of literature which the believer must read, believe, and apply to his or her life. If a religious educator emphasized this perspective of the Scripture, then the starting point of each educational activity is always the Sacred Scripture. In other words, certain passages of the Scripture could be read and their inferred applications to life could be made.

Yet, when the life of the Israelites and the life the early Christians are studied, it is quickly discovered that the starting of their life with God is not the written word of the Bible. Rather their starting point is the religious experience with God. Consequently, for the purposes of this chapter a better definition of the Bible is that it is normative literary articulation of the religious experience of the Israelites (Old Testament) and the early Christians (New Testament). This definition encompasses the nature of the Bible and opens many avenues for use in religious education.

The Bible came into existence only after the people had a religious experience with God at some particular time in human history. The Bible describes that experience. The religious experience is the real encounter of God in life, either in the life of an individual or in the life of the community. The religious experience is the discovery that God is actively involved in human life and human history and comes from God's manifesting himself in history and from the community's discovery of that revelation through reflection and religious activity.

A close examination of the Scriptures reveals that it does describe a religious experience. In the Old Testament it is the religious experience between God and Israel. Throughout the Old Testament, the authors are convinced that God, whom they know as Yahweh, is a part of Israel's history. When the people of Israel are freed from the slavery of Egypt, they discover Yahweh's salvific hand at work. (Ex. 15:1–18) The law that Moses proposes to Israel is understood as coming from God himself (Ex. 20:1–17). The narratives of Israel's wandering in the wilderness are marked with dialogues between God and the leaders of

Israel (Nm. 14:10b–13). The entrance into the Promised Land is hailed as God's intervention in favor of his own (Jos. 1:13). The subsequent exiles from the Promised Land and also the reentries into the land were always interpreted as the activity of God in Israel's history. The perception that God is acting in Israel's life is in an important sense religious experience in its own right.

Besides these interventions of God in the history of Israel, the Old Testament also records quite a few religious experiences of individuals. The call naratives of the leaders of Israel are always an encounter between the individual and Yahweh. Among the most noted examples are the call of Moses (Ex. 3:4–22) and the call of the prophets (Jer. 1:4–10, etc.).

The story of Elijah's search for God (1 Kgs. 19:9ff) represents a profound religious experience. The desire of Elijah to know God moves him to search in many places. Elijah ultimately finds him in the quiet breeze. This dynamic of search and discovery is the religious experience between God and individuals.

The Old Testament also records the community's and the individual's response to God's movement in human experience. Nowhere is this more beautifully manifest than in the Psalms. The psalmist writes: "O Lord, my God, I cried out to you and you healed me" (Ps. 30:3), and "The Lord has done great things for us; we are glad indeed" (Ps. 126:3). Psalm 136 is Israel's ultimate song in recognition of God's movement in its history. Through stories and images the authors of the books of the Old Testament describe Israel's religious experience.

At the same time the New Testament records the initial religious experience of those who encountered Jesus. The Risen Lord is understood as the ultimate intervention of God in human history. He is the culmination of revelation. The author of the letter to the Hebrews writes: "In times past God spoke in fragmentary and varied ways to our fathers through the prophets; in the final age, he has spoken through a son" (Heb. 1:1–2a). The religious experience of the New Testament is to discover that Jesus is truly God among us and through maintaining a relationship with Jesus, the believer has seen the Father himself (Jn. 14:7).

By now it should be clear that what lies behind the words of the Bible is the religious experience which constitutes the data of the Bible. The Bible came into existence from the recognized encounter between God and his people. The religious experience produced the

Bible, not the other way around. Perhaps a diagram would help in understanding this fact:

God
  } ———→ the religious experience ———→ The Story
People   (Bible)

The Bible is the story of the religious experience. The task of the biblical writers was to find the right words, phrases, images, and symbols to communicate their experiences. It is the task of any writer. For example, a newspaper reporter tries to communicate what he or she witnesses as accurately as possible, trying to connect words and events. This is not as easy to achieve as it may seem.

The task is complicated even more when a writer tries to communicate an experience that is not so objectively concrete. Any experience that goes beyond the concretely verifiable is often difficult to communicate to others. For example, the experience of love is understood by the lovers. Yet when one asks them to articulate that real and indeed objective experience they may have difficulty and be forced to revert to a special language, particularly symbols and images.

The Sacred Scriptures record the religious experience between God and his people, a real experience, one that can be fruitfully passed on by employing the special language of storytelling. Biblical research during much of this century have been dominated by the assumption that the biblical stories reported history. This approach of course recognized the inaccuracies in some accounts, but nonetheless thought historical events to be at the base of the accounts. Biblical scholars attempted to reconstruct the underlying history. Today, however, there seems to be more emphasis on the Bible as story, instead of the Bible as history. [3]

Religious educators, however, may be tempted to use the Scriptures primarily as history. After all, there is a fascination among many believers to accept the narrative in the Bible as historical events. This approach produces a "how marvelous it must have been" mentality. In other words, the believer's faith is based upon accounts reported as historical events that appear incredible, such as the dividing of the Red Sea, the spectacular events on Mount Sinai as Moses received the Ten Commandments, the moving star leading wise men to Jesus, the walking on water by Jesus and momentarily by Peter. When the believer puts such emphasis on the historicity of these events, then the believer's faith remains in the past. How often have religious educators heard phrases such as, "Would it not have been great to have seen the Red Sea open or to see Jesus walk on water?"

This approach to the Scriptures could even cause some serious doubts among the believers. He or she may wonder why such events do not happen now. "Why doesn't God act in the same dramatic way that he apparently did in the past?" What is wrong with God, or more probably the question becomes, "What is wrong with my faith?" Once the catechist and student are brought from perceiving the Bible as history to perceiving it more as story, they are freed from these questions. The fact is that God does still act in the life of the world and nothing may be wrong with the believer's faith. What the catechist and student are challenged to do is to become involved in the biblical story so much that the religious experience expressed in the story becomes clear. What the religious educator and student will probably discover, is that the religious experience of the biblical stories are parallel to the religious experience today.

One of the authors who has done much in the whole area of storytelling in religion is John Shea.[4] Shea has analyzed the phenomenon of storytelling and concludes that it has an important place in the human experience. Storytelling causes a dynamic within the listener as he or she is moved from the contemporary moment into the situation of the story with its exciting plots and resolutions and then back to the listener's own reality with new insight. As Shea himself says: "At any age people hunger to move 'outside their own skins' and to return within them slightly different for the journey. And since storytelling can accomplish this redemptive going forth and 'returning home' it flourishes."[5] Throughout the ages believers have related their significant religious experiences in story.

A story of a religious experience tries to capture the deepest significance of the experience, so that it can be communicated to others. This dynamic is a rather obvious fact. People who have had a religious experience realize that their lives have been affected by the experience. Something has happened to change them. This significant event must be communicated to others.

The experience is told in story form. How often we have heard the phrase, "One day I was . . ." and then the intriguing story of some religious experience. The story is told over and over again each time changing a bit until the deepest aspects of the original experience are captured. The details of the story will change as long as new insights of the original experience are discovered and reflected upon.

The Bible contains the significant stories of the Judeo-Christian experience. The Bible as a whole can be understood as the story of faith. What lies behind the stories is the religious experience of the community. The stories were first transmitted by word of mouth. They were told over and over again being modified so that the ultimate meaning of the religious experience could be passed on to and received by others. The story becomes the medium by which some religious insight into life is transmitted.

Two Examples of Biblical Stories

Two examples, one from the Old Testament and one from the New Testament will help in illustrating the point. One of the great stories in the Old Testament is the story of Job. It is a literary masterpiece which wrestles with the constant question of human suffering.

The story begins as many stories do with the phrase "There was once a man. . . ." The main character, Job, is introduced as a good and honest person who "feared God and avoided evil" (Jb. 1:1). He apparently is wealthy and has a large family. Then all of a sudden Job's world begins to crumble. He is stripped of his family and wealth for no apparent reason. His worldview was simple: The good prosper and the bad suffer. Yet, his personal experience was different. He, a recognized upright person, was suffering. Job's suffering is reported in the most extreme and absolute terms. Job loses everything. Nothing is left for him to fall back upon. This absolute description of Job's suffering signals to the listener that a story is being told and causes the listener to enter into the problem of the story. How will Job face this dilemma. Chapter 2 may tempt the listener to take the easy answer to the problem. In this chapter Job is presented as a patient person taking his problem with a spirit of stoicism: "We accept good things from God; and should we not accept evil?" (2:10).

Yet chapter 3 expresses the usual human response to human suffering. In the most extreme terms he asks the question why. Job desires to vanish. He questions his very existence. "Perish the day on which I was born" (3:3a). "Why did I not perish at birth?" (3:11a). "Why is light given to toilers and life to the bitter in spirit?" (3:20).

The key to understand Job's profound response to his dilemma is found in Job 3:4. He says, "May that day (of his birth) be darkness, let not God above call for it, nor light shine upon it." His use of the symbols of light and darkness brings the reader back to the opening verses of Genesis. There the author states that "darkness covered the abyss" (Gn. 2:2), and earth is described as a formless wasteland. To bring earth out of its darkness and chaotic state God creates light (Gn. 3:3). Job's statement that his day of birth be darkness and no light shine upon it represents his intense desire to return to chaotic state of nonexistence. Better yet, his implied judgment is that life is without order or meaning; it is absurd.[6]

By now anyone who has suffered or ministered to suffering people has entered into the story of Job. The story of Job is the real story of any sufferer, his dilemma is the dilemma of any sufferer, his question is the question of any sufferer. The book of Job in its first three chapters stated in exceptional terms and painted in vivid imagery human suffering and how the human person tries to cope with that reality. It is a universal story.

Indeed, if an author today wrote about the phenomenon of human suffering, he or she would describe the experience employing contemporary imagery and examples. Perhaps the author would use the image of some cancer illness which slowly and painfully destroys a human being. Perhaps the author would paint the picture of a family whose young baby has just died for no apparent reason. Perhaps the author would represent the dilemma by portraying a person whose loved one has been suddenly killed in an automobile accident. In all of these stories the underlying cry is the same as the story of Job: Why me?

The Book of Job proposes to answer that question, as people in every age do. Different insights are presented through the three friends of Job. All three explain Job's suffering with the traditional Old Testament concept of retribution: Job suffers because he has sinned. Even though Christian theology questions this belief;[7] nonetheless, the Christian believer can still identify with the story because Job's claim to innocence refutes this explanation.

So what is the answer? When the reader finally arrives at chapter 38, he or she may expect to find the answer in God's theophany. Job 38:1 states: "Then the Lord addressed Job out of the storm and said. . . ." (Actually the Jerusalem Bible reads: "Yahweh gave Job his answer.") The drama of the story intensifies as God himself will speak. There may be an answer.

Yet, the careful reader of the Bible has a clue that perhaps an answer *per se* may not be given. Job 38:1 states that God spoke out of a storm. Usually whenever God's presence is explained in terms of a storm, God will pronounce judgment, as seen in Psalm 50. Consequently, a close reading of the speeches by God reveals that a definitive answer is indeed not given.

Rather God questions Job. He asks: "Who is this that obscures divine plans with words of ignorance" (38:2) and "Would you condemn me that you may be justified?" (40:8). While these questions may seem harsh they do reflect the ultimate reality of the religious experience in regards to suffering. The first is ultimately stating that the human person cannot perceive the bigger picture as God sees it. The second question gives the reason why this is so. Indeed, one's individual experience cannot be the primary component to evaluate and perhaps even to create God's universal and all-encompassing plan. God does not answer the question; rather he questions the question. The story of Job ends without an answer. That is the way most stories concerning the apparent absurdity of human suffering end. To pursue the question of why to its most extreme point results with more questions. The story of Job captures this experience. Indeed, it is not until Christ accepts human suffering with all of its absurdity does the human person begin to be freed from the question of why.[8]

The story of Job concretizes the experience of human suffering. It does not speak of suffering in the abstract; nor does it debate the problem in lofty terminology or philosophical logic. Rather, the reflection on this experience is presented in the most specific and concrete terms. However, even though Job is an individual figure, the reader can immediately identify with him and his dilemma. He can identify with the situation the author has masterfully portrayed. Through the medium of story a significant reflection on human suffering is communicated to the listener and reader.

The New Testament story, Luke 16:19–31, also illustrates the point. This narrative is in the form of a parable, the favorite medium of Jesus in his teachings. Parables have all the dimensions of a good story, above all drawing the listener into the drama of the story. The listener of a parable can never remain neutral, as he or she is forced to make a judgment on the situation that the parable narrates. From this judgment the listener is no longer a mere on-looker, but now is forced to act.

The story of the rich man and Lazarus is a well-known parable that has usually been interpreted to mean that it is essential for us to share with the poor. Obviously this interpretation is true. Yet a complete immersion in the story causes the reader to go beyond this interpretation.

The story is easily understood. The characters are clearly defined. The rich man is portrayed as totally rich. The poor man, Lazarus, is portrayed as completely poor. After their deaths, the rich man goes to the abode of the dead in torment; Lazarus to the bosom of Abraham. The desire of the rich man to be refreshed by water from Lazarus cannot be fulfilled since there is great distance between the two.

Thus far in the story the elements indicate a retribution-type paradigm. In other words, the rich man ultimately ends up in punishment while Lazarus is vindicated by God with the riches of afterlife. Consequently, the listener is forced to reevaluate his or her response to the needs of the poor.

Yet, the story does not end there. In fact, it goes on to give the listener a profound insight on how to evaluate an appropriate response to the poor. Verses 27–31 relate another desire of the rich man. He wants Lazarus to return to the rich man's family home to warn his brothers. Stating that they have Moses and the prophets to tell them what to do he denies the request. The rich man however insists that someone who would come back from the dead could have an effect on their lives. Abraham thinks differently, he denies the request. Giving the reason for this denial, Abraham states what is the key to the story's message: "If they do not listen to Moses and the prophets, they will not be convinced even if one should rise from the dead" (16:31).

It is this last verse that draws the listener into the story more than any other. Abraham's reasoning seems to be so unusual to the average person. After all, if someone did come back from the dead to tell us to get our life in order, it probably would effect us very much, if for no other reason than out of fear! Therefore the listener is drawn completely into the story and is forced to come up with an explanation since verse 31 seems to contradict experience.

Verse 31 however is the clue to the story. Here the evangelist changes the rich man's words. No longer is it simply Lazarus' going from the dead to talk to the brothers. Now, it is "one risen from the dead," clearly referring to Christ, the only one risen from the dead.

Consequently, verse 31 could now read, "If they don't listen to Moses and the prophets, they will not listen to Jesus."

The message of the story is beginning to emerge. Moses and the prophets represent the law of the old covenant while Jesus represents the new law, the law of love and the beatitudes. The law of the Old Testament requires only minimal action. For example, the fifth commandment states, you shall not kill. Nothing is said or even implied about one's relationship with others. In other words, the law is not concerned if one loves the other person, just don't kill him!

On the other hand, Jesus' law requires the maximum action and is concerned with one's relationship with others. If one loves others then to kill or not to kill is not even a question. The beatitudes require maximum living in that the Christian is called to love all.

Therefore, on one end of the spectrum of moral living is the old law (minimum living); on the other end is the new law (maximum living). Now verse 31 could be rewritten again: "If you are not doing the minimum how can you expect to do the maximum." here the listener connects with the meaning of the story. The listener has experienced the fact that moral development is gradual, moving through various stages. Consequently, the listener must determine where he or she is on this moral spectrum between minimum and maximum Christian action.

These two stories represent specific stories in the Sacred Scriptures. They both reflect the best in storytelling. A penetration into the stories recorded long ago allows the reader to discover the ultimate experience expressed in the story, experiences which are not very far removed from the experiences of today.

The One Story of the Bible

Is it possible to think of the Scriptures as one story? This question is somewhat of a variation of the question that has plagued biblical theology in recent times, particularly in regard to the Old Testament. Several authors have attempted to come up with a unifying principle, theme, or concept that would bring the books together as a whole.[9] The debate will probably continue for some time. The question proposed here is somewhat different. Instead of attempting to discover a specific detail in the narratives themselves that brings the Bible together, here we are more interested in trying to discover a religious experience that lies behind most, if not all of the biblical narratives.

The ultimate religious experience that the Bible records is the death and resurrection of Jesus. This experience could be considered as the religious experience which unifies the Sacred Scriptures. The resurrection narratives relate the concrete story of the early Christians' experience of the resurrection of Jesus who was crucified on the cross. It is the cornerstone of Christian faith. What the early Christians experienced was a quite profound event: Jesus who was crucified, who died and was buried, was actually alive. He had been raised by the Father.

What lies behind the story is the real human and religious experience of dying and rising. It is this experience that ultimately lies behind the biblical narratives. The concrete expressions of this paradigm are of course different in each story, but they can always ultimately be understood in terms of dying and rising. There are several examples. In the Old Testament there is the Exodus story in which the Israelites move from slavery (dying) to freedom (rising). They wander through the desert (dying); they enter the Promised Land (rising). When they break their covenant by sinning they are led into exile (dying); they repent and are led back into their land (rising).

In the New Testament examples abound as well. This paradigm could be applied to all the miracles of Jesus in which he raises someone from a horrible state of existence (death) to a new state of existence (resurrection). The parables of Jesus have as their goal to invite the listener to enter the kingdom of God. To do that the parables narrate a story from which the listener must die to self (death) so that he or she might live for God and others (resurrection). Even Paul describes the primary rites of the Christian community using the paradigm, The Eucharist (1 Cor. 11:26) and baptism (Rom. 6:1–11) are explained as being united with the death and resurrection of Christ.

This cycle of dying and rising is the cycle that best represents the human experience. Just as Israel in the Old Testament and many in the New Testament participated in this experience, so does every human being. It is the story of everyone's life. Yes, the details are different for each person. For some, dying is experienced in being rejected or hated; for others in being ill or sick, and for others in being confused or lost. Yet, just as much as death is experienced, so also is resurrection experienced. It is the story of life; it is the story of the Bible.

To approach the Scripture as story means that the religious educator must examine two stories: The multiple biblical stories and the diverse stories of contemporary Christians. Behind each story rests the religious experiences which should parallel. Therefore, the religious educator must always encourage the students to tell their stories of faith, since their stories are relating their religious experiences.

The Bible as Normative

If the ultimate religious experiences are expressed both in the Bible and in present-day stories of faith, then what is the importance of the Bible? Christian tradition has always held the Bible in high regard and has given it a certain normativeness in the life of the church. The Second Vatican Council of the Roman Catholic Church emphasized the importance of Scripture in the church. In the document on divine revelation the Fathers of the Council wrote:

> The church has always venerated the divine Scriptures as she venerated the Body of the Lord, in so far as she never ceases, particularly in the sacred liturgy, to partake of the bread of life and to offer it to the faithful from the one table of the Word of God and the Body of Christ. She has always regarded, and continues to regard the Scriptures, taken together with sacred tradition, as the supreme rule of her faith. [10]

For many people, their understanding of the authority of the Bible is based on their conception of the Bible as inspired literature. [11] For the fundamentalist the Bible, because it is inspired, expresses the exact, total, and absolute word of God. The Bible, as it is written, is without error, and since it is immune from error it is accurate in all of its details. Consequently it must serve as the absolute authority of Christian tradition.

Yet a careful and studied reading of the Scriptures reveals that the Bible does contain some historical, scientific, and even grammatical errors. There are also some discrepancies in the Bible. Therefore, to base the authority of the Bible on the belief that the Bible is totally without error of any kind is actually to minimize the authority of the Bible. A fundamentalist approach to the Bible causes the Christian to become involved in debates that are of marginal consequences in relation to the overall message of the Bible. The fundamentalist simply fails to come to terms with the human aspect of the written word and therefore never really penetrates into the authentic message of the story. The authority of the Bible does not come from the supposedly inerrant nature of the Bible.

The problem of inerrancy was much discussed at the Second Vatican Council. When the question of inspiration was debated at the Council the original draft insisted that the result of inspiration was inerrancy. The first draft (schema) read:

> Since divine inspiration extends to all things (in the Bible) it follows directly and necessarily that the entire Sacred Scripture is *absolutely immune from error*. By the ancient and constant faith of the church we are taught that it is absolutely wrong to concede that a sacred writer has erred, since divine inspiration by its very nature excludes and rejects every error in every field, religious and profane. This necessarily follows because God, the supreme truth, can be the author of no error whatever (emphasis added).

The concept of biblical truth as formulated in this first draft insisted upon the notion of absolute inerrancy, a concept very near the fundamentalist perspective. Actually this proposal was ignored in subsequent drafts, nonetheless the word inerrancy was retained in both the second and third drafts of the schema.[12]

The fifth draft was the one finally approved by the Council. It states:

> Since, therefore, all that the inspired authors or sacred writers affirm should be regarded as affirmed by the Holy Spirit, we must acknowledge, that the books of Scripture firmly, faithfully, and without error teach that *truth* which God *for the sake of our salvation* wished to see confided in the Sacred Scriptures (emphasis added).[13]

The teaching in this document is significant because it removes the notion of inerrancy from the important concept of biblical truth. The truth of the Bible and therefore its normative nature is not a result of the Bible being immune from all error.

Rather, the truth of the Bible is qualified by the Council. It is that truth "for the sake of our salvation." Consequently, only a particular truth is guaranteed in the Bible, not all truth. The Council does not give a definition of the phrase "for the sake of our salvation." Neither does it list certain passages of the Scriptures that would be considered true for the sake of our salvation.

Salvific truth lies in the message of the biblical stories. It does not lie in the scientific or historical accuracy of the stories, but rather in the message that the sacred writer wished to communicate by using the literary devices available to him. The goal of the student of Scripture and reader of Scripture is to discover the message. It is the message that is normative for the believer.

The normative nature of the Bible also rests in the fact that these stories are the original stories of the Church. Karl Rahner understands the Scripture to be a constitutive component of the Church.[14] The stories in the Scripture gave the Church an identity by articulating in word the original faith experience of the community. The new church would see in these stories the reality of its lived faith.

Even though there were many other stories written[15] only those in what we now know as the Bible were preserved by the church. They were perserved because the ultimate faith experience contained in the stories resonated with those who first encountered the risen Lord.[16] The Scriptures then become the original documents written by the founding fathers, those who participated in the original experiences of faith. It is to this document that subsequent generations refer to give them identity and to guarantee an authentic and true expression of faith. The challenge of each new generation of Christians is to make sure that their stories of faith resonate with the original stories of faith.

The normative nature of the Bible lies then in the fact that it contains the original stories of faith whose message is true.

Interpreting the Scripture

The final question of this chapter is to explore the way to interpret the Bible. If it is true that the message of the biblical stories is of primary importance, how does one discover the message? How should religious educators approach the Scriptures?

The stories of the Bible were written in a particular time, in a particular language, with a particular cultural background. The task of the religious educator who uses the Bible is to discover the influence which these particulars had on the authors who wrote the stories. Obviously, the particulars had a great influence on the expression of the biblical truth contained in the stories. In fact, the authors could write their stories using only the literary devices available to them. The reader of the Scripture must understand the authors' particular literary devices in order to determine the message of the stories. Actually, the believers today must go back and discover how the believers of biblical times expressed their experiences of faith.

In 1943 Pius XII, in his encyclical *Divino Afflante Spiritu*, approved the approach to Scripture that searches for an understanding of the literary devices employed in the biblical stories. He wrote:

> What is the literal sense of a passage is not always as obvious in the speeches and writings of the ancient authors of the East, as it is in the works of our own time. For what they wished to express is not to be determined by the rules of grammar and philology alone, nor solely by context; *the interpreters must, as it were, go back wholly in spirit to those remote centuries of the East and with the aid of history, archaeology, ethnology, and other sciences accurately determine what modes of writing, so to speak, the authors of that ancient period would be likely to use; and in fact did use* (emphasis added). [17]

The conciliar document *Dei Verbum* teaches the same:

> Seeing that in Sacred Scripture, God speaks through men in human fashion, it follows that the interpreters of Sacred Scripture, if he is to ascertain what God has wished to communicate to us should carefully search out the meaning[18] which the sacred writers really had in mind, that meaning which God had thought well to manifest through the medium of human words. In determining the intention of the sacred writers, attention must be paid, *inter alia*, to "literary forms, for the fact is that truth is differently presented and expressed in the various types of historical writing, in prophetical and poetical texts," and in other forms of literary expression. Hence the exegete must look for that meaning which the sacred writer, in a determined situation and given the circumstances of his time and culture, intended to express and did in fact express, through the medium of a contemporary literary form. [19]

What both of these statements encourages us to do in order to discover the message of the stories is to return to the cultural, linguistic, and literary particulars of the authors. Through this process of determining and studying the particulars we discover the message. Our diagram on page 4 can now be expanded:

God ⎤
  ↕ ⎬→Religious Experience → The Story   ↗Religious
People⎦   Bible   Experience
                                               Today

The arrow from the religious experience of today to the Bible represents the challenge of biblical study.

In order to study the particulars of the biblical stories, one who uses the Scripture in religious education must apply the principles of literary criticism to the texts. Literary criticism of the Scriptures applies the very same critical questions to the biblical books as are applied to other pieces of literature. These are the questions of literary form, structure, and language.

The most important question is that of literary form. Literary forms are those types of writing through which the message that the author intends is communicated. There are several literary forms with which we are familiar: history, novels, comics, biography, science-fiction, etc. All of these communicate a message. We approach different literary forms in different ways in order to reach its message. For example, we approach science-fiction differently from the way we approach historical writing. Both are communicating a true message but in different forms. Thus the very first thing the reader of Scripture must determine is the literary form since "truth is differently presented and expressed in the various types . . . of literary expression."[20]

Another important question is that of language. The Bibles that are used in various religious education settings are translations. Most of the Old Testament was originally written in Hebrew; while all of the New Testament was originally written in Greek. As any student of languages knows, in some cases translations from one language to another require an interpretation of meaning. The meaning of a word that is translated into English can often have much more significance in the original Hebrew or Greek. To know the meanings of the words in their original language usually sheds much light upon the interpretation of the text.

Another aspect of language that must be studied is the images and symbols employed by the authors. The stories of the Bible are communicating religious truth that by its very nature must be expressed with symbols. For example, when we try to express the experience of love we ultimately resort to symbols (rings) and images (love is a rose). The reader of Scripture must acknowledge the presence of symbolic language in the Scripture, after all, his or her own religious stories will probably contain symbolic language as well.

Literary criticism also seeks to discover the structure of the story. In other words, how the author organized the story can often give a clue to the meaning. When reflecting upon a particular passage, it is always good to know what comes before and after the story. Also, one should know the overall context of the story, that is, where it fits in the organization of the book itself.

There are many other questions that literary criticism poses to the stories of the Bible, but these are the most significant for our purposes here.[21] However, even the mention of these questions may somewhat frighten the average religious educator. After all, how many of us are literary critics? How many of us actually know Hebrew or Greek? How many of us are structuralists? But to be an expert in these fields is not necessary. Rather, we should consult good resources on these questions.

First and above all, a good translation of the Bible should be used. Historically speaking the most widespread English versions of the Bible were the King James version (1611) for Protestants and the Douay-Rheims version (1582–1609/10) for Catholics. Both of these versions were later revised, the King James in 1901 in America and the Douay in 1749. Both of these heavily employ old English.

However, since the advancement of biblical studies and a better knowledge of the Semitic and Greek languages, newer English versions of the Bible have appeared. The *Revised Standard Version* attempts to translate the Bible word for word from its original language. It does not paraphrase or necessarily use modern modes of English. For a student of Scripture who must work with the original languages it serves as a good resource.

The Jerusalem Bible was originally published in French. The English translation under the direction of Catholic scholars is from the Hebrew and Greek with a constant reference to the French when questions arose in the translation. The translation does employ the language of today but tries to reflect the original Greek and Hebrew. This edition is also excellent for its introductions to the various books of the Bible and its footnotes on key lines and passages. These introductions and footnotes represent the best of modern biblical scholarship.

The New English Bible is a translation undertaken by some of the best Protestant biblical scholars. The purpose of this version was not to translate from the original, word from word, but to understand the sense of the original text and translate that into the best possible English. Although it is not a paraphrase, Greek and Hebrew structures are replaced by modern English structures. A translation that is truly a paraphrase of the original is the *Good News Bible* (sometimes called *Today's English Version*). Its purpose is very simple: translate the original texts in a common everyday English.

Another English translation of the Bible is the *New American Bible*. This version was the undertaking of Catholic scholars in collaboration with scholars of other denominations. These scholars translated from the original texts aiming "to convey as directly as possible the thought and individual style of the inspired writers."[22] At the same time, the translation is in very readable English.

It is difficult to say which particular translation is the best for religious educators to use. For different situations different versions should be employed. For example, in planning a class, a careful study of the text is required; therefore, the *Revised Standard Version* giving the closest possible translation of words would be a good resource, or the *Jerusalem Bible* with its footnotes would be excellent. On the other hand, the version used in the classroom might be the *New American* since the English in this version is more understandable and smoother.

Besides the various translations, the teacher of religious education should be aware of the numerous resources available for biblical studies. It would be impossible to list all of them here. Yet, an acquaintance with the most outstanding would be valuable.

Among the best commentaries of the Sacred Scriptures is the *Jerome Biblical Commentary*.[23] Edited by three of the most renowned biblical scholars in the United States, Raymond E. Brown, Joseph A. Fitzmyer, and Roland E. Murphy, this commentary was published in 1968. It has excellent introductions to the books of Scripture and articles on biblical themes. Above all, it gives an explanation of each line of Sacred Scripture. It still stands as the best single-volume commentary available in English.

Another excellent commentary on the Bible is *The Interpreter's Bible*.[24] This multi-volume commentary also explains the passages of Scripture. A valuable dimension to this commentary is its theological and spiritual reflections on certain passages of Scripture.

Both the *Jerome Biblical Commentary* and the *Interpreter's Bible* are somewhat technical. There are two good commentaries on the Scriptures that are less technical and more of a biblical-theology commentary. The first is *The Daily Study Bible*[25] by William Barclay. It was first published in 1956 and revised in 1975. Dealing with only New

Testament books, the aim of Barclay's guide is to convey the results of scholarship to the ordinary reader. Like Barclay's works, *The New Testament Message*[26] series, published in 1980, tries to bring "to the fore in understandable terms the specific message of each biblical author." The *Old Testament Message*[27] series was published after the New Testament series and has the same goal as the New Testament series.

Besides commentaries, Bible dictionaries are also a helpful resource. A biblical dictionary allows the student of the Bible to penetrate deeply into the meaning of specific biblical terms, words, places, names, and concepts. Among the best are *The Interpreter's Dictionary of the Bible*,[28] *The Dictionary of the Bible*,[29] and *The Dictionary of Biblical Theology*.[30]

Once a step has been taken back into the biblical world in order to discover the message of the biblical story, another step must be taken. The message of the text that has been uncovered through study and reflection must be brought to the present day Christian. Now we must add another arrow to our diagram:

That message should resonate with the Christian community of today. It is the same God who constantly reveals himself to his people. It is people who share the same desires of their ancestors in faith to enter into relation with this all-loving, self-revealing God. Consequently, the religious experience remains essentially the same.

Yet, to make that leap requires of the teacher of religious education two things. First, the religion teacher must be able to articulate the message of the stories in the language of today. He or she cannot remain at the level of the language of the commentaries or dictionaries. Rather the religious educator must be able to state that message in words, images, and symbols that are understandable in today's world. In short, he or she must write new stories of the religious experience.

Second, the educator must be attuned to the present-day experience of faith. This requires of the religious educator prayer and meditation. It is through prayer that we become sensitive to the reality of God in our human journey. It is through meditation and reflection that we are able to perceive the presence of God in life. Through these exercises we discover the religious experience of our life and time. Also the religious educator must be familiar with the religious experience of the students and their stories of the experience.

Conclusion

Because the Bible is the normative literary expression of the Christian faith it will always be in the center of religious education. Yet, as this chapter has tried to show, the challenge that is before the religious educator is to continually uncover its message. This process is not an easy one, but it certainly is exciting. Once a person approaches Scripture in the way proposed in this chapter, unlimited possibilities for the use of the Bible in religious education lies before him or her. As with every good story, the message of the Bible is always alive and always being presented to each new generation of Christians whose story is so much like that of the Bible.

Notes

1. St. Jerome, *Commentary on Isaiah.* Jerome also urged that children's games should be based on biblical themes. Many other early Church Fathers saw the necessity of the Scripture in enriching the Christian's life.
2. Raymond E. Brown in *The Critical Meaning of the Bible* (New York: Paulist Press, 1981), chapter 1, "The Human Word of the Almighty God," explores this question in more detail. He insists that the human aspect of the word must be taken into consideration.
3. This is not to say that we must abandon the historical-critical method of biblical analysis. Rather, this shift in emphasis can be understood as a logical development of the method. For a more detailed account of this shift see John J. Collins, "The Rediscovery of Biblical Narrative," *Chicago Studies* 21, No. 1 (1982), pp. 45–58.
4. John Shea, *Stories of God: An Unauthorized Biography* (Chicago: The Thomas More Press, 1978) and John Shea, *Stories of Faith* (Chicago: The Thomas More Press, 1980).
5. John Shea, "Storytelling and Religious Identity," *Chicago Studies* 21, 1(1982), pp. 23–24.
6. For an excellent treatment on the Book of Job see Dermot Cox, *The Triumph of Impotence* (Rome: Univerità Gregoriana Editrice, 1978).
7. Cf. John 9.

8. Cf. Romans 8:18.

9. For some excellent insights into this question, one could consult the following resources: Joseph Barr, "Biblical Theology" *The Interpreter's Dictionary of the Bible. Suppl.* (Nashville, Tenn.: Abingdon, 1976). Brevard S. Childs, *Biblical Theology in Crisis.* (Philadelphia: Westminister Press, 1970), pp. 36–39. Gerhard F. Hazel, "The Problem of the Center in the OT Theology Debate," ZAW 86 (1976), pp. 65–82.

10. *Dei Verbum* (Dogmatic Constitution on Divine Revelation), paragraph 21. (In the future cited as *DV*).

11. It is not germane to this essay to go into the various theories of inspiration.

12. For a more detailed explanation of the history of the schema see Bruce Vawter, *Biblical Inspiration* (Philadelphia: Westminister Press, 1972), pp. 143–150.

13. *DV* 11.

14. Karl Rahner, *Inquiries: Inspiration in the Bible,* trans. W. O'Hara (New York: Herder & Herder, 1964).

15. Among the noncanonical gospels are the Gospel of the Ebionites, the Gospel according to the Hebrews, the Gospel according to the Egyptians, and the Gospel of Peter.

16. This of course includes the Old Testament. The Old Testament is the beginning of salvation history. Together, both the Old Testament and the New Testament give testimony to salvation history.

17. *Divino Afflante Spiritu* (On Promoting Biblical Studies), paragraph 35.

18. Using the concept of story could we understand the "meaning" here to mean message as applied to the contemporary believer?

19. *DV,* 12.

20. Ibid.

21. For an overall treatment of this question see: Daniel J. Harrington, S.J. "Interpreting the New Testament," *New Testament Message,* Vol. I (Wilmington, Del.: Michael Glazier, 1979).

22. "Preface," *New American Bible* (Nashville, Tenn.: Nelson, 1971), p.v.

23. Raymond E. Brown et al., eds., *The Jerome Biblical Commentary* (Englewood Cliffs, N.J.: Prentice-Hall, 1968).

24. George A. Buttrick et al., eds., *The Interpreter's Bible* (Nashville, Tenn.: Abingdon, 1978).

25. William Barclay, *The Daily Study Bible Series,* revised edition (Philadelphia: Westminister Press, 1975).

26. Wilfrid Harrington, O.P. and Donald Senior, C.P., eds., *New Testament Message* (Wilmington, Del.: Michael Glazier, 1979).

27. Carroll Stuhlmueller, C.P. and Martin McNamara, M.S.C., eds., *Old Testament Message* (Wilmington, Del.: Michael Glazier, 1982).

28. George Buttrick et al., eds., *The Interpreter's Dictionary of the Bible,* (Nashville, Tenn.: Abingdon Press, 1962). Volumes 1–4. Also, Keith Crim et al., *The Interpreter's Dictionary of the Bible* (Nashville, Tenn.: Abingdon, 1976). Supplementary volume.

29. John L. McKenzie, S.J., *Dictionary of the Bible* (New York: Macmillan, 1965).

30. Xavier Léon-Dufour, ed., *Dictionary of Biblical Theology*, trans. P. Joseph Cahill, S.J. (New York: Seabury Press, 1973).

PART II

Specific Themes

CHAPTER 3

The Discovery of God

Dermot Cox

Surely the discovery of God is a crucial process and goal in the task of religious education. My essay will center on this process and goal, with the intention that the religious educator will be thus empowered to assist the person he teaches to make this glorious but sometimes difficult journey himself.

The God of the Bible is essentially a God *who reveals himself,* not one who is discovered by purely human effort. One may indeed come to know him, but the primary stimulus comes from outside, being a divine initiative. Only by God's choice does any person find him. From the evidence of the Bible itself it is clear that Israel did not arrive at a knowledge of God by reason or philosophy; its history is a history of personal encounter, and it is in encounter with a personal God that biblical man discovered the face of the divinity. One finds God in what he says and does. Thus the earliest texts of the history of salvation take the form of a divine revelation that comes through encounter.

Genesis 12, for example, presents to each reader a meeting between God and one individual—Abraham—that decisively marked the future path of God's self-revelation to humankind. Yet in the biblical tradition this discovery takes many forms. It can be a direct "meeting" with Yahweh, as that experienced by Abraham. But it can also be a discovery of God, or even of the divine, in the depths of the human mind: in suffering; in one's personal awareness of the inadequacies or even cruelties of life; and in everyday situations of joy and sorrow, the changes of seasons and the passage of time. God has always used human language and reason to initiate the adventure.

The Witness of the Old Testament

The Old Testament presents a long and complex evolution in the process of mutual discovery between God and man that is the central dynamic of the history of salvation.[1]

a) An Innate Sense of the Divine

Man is a questioning animal that must always have a cognitive relationship with the environment. Involved as he is with the world of human experience tbe question "why?" is never far from his thoughts. One of the most primitive passions of the mind is the desire to touch some transcendent that can satisfy the need to understand what, or who, lies behind the mysterious phenomena of nature. Psalm 29 may be one of the earliest efforts at plumbing the mystery of the world that surrounded primitive man, and of perceiving the face of the divinity in the experience of the storm: "The voice of the Lord breaks the cedars, the voice of the Lord strikes fiery flames." (vv. 5, 7), and in the phenomenon of the storm the author finds the face of his divinity. This primitive quest for the numinous at *some* level is natural to humankind, for it is an integral part of human existence, as natural as the search for first principles. This desire is in fact a movement of liberty that carries one towards the "other," but it demands a commitment of knowledge that must be articulated until it becomes the *known* as well as the *felt*. For the Bible, the initial experience is a starting point on which the individual must build. The internal dimension of mystery as felt must be intellectually realized, for the very nature of human life implies intercourse, an interlocutor, an "other" to whom one can speak. Psalm 8 is a more sophisticated intellectual exercise that moves from the simple perception of the created world (vv. 1–3) to man as perceived (v. 4) to the intelligible "Other" that *must* lie behind the phenomenon and be related in some way to it (vv. 5–8).

It is not enough to say that the initial step is one of self-revelation on the part of the divinity. There must be some coherent form of communication: What does the other *say* to us; under what guise does it manifest itself; what can it imply? Given the primary experience of the divinity one must work out humanly acceptable and perceptible categories that carry us to the *person* beyond the mystery. In his autobiographical writings Julian Huxley speaks of an experience of the transcendent in nature—something he evidently could not further articulate. The Old Testament does. Quite often in the texts it can be seen how knowledge of God is to some degree based on just such a "feeling"—an intuition common to the species that something lies beyond science. Yet if this remains significant only at the affective level it is not discovery of God, for he is a person one can know. The authors of the biblical tradition realized this, and set themselves to the task of communicating the implications of this experience to those who wished to learn.

Sirach 42:15–25 reflects such a process of discovery, as the author moves from the primal awareness of the transcendent to a knowledge of the person. Acceptance of the mystery is an acceptance of the fact that life has *meaning*, that this meaning is imposed on it by another; therefore life is a *gift*, and this is a preliminary to the discovery of a God who is responsible. The editor of the Abraham narrative carefully sets Genesis 11:31–32 over against Genesis 12:1–5: Abram the primitive theist, and Abraham the adventurer sent out on his travels towards a relationship with the God who so unexpectedly entered his life.[2] This surrender to the grace of divine self-communication—numinous as it was in its initial stages—depended on an openness to reality that goes beyond the more reasonable openness to the provable. It must be seen as a test of Abram's humanness, this willingness at least to listen to something that is primal and precedes the more rational reactions. Yet it is essential to forge on beyond this step: Abram had to "go forth" as the Lord told him. There must be some evidence to satisfy the mind, for the mind is preeminently human and nothing can remain alien to it. Knowledge of the infinite must leave traces at the level of human cognition if it is a human phenomenon—and indeed Genesis 12–23 shows the reader a very human Abraham who seeks to rationalize, and so control, the revelation of God he has received. He applies human reasoning where the reasoning of God seems inadequate, and has a child "before it is too late" (Gen. 16) only to discover that this is not the mind of God. If God has communicated, it must be comprehensible. This one factor is a determinative mark of biblical religion—the search for the comprehensible face of God.[3]

b) The Biblical Method of Communicating the Experience

As regards a "natural religious sense," Israel seems historically to have differed from contemporary peoples.[4] In other religions god reveals himself to the inner consciousness of man. This, of course, also happens in the Bible, but it is only an opening gambit and is predominantly historical in scope. The primary, inner awareness of God is firmly anchored to real historical categories, and the arena in which individuals are called to respond is a "now" of existence clearly definable by reason and history. The inner knowledge of God is made concrete and definite, objective and not merely subjective. The discovery of God is a human project, correlated to human categories and a human moment in which God has bound himself to act. Indeed, while God may be known in his own self-revelation, for the Bible this knowledge must result in a human effort of thinking and searching. God uses man's own nature to start the process, but he expects man to use his own mind in prosecuting the affair. The task of the catechist, as indeed the task of God in both Old and New Testaments, is to activate and exploit the initial sense of the numinous. Here the role of the "witness" is paramount. Few can recognize the divinity—creator, redeemer, or helper—without testimony. This is suggested by John 1:6–8, a text that at first sight seems to be an intrusion into the Johannine prologue. Yet it is clearly an integral part of John's conception of the discovery of God. A witness is necessary, whether this be directly divine, as in the prophetic formula "thus says the Lord," or mediated through a human teacher, as in the tradition of the Sages of Israel who spoke from the teacher's rostrum (Prov. 3:1; 4:10) but wielded the same ultimate authority.[5] The reason is that God is not simply an object of perception, but the subject of testimony.

The question now remains: How in the biblical tradition has God actually done this? What strikes one most is the fact that the nature of God is not presented abstractly, as a doctrine in itself. He can be personally known, and then described within that personal, temporal, and situational relationship. One cannot describe God; one can explain how one individually finds him. This is brought out by the fact that the earliest "confessional" statements, or as we would say, professions of faith, about God are recitals of divine intervention.[6] The classic text for generations of Israelite pupils was Deuteronomy 26:5–10. This text, along with such similar texts as Psalm 78 (a poetic re-statement of Dt. 26), Deuteronomy 6:20ff and Joshua 24:2ff, makes it clear that it is precisely within the personal context of one's *own* history that God is discovered and known. In fact, this is brought out by the very nature of the Old Testament message and its communication to successive generations. The text stands as a form of catechesis, but not merely by communicating the *content* of a message. It is meant to reevoke the inner reality of the event narrated, so that each generation can, in its turn, experience the divine intervention and so know God for itself and work out its own form of commitment. Joshua 24 is a clear example. A full generation after Sinai, with all those who had actually been there dead in the desert, a new people who had never met the God of the Covenant are told, in the context of a recital of the event (vv. 2–12), to "choose *this* day" the mode of their service of God (v. 15). Here the relationship that already existed between Israel and God, and is now renewed for the followers of Joshua, is offered to the people of Shechem by allowing *them* experience through recitation the actuality of the divine intervention and make their own choice.[7] This is a classic example of a Covenant renewal ceremony, where the text itself, the narration of a biblical event, becomes the challenging ground and point of encounter for generations far removed from the historical event.

What the Old Testament does is present a fact. The Israelite listens to the narration and by means of the unity of salvation history participates in the saving act of God. It is in this way that the Old Testament introduces God. It follows that the people who experience God thus and grow to know him themselves become the medium through which others can discover him.[8] This, again, is clearly suggested by the text of Genesis 12 and is further seen in the vocation of the people narrated in Exodus 19.[9]

The Meeting of God and Man in the Old Testament

Something that the Old Testament is insistent upon—and that facilitates discovery—is a twofold characteristic of God: he exists (Ex. 3), and he can be known (the prophetic insight).

Situated at one remove from the historical event itself, it is evident that God is now to be found *in the word*, as that impinges on the human situation and on history, rather than directly in an immediately perceptible experience. This is obvious from the fact that he is a God who is creator of all and who transcends "place," whether this is the temple or some other "holy place" (Jn. 4:21).

In practical terms, therefore, the first step for biblical man is normally an encounter with the "word," which is experientially the primal manifestation of the divinity. Thus, for the heirs of the biblical tradition God is primarily discovered *in the text*, which remains a crucial way of discovering a *personal* God as distinct from a vaguely perceived divinity. What are his characteristics? The fact is that the discovery of God in the Old Testament is not a single experience. It may indeed begin with that—the experience of a particular aspect of

God; creator, tyrant, savior or the aloof deity, above man's battles (as in Job)—but in reality this discovery is an ongoing process. To a great degree also it is mediated to us through the interpretation of other people's experiences (Abraham, Moses, etc.), as one discovers, one after the other, the various dimensions to the Godhead. He is the "other" (Ps. 24), the holy (Is. 6), the just (Ps. 73) and the liberator from the toils of the historic and personal now (Ps. 25; Ps. 51).

a) The God of Abraham

The Yahwistic faith of the earliest books of the Old Testament canon is built upon personal experience of a particular kind. One meets individuals who themselves have encountered a personal God and whose experience is passed on: Abraham, Moses, Elijah, and others equally chosen like the writing prophets.

At the most basic level of perception, these experiences can be classified as "gift," or the divine initiative of self-communication. But the second level reveals a personal apperception that can be communicated. In general, the God of these first adventurers into the world of religious experience, the patriarchs, is a brusque, peremptory divinity.[10] He emerges from the background of primeval beliefs and consciousness and issues commands arbitrarily and without explanation, as we find in the mythical narratives of Genesis 2:15 and Genesis 3. The overall design, if indeed there is one, he keeps strictly to himself. But of course a closer appreciation of the actual human background explains much of this. The early editors of the biblical material experienced life itself as arbitrary and contingent, and this experience determined their understanding of God. The world Abraham knew could be very capricious: flood and famine and death waited on no logic; the ways of rulers, as of ruled, could be erratic. So the picture of a "jealous" and even willful God often reflected the known world, and so could find its forensic voice in such texts as Exodus 20:3: "You shall have no other gods before me."

This attribution of qualities to a divinity is a very human process, being the perception of an intelligence rather like man's own, but comparatively and appropriately more powerful and arbitrary as befitting the known world and capable of explaining why it was such a world. As it were, the world became the logical mirror of its ruler and creator.

This is the background of the Abraham Cycle of Genesis 11–23, where the traditional perception of God becomes startlingly modified by means of a personal communication. As one enters into the text of Genesis 11:31 the familiar atmosphere of the known is palpable. The recognition of a divinity is one thing, and is a familiar enough experience. But the biblical recognition of Yahweh the personal God that is now introduced in Genesis 12:1 is quite different. This came to Abraham, not initially by force of reason, but by divine initiative. Seemingly, it had also come to Melchizedek in some similar way (Genesis 14). Certainly, for both it was the discovery on a personal level of one who by nature was totally other and totally unreachable; a person who was beyond all humanly knowable things—"God most high," as Genesis 14:19 formally states it. The transcendent as creator and liberator (vv. 19b–20) making himself known. Clearly, the God of Genesis 12–14 is one who cannot be known by human initiative, for he is *'el 'elyôn*. Yet he has, by one historical act, revealed himself. And thus he can, through a historical event, be *known of*, if not immediately known on a personalized level.

In this way the Abraham experience, seen as a discovery of God, shows two dimensions that are to dominate the rest of the biblical tradition:

1. It is based on a human experience that enriches one subjectively and, no matter how inchoate at first, leads to knowledge;
2. It is a revelation of a personalized transcendent.

A synthetic approach to Genesis 12–14 reveals a psychological and intellectual process at work in a historical individual. It begins with a universal awareness of mystery shared with contemporary peoples; then God, hitherto the unknown element in human existence, invades an individual's life. Thus the mysterious "divinity" is perceived as a "God in history" and a God who not only can, but does, communicate. This ensures determined historical categories for the discovery of God. He is not an element of the subconscious, nor is he merely a subjective phenomenon. He is now a person. Yet quite clearly this situation did not remain static; Abraham must have grown in knowledge through the ordinary historical events that followed: his meeting with another "discoverer," Melchizedek; the clarification of vocation (Gen. 15 and 17); the renewal of the promise and the weakness of faith

(Gen. 18); and the harrowing test of Genesis 22. It is possible that behind the editorial hand we can see how this growth came about by the interpretation of each of these events in the light of the primary experience—"could this make sense if God really . . . ?"—may lie behind the very human lapse of Genesis 16 and the birth of Ishmael. What happens to an individual is modified by his subsequent experiences and leads to a clarification of meaning.

Abraham had to rethink everything new that presented itself to him in terms of the primary, catalystic experience. Nothing in life could be considered apart from it, so he was "on the lookout"—sensitive to his environment and his history—to see God and discover him in whatever subsequently occurred. After his first experience, everything that happened that was anyway human—pain, doubt, loss, death—added to his knowledge of that person who had entered his life so long ago. Humanly speaking, Abraham's search for God, as the Old Testament presents it, must have begun with the primary gift of God's self-revelation, so if any evidence exists as to how this subsequently developed it may be found in the Abraham Cycle. But it is the first event that is determinative, the first human experience in history of a divine intervention to communicate. It is this that resulted in a discovery of God for the father of God's people. With Abraham a major event took place: A *fact* is presented that has permanent value, and a human being responds. What he had discovered, what was powerful enough to change human history, was to take many more centuries to reach its fulfillment.

b) The God of Moses

Exodus 3 is certainly the discovery of a personal being, a living or existent God, as opposed to a god created in the image of man or inferred from nature. Moses was approached by a preexistent and eternal God, himself the source of life and the master of history (as also in Ps. 105 and Ez. 37).[11] It is possible that Moses was in the religion of the fathers (cf. Ex. 2:11)—that atmosphere of vague, ill-defined theism of the patriarchs—and by means of the religious experience narrated in Exodus 3 identified the "divinity" with the personal God of Abraham whose name is now revealed as "Yahweh." From the structure and language of Exodus 1–3 it appears that Moses did not know this God or his "name" until told by God himself. Clearly, he is a personal God to those who, like Moses, discover him. He is also a liberating God, as

Exodus 13–15 will subsequently disclose. This he had also been for Abraham (Gen. 14), but from now on he is seen to be the God of a *people* rather than the semiprivate property of a family. [12]

Exodus 3 exhibits many of the same characteristic elements of encounter and learning as did Genesis 12–23. The divine statement contains two imperfect forms of verb that adequately communicate the divine nature. "I am with you" in v. 12 expresses a feeling of continuity and permanence, and this is reinforced by "I am who I am" in v. 14. Both communicate a sense of the transcendent God making contact with humankind in a covenant; a God of power and authority calling for a response. The God of Moses is at once a God of moral action and the source of moral authority. As such he invites man to participate. [13]

What follows this covenant—the conquest of the land of Canaan that is depicted in the biblical narrative from Exodus to Samuel—is in fact a community growing in knowledge of this covenant God. [14] Historically, the rise of the monarchy under Saul and David may have been inevitable, as indeed the confrontation depicted in 1 Samuel 8 suggests, yet that historical process represents Israel thinking in terms of the primary grace of intervention experienced by Moses in Exodus 3. By interpreting the way this was worked out in history Israel came to a new knowledge of the God of Horeb. The history of a people of God bears in it the seeds of a knowledge of that God, for he is inevitably part of it all, in war and peace and growth.

In a different way the cry of the Hebrews in Exodus 3 is repeated by each individual in his own history. It is stated formally in Deuteronomy 26, and reiterated by each generation in its own historical context. "Out of the depths I cry to you, O Lord" (Ps. 130) is a cry of recognition of God *now* with me that resounds throughout the Old Testament (see Ps. 3; Ps. 4; Ps. 5, for example). In the human experience of Old Testament history, God makes one feel he exists, but that would not be possible unless man felt the need of something—fulfillment, peace, liberation: all names for God. This, implicitly at least, the Hebrews of Exodus 3 felt: "The cry of the people has come to me" (v. 9). It was a cry to an, as yet, unknown God, and his first response was to make himself known as the one who exists: "I am" (v. 14), and then as the liberator who sees the condition of a suppliant and answers a need that may not as yet be fully comprehended (vv. 16b–17). Thus, for Moses, God was no longer a concept, but a presence that offers itself to the individual as an "I" with existence and a purpose; and Moses is drawn into that, becomes involved in the divine plan.

c) The God of the Prophets

Given the initial grace of revelation, the rest follows. By continual teaching and writing a people can be brought from a shadowy awareness of the divine to a knowledge of God. The central dynamic of the prophetic teaching is the conviction that *God can be known*.

The educational work of the writing prophets carried Israel from the monolatry of Elijah and Eliseus (1 Kgs. 17–2 Kgs. 9) to monotheism. It is readily understandable. People who are as strongly convinced that they carry God's word as were the prophets can impress others.

The prophets did not present religious instruction as such, but an intimate experience of a personal God whom they had met, and whom they had found to be "holy." This concept of a holy God can draw the attention of a thinking people to a problem of human existence, and thus to a new perception of the interaction of human and divine.

The person of Elijah (found in the cycle of stories that runs from 1 Kgs. 17 to 1 Kgs. 19), especially the central episode of the Sinai experience (1 Kgs. 19), marks a discovery of God from direct encounter to growing awareness. This encounter, like previous ones in the tradition, was related to a new stage in the history of the people, and thus a new problem in the perception of God in the life of Israel. It called for—and found in the "still, small voice" of theophany—a new, prophetic, experience. This was no longer the stunning theophanic experience of the "burning bush" of Exodus 3, but instead a "quiet voice." The modality of God's revelation is different. This new act of self-communication *by the word* was to dominate the rest of the biblical tradition. Indeed, a classic example, in totally different circumstances, can be found in Job 4:15. This new modality of discovery may well stand for a different, new, spiritual aspect of God, perhaps the interiority of a learning attitude necessary in the changed circumstances of a people already part of an established society. (At the end of the tradition, John 4:23 maintains something of the same character.) By means of this Sinai experience Elijah learned that God was still God of the covenant, but that the modalities were changed for good. He was also, and preeminently, a God of the individual's inner experience; a universal God.

One century later Isaiah 6 presents another prophetic experience of

God. The "vision" in the temple discloses a God who remains the transcendent God of Abraham—powerful, universal, fearful, and above all holy. And from this stunning revelation man learns something of himself—he is sinful; and he infers something about God—God is forgiving, the one who purifies man of sin. Awareness of human need leads thus to an awareness of the nature of a God who answers that need.

More subtle, and infinitely more humanly appealing, was Hosea's experience of God. This was not an immediate experience of the divine, as was Isaiah 6, but almost exclusively *an inference*: God, as it were, seen through the human plight of the prophet; God perceived in man's image. Hosea 1–3 presents the reader with a parable of discovery. Not a direct encounter with the divine, but an interpretative voice that reveals the lover-God, viewed in the mirror of the prophet's own alienation from his beloved wife and his loss of love.[15]

Jeremiah's prophetic failure revealed to him yet another face of God, felt rather than seen. A psychological problem with vocation and life made him the perfect foil for God's self-disclosure to his people, and a singularly clear prototype of Christ in his alienation. In the sections of the Book of Jeremiah frequently called the "Confessions," the reader discovers a sensitive man, at times almost pathologically schizoid as a result of the pressures placed on him by God. By this means one gets a new perception of a God who was capable of such seeming cruelty (esp. 11:18–23; 12:1 6; 15:10–21; 17:12–18; 18:18–23; and 20:7–18). Yet through this prophetic experience of alienation one perceives that God himself is also alienated. The life of Jeremiah, with all its vocational tensions, is in fact a mirror held up to the tensions that exist in the emotional life of God himself: He does not want to destroy Israel, but if he does not do so there will be no chance of her survival.[16] A comparison of 5:7–29 and 9:8–9 is suggestive: God's words betray the same inner tension that Jeremiah's betrayed when he spoke of his own failure as a prophet. And God, as it were, stands revealed as a suffering God, for it is not really the anguish of the prophet that gives this book its real strength, but the reader's insight that this human anguish, this conflict between duty and personality, is but a reflection of God's own all-too-human predicament. "O daughter of my people, gird on sackcloth, roll in ashes. Mourn as for an only child with bitter wailing"; but the "only child" we are to grieve for here in 6:26 is God himself.

The prophets had a remarkably clear and acute perception of events and of the fact that God was present with mankind in these same events. Theirs was a supernatural penetration, an intuition that enabled them to perceive the inner meaning of their own limited experience of God and so present God in the events of every hearer's own "today."

The Intellectuals Make Their Own Discovery of God

Direct religious experience is not too frequent in most lives, so the question arises as to whether God can be found in ordinary human experience and through the expression of everyday human values, independent of direct revelation. The sapiential literature of the Old Testament set itself to this particular task.[17]

a) The God of the Sages

Perhaps the situation in which the Wisdom tradition evolved was in part responsible for this new trend. It represents a pluralist, secular society in search of fundamental human values, and such tends to find a "faith" that is largely independent of confessional theology. A God so discovered would tend to be one who is a natural part of the human environment.

There is an unstrained, even necessary, relationship between the divine and the secular. Indeed, to say "human" is in some way to say "divine," so to find a truly human value is to find a divine characteristic. According to the sages of Israel, God can be found in the human search for wisdom itself, for even purely human wisdom is a trace left by God on the face of the world, simply because "the spirit of the Lord has filled the world," as Wisdom 1:7 perceives.

Perhaps one of the most remarkable insights into the nature of God is the concept of personified Wisdom found particularly in Proverbs (8 and 9), Sirach (24) and Wisdom (7–9). In these texts wisdom is presented almost as the feminine dimension of the deity—and so a call for mutuality and reciprocity. But the primary sapiential insight is simpler. Man is surrounded by a world that will always remain alien, even threatening, if it cannot be controlled, and the way to this end is by controlling its point of origin—that is, by arriving at a knowledge of a responsible creator and an understanding of his mastery. Thus the search for God becomes a quasi-philosophical quest for a personal creator.

Peoples of all races shared one particular experience of the transcendent—that of the mysterious and the spectacular in their environment as well as the contingent in human life. Israel was no different. The sense of the numinous which led them to God can be found in the older strata of folk-religion and folk-wisdom such as Proverbs 16 and Psalm 29. More explicit, however, in the Wisdom tradition is the experience of a *common humanity*. One naturally shares so much with others of a different cultural and educational background that one moves, imperceptively at first, to appreciate the existence of, and hence the value of, different beliefs and different norms. Are they not all created by the same God? (Prov. 25; Sir. 4:1–10). Such an appreciation of the common human denominator can lead to an openness to truth, however presented, and an awareness of its source. In fact, it is clear that Israel met God in history, and at the primary level this means the sphere of the secular: concrete events and interpersonal relationships. So Israel came to discover God right there where it lived—in the world. The Wisdom writers reflected on the basis of this personal experience and their concept of God is what might fittingly be called intellectually existential. That is, the experience of God found in Israel's sapiential tradition tends less to be based on divine intervention than on human perception and excogitation. Since a feeling for the numinous is natural to humankind, the environment is inclusive of the divine dimension at one or other of its dimensions—explicit or implicit. The Book of Proverbs furnishes many examples of this: the sense of mystery, 30:18ff; the absurdity of life, 16:1ff; the interplay of sorrow and joy that perhaps reaches to the very roots of life, 14:10–13—for "even in laughter the heart is sad, and the end of joy is grief." That speaks for all; that leads us beyond the known. It is no more than a step from this perception to God.

Behind it all lies the poverty of human desire and the natural feeling of unfulfillment that drives the individual to seek the absolute in some form. Life as experienced *is* inadequate, emotionally and intellectually. There are far too many human areas that escape comprehension. Thus one's natural human environment creates an internal space that needs to be filled by some form of personal encounter. Thus the very problem of human existence, and the concomitant problem of God as one who exists, can supply the stimulus that initiates the search for God. In fact, both Job and Qoheleth apply a critical analysis to human existence as such, though in different ways. Job proceeds from a worldview in which man is absurd, inherently contingent. So reason forces one to see God as cruel or disinterested. Even so, *he exists*. This is the problem as it appears to those who belong to a tradition of faith, and run into problems. But the problems themselves force such a one to face, directly, the personal task of working things out. The belief in a God, of whatever sort, is a starting-point for an encounter with a real God, honestly perceived. He may well be an awkward sort of God, but he is authentic. Such a discovery of a *real* God must result in a transformation of apperception. The protagonist of Job began with the same beliefs as the three friends of the Dialogues (chapters 3–31), but he is forced by pressure of intellectual honesty to pass on to a different, and unorthodox, concept of a God who is difficult to live with (chapters 38–42) but for all that is a reality one can be sure of. Comfort in religious platitudes is replaced, perhaps not too consolingly, by discomfort in truth. Thus even a rational refusal to accept the traditional face of God must, almost inevitably, lead one to some acceptance of God.

It is in this sense that the Book of Job is timeless, since one of the most pressing questions for any intellectual believer is the problem of *meaningless* suffering (for suffering of itself can make sense at times). What forces the mind out of its accustomed grooves is the way the young or the good seemingly become playthings of an absurd God. Anyone who thinks seriously about the human situation must tackle this problem of God. Yet a negative—or even inimical—attitude such as Job's can be a positive element in getting someone to discover for himself a personal God. This is what the last part of the Book of Job (chapters 38–42) purports to do.

A search for the divine at this level is a natural corollary to the fact that the human person can feel isolated, a stranger in his own world. Relying on his own resources he frequently feels inadequate; faced with death's inevitability he feels impotent. Job shows how this very feeling of impotence and intellectual rebellion against a soporific "faith" is a first step towards discovering God in the natural conflict of faith and reason. In the book as it now stands the three friends present faith and theology, while Job presents experience and the cutting edge of human intelligence.[18] What is the conclusion? There may be as many conclusions as there are readers, for God is discovered, even here, through personal experience, in this case the personal experience of intellectual unease. Certainly, the author of Job was driven to an appreciation of the transcendent as the only answer, simply because without the transcendent there is *no* answer. And Job continues to believe, even though the theophany affords no truly satisfying answer to life's problems. One is forced to ask—if there is no answer in the Book of Job, what is its value for the reader?[19] It articulates problems that are common to all thinking people; it shows how one is not alone in any sterile search; and above all it forces each individual to work out an intellectually viable answer for himself, free of confessional restraints.

The Book of Qoheleth offers a more placid, perhaps even a hedonistic, answer to the problem of God and the world of humankind. Life appears absurd; the framework of the book stresses this empirical fact (see 1:2ff in parallel with 12:8). But life is good, and it is after all the only stable value mankind knows. So one presumes, despite whatever contrary evidence there is, that a God who in some way can be seen to be good is responsible for the pleasure and the simple joy of existing, finite though that gift may be. Qoheleth may be able to say that "all go to the one place" when life's race is run (6:6; see also 2:1ff; 3:11ff; 5:18ff), but he also knows that it is a sweet race, and presupposes a God who "has made everything beautiful in its time" (3:11)—perhaps nothing more beautiful than the eternal lust for life.

In a more traditional vein, at peace with his intellect and his tradition, the author of Sirach suggests that—most naturally, perhaps—one can discover the real face of God through the contemplation of his marvelous creation (cf. Sir. 42:15ff), an idea that is so congenial to noncontestatory personalities that it is taken up frequently in both Testaments (Ps. 8; Wis. 13:3–5; even Rom. 1:19ff). It is a valuable insight on this adventurous road to the divine. All that is truly human leads most naturally to the creator: justice and a love of humanity (4:1–10); friendship itself (6:5–17); the love of learning (1:1–4). God has inserted into man's relationship with the environment the seeds of discovery (17:1–15). For to Ben Sira the ultimate principle is that all human wisdom comes from God and leads back to him (1–10): "All wisdom comes from the Lord and is with him forever."

Thus for the Old Testament God is discovered, even without direct religious experience, in the limits of human reason and even of religious faith—the limits to what one can really know and accept. It is a natural intuition regarding one's basic finiteness that forces one to stretch out to something that is infinite. And this is essentially a very human openness to, and need of, the "other." Ultimately, even the mystery of death itself can lead man to a conception of both divine and human nature that transcends human limits: "For God created man for incorruption and made him in the image of his own eternity" (Wis. 2:23–3:9).

b) The Passionate God of the Psalmists

The language that comes closest to the bone of humanity in the search for God is found in the Psalms. Here one may retrace the whole process of discovery as the Old Testament knew it.

Central to the anthropology of the Psalter is the belief that in some real, though perhaps indefinable, way man is "image of God," and that this is the key to his being. It is a human call for reciprocity. This concept runs like a living stream through the Old Testament, from Genesis 1 to Sirach 17 and the final, great theological synthesis represented by Wisdom 2:23. Thus man's religious and intellectual life is an effort at breaking through the dark cloud that lies between God himself and the divine in man. In a sense, both God and man have a common inner being, so in discovering man one discovers God, and thus discovers the core of one's own nature. It is a very human trait indeed— that need of the person for an ideal companion, a perfect complement to oneself, emotional, intellectual, and physical. This can drive the individual to seek God at a deep level of union, of human colloquy, and of intimacy.

Prayer is a natural response for all theists, and this can be met in Israel's tradition of psalmody. One discovers God in the depths of one's own being (Ps. 144), in one's human needs and the pain and alienation that is fellow traveler to everyone (the lament form, particularly the individual lament such as Ps. 6; Ps. 13; Ps. 28, etc.). On a different level, one meets the divine in a personal, mystical relationship that is the summit of all individual research for God.

The classic Psalm that was placed at the very beginning of the Psalter as a sort of superscription speaks of a relationship to God that is the summit of the religious adventure and the fruit of a lifetime's search. It is described in terms that one would sooner expect to find in an openly erotic work such as Song of Songs, and therefore it rivets the attention. "His *delight* is in the law of the Lord," the second verse of Psalm 1, uses a vocabulary that suggests the sensual and affective love that belongs to human intercourse. The Old Testament was no stranger to this idea of an intimacy of union with the divine. In the toils of a personal crisis of faith and of intellect the author of Psalm 73 could recover the same ecstasy of fulfillment: "Whom have I in heaven except you? And there is nothing upon earth that I *desire* besides you" (v. 25). Here the verb is one normally associated in the Bible with passionate love. On parallel lines the author of Job represents the same relationship as being an integral part of the religious tradition of Israel, when he describes the reward of the just: "you will *delight yourself* in the Almighty" (Job 22:26). It is worthy of note that this is a conservative statement of traditional theology where only the vocabulary alerts the reader to the high emotional content.

The human need of friendship can take many forms. It can be the savage alienation of pain and suffering that challenged Job, but it can also be the quotidian search for value and meaning, and the appreciation of the holy in simple, created things. But there always remains the discovery of God in intimacy.

Perhaps this is the final objective of the search.

On the whole (apart from such Wisdom Psalms as 37 and 73), the world of the psalmist is not one of contestation. These writers expand an already existent faith by deepening the comprehension of God and the proximity to him on a personal level that at times reaches the state of mystical union, where God is discovered totally, as a person.[20] Indeed, one of the things that determines the faith of the psalmist, as this impinges upon his relationship with God in prayer, is the Old Testament belief in his nearness to man. This is a theological faith, based on experience. God is present to his people (Dt. 4:7). In the experience of prayer, especially in the prayer of the Psalms of lament (such as 6; 13; 17; 28; 51, etc.), he is known to be close and active; indeed he is considered to be obliged to make contact with the one who prays.[21] An analysis of Psalm 42:2 and 73:23 in tandem is suggestive. In the recitation of these Psalms the great encounter with God that Exodus and Sinai signifies becomes a living reality to be encountered anew by each suppliant, in each new generation. In fact, this is the way Old Testament man would have understood "catechesis"—as the re-presentation, liturgically and by recitation, of the objective reality of the primary event of divine intervention in human history. Preeminently, it was by a liturgical reliving of the divine event through recitation of the text that, generation after generation, Israel grew into an awareness of its God.

The Old Testament Way to Discovery

The road to discovery has been clearly mapped by the cumulative witness of the biblical texts. Given the internal value of this testimony, one can accept as normative, for the Scriptures, a distinctive way of finding a personal God.

a) The Presentation of the Reality of God

The Old Testament does not set out to present a systematic body of doctrine about God or the world of man. The basic thrust of the biblical tradition is God's revelation of himself *through his acts in history*—word and deed.[22] It is existential, presenting an objective reality and not a subjective "sentiment." Externally, this self-revelation of God is a progression of interventive acts and events, with an inner dynamic of a continual development of supernatural perceptions that thrust towards an eschatological terminus. Discovery of the divine is facilitated by the accepted unity of salvation history thus formed, and the many levels that constitute the Old Testament are all united by this dynamic of expectation and fulfillment. Thus religious education in Israel takes on a distinctive coloring. "Catechesis" is primarily the presentation of an experience which may then be followed by a clarification of the implications of that experience.

A classic example remains the "Passover Renewal Covenant," presented by Josiah in 2 Kings 23:22 as a means of recovering the past event and its full implications.[23] In fact, Israel only gradually came to know and understand the God of Exodus as, generation after generation, the people reenacted liturgically that primary event and so "grew into" an awareness of its full implications, even in changed circumstances. Thus the process of discovery of God must, at least at its primary level, approximate the process used in the Old Testament texts: first, the presentation of an event that is personal (and not communitarian); then the human response to that grace of self-communication. If the act is *directly* divine (as e.g. Ex. 14:19 or Ex. 19) then the act of recitation provides an arena of encounter; if indirectly divine (mediated through the human dimension of reason or need) the dimension of "divine presence" (as in the lament form) may serve. Here the Hebrew concept of "knowledge" is crucial. It is not mainly an intellectual faculty. Because the whole of reality is constantly determined anew by God, all dealings with it are simultaneously an encounter with him.[24]

b) The Intellectual Development

From a primary *experience* of God (however historically presented) one must move to a self-awareness and subsequently to an awareness of the intrusion of the divine into the sphere of the "I" that results in a special relationship to the world. Emphasis must be placed on the nature of the biblical tradition as a means of reevoking an event, and on catechesis as encounter. God is known through experience. And the first result of this perception of God as revealed in Old Testament history, and reexperienced in the "now" of the reader, is an awareness of the fact that *one is chosen*. God is discovered because God gives the gift; *he* chooses those who are to know him. So one grows aware of the first implication—that God must have had a reason for so choosing. In this way discovery of God is recognition of grace and of vocation. Now while the Israelite came to a knowledge of God by this divine initiative of self-giving, the human dynamic—need, reason, etc.—can begin the process and bring one further on the way. The last step will often be taken by God—towards the searcher (as witness the theophany of Job 38–42 and the mystical insight of Psalm 73). The primary assumption is that human existence itself, and human history, remains the place where God is discovered, for in the Old Testament history is the arena of revelation. Of course, there is also the question of Israel's collaboration: a people set to interrogate religious beliefs, their own and those of contemporaries, and so moving—perhaps from agnosticism—to a personal conviction, even if this is not too strongly presented.

Witness the "confession" of Agur in Proverbs 30:1–4. Here a religious skeptic presents his argument, based on experience, that God is at best an absentee divinity, only to have the statement lead to an act of faith in vv. 5–9. Qoheleth, in his own way, can be seen as a proclamation of "moderate belief." Historically, this is presented by the recurring choice placed before Israel. Israel came into the Land of Canaan and found this new experience was a confirmation, a clarification, of faith, as well as a process of weeding out. The Elijah Cycle in 1 Samuel 17–19 is one further step in the people's search for meaning, as is the rise and fall of the monarchy in the Books of Kings. Thus running through this process of growth towards knowledge is the awareness of the historical perspective; not history in the sense of a sequence of ideas so much as history as an arena in which God acts and may be encountered.[25] By history in this sense is meant the "now" of every one and every generation. The Exodus event is not merely a historical event in that it happened in a determined past, but also in the sense that it is happening now; it is re-presented and experienced now.

Thus, while knowledge of God is primarily a gift of self on his part, both revelation and discovery are central to biblical religion.[26] They are not *two* approaches: The first, as it were, lights the fuse for the second; the first is a catechesis for the second—encounter calls for response. The biblical tradition presents us with a growing awareness of God in all that pertains to human history. It presents a knowledge of God that is intuitive; a concrete knowledge of significant events within which God is apprehended.

The Witness of the New Testament

Because of the nature of God's self-revelation—encounter—it is clear that Christ cannot be seen mainly as a teacher of "truth" or of ethics. His coming was an *event*, the final event of the history of salvation.[27]

Therefore God, in the perspective of the New Testament, is not primarily discovered through the teaching of a doctrine or a code of observance. He is discovered in *Christ as event*, for Christ is the mid-point of history between the "then" of the Old Testament and the "now" of our history. He is the arena of encounter.

In fact, the First Epistle of John gives us an insight into the changed categories of the New Testament.[28] Knowledge of God is of a special order. It was necessary for Jesus to come for mankind to arrive at it— for only the Christ-event gives us the categories necessary for full discovery: "And we know that the Son of God has come and has given us understanding, to know him who is true" (1 Jn. 5:20).

So we are dealing with a different order of knowledge. The process of discovery is not quite the same as it was for Old Testament man— for in spite of all philosophy, all intelligence, the pagans could not reach it independently: "See what love the Father has given *us*, that *we* should be called children of God" (1 Jn. 3:1). Only those "chosen," as recipients of the primary grace of sonship, can proceed further on the way of discovery. Yet it is not just those first few who met Jesus in the flesh that can be said to know God. The recipients of the First Letter of

John never met the historical Jesus, yet they *know* him. They know him because he *lives now*, and through him (after the glorification) they will live (Jn. 14:19). Only when they fully possess the life of Christ will they discover God in his fullness. Thus discovery of God clearly comes as a result of a life-union with the Christ. The Spirit that has come upon the baptized (1 Jn. 3:24b) "introduces" them to God. This primary experience brings them "into the family," as it were.

Therefore, it is essential to understand how the New Testament saw this sequence from *gift* to *new birth* to *sonship* finally flower into *knowledge*, on both the theological and the psychological levels.

The Evidence of the Synoptics

Jesus' own thinking about God can be perceived in those elements that distinguish his teaching.[29] The inbreaking of the reign of God dominates the opening of Christ's own active mission (cf. Mk. 1:14ff and Mt. 3:2), and thus underlines the radical exigence of divine vocation. It comes across as a challenge: to overcome the evil in the world and to build a new creation. All this is achieved by means of a new intervention of God that manifests the radicalism of God's love.

Jesus presents God as a father in a special, new way, and the concept dominates the New Testament view of God.[30]

Not only is he father, he is a father *who forgives sin* and liberates man. Therefore, one who has been liberated should be able to come to a closer knowledge of God through that very state of liberation. The idea of discovery precisely as discovery *of a father* comes from Jesus' own teaching. Even his ethical instruction is basically founded on the so-called "entrance liturgies" of the Psalter,[31] the interiorized ethics of the Old Testament, and this is inherently related to the conception of God as father—a child genuinely shares the father's nature, and does not need an external code of laws to determine filial response. So Jesus' teaching does not so much tell us *about* God as, by word and act, leads us to an experience of God and so to a lived relationship that, itself, leads to existential knowledge.

In all of this Jesus used the Old Testament categories of experience and apperception, adding the newer perception of God as a father who forgives. So the gift of sonship not only contributes to the discovery of God but is the constituent means thereto—as the unusual Matthaen text of 11:27 suggests: "All things have been delivered to me by my

Father; and no one knows the Son except the Father, and no one knows the Father except the Son and anyone to whom the Son chooses to reveal him." What this means is that God has given the full revelation of his own nature to Christ; and just as only a father *really* knows his son, so only a son really knows his father (see also Jn. 10:15); thus only a son can, by reason of this onthological relationship, pass on this knowledge of the divinity. This sequence of gift, knowledge, and discovery of relationship is crucial to any understanding of Christ's mission. In fact, the Greek text suggests that this full revelation, by which God allowed Jesus to participate in complete divine knowledge, has to do with the primary, complete experience of the godhead through Baptism.

The Pauline Synthesis

Paul, a Hebrew born of Hebrews (Phil. 3:5), writing according to Old Testament categories,[32] shows how God can be seen as revealing himself in two ways:

1. Through events of salvation history interpreted by the "word" of the experiencing community (Rom. 4:1ff; 9:1–5; 1 Cor. 10:1);
2. Through a new experience that he, himself, is living out in the "now" of the eschatological age.

This process of discovery is determined by the decisive event that reveals the "good news." One sees how this is communicated through the early community's interpretation of the Damascus event (cf. Gal. 1), an experience that reflects an aspect of the divinity that is to remain important to Paul: God acts through the Christ, and Christ is always the presence of God. Hebrews 2:14 offers a particularly Pauline conception of the good news from this point of view: "Since therefore the children share in flesh and blood, he himself likewise partook of the same nature, that through death he might destroy him who has the power of death," and this is peculiarly reechoed by the extended missionary speech of Acts 17:22ff.

As Paul views the Gospel, even the pagans could, to some extent, discover God in their own experience of his creation (Rom. 1:19). Here he is being particularly true to his Old Testament tradition. But he knew that this needed to be infused by an interpretation of that primary "experience," and this—as John was to perceive—comes only through the Spirit. Indeed, for Paul it is preeminently the gift of the *"pneuma,"* the spirit, that inaugurates the age of eschatological existence: God, *through* Son, *to* disciple is more often associated with John's theological synthesis, but in its own way the journey of the disciple to God through the Son is seen in a very Pauline light in 1 Corinthians 3:23: "And you are Christ's, and Christ is God's."

The Johannine Synthesis

John, perhaps to a degree unknown to other New Testament writers, is fascinated by the psychological progress from experience of the divine to discovery of God. One immediately thinks of texts such as John 6; 8; 9; 17, etc.

a) The Journey from "Logos" to God

The prologue to the Fourth Gospel puts the whole search for God in concrete terms with the concept of *"logos,"* word—at once Greek and Jewish, philosophical and theological. The use of the term *logos* represents a kind of *lingua franca*, suggesting both the creative aspect of divinity and the principle of a self-communicating universe. Because it is the nature of the *logos* to reveal itself, the world comes to existence through its instrumentality.[33] Therefore the created world has an inherent need of it, and it thus becomes the arena of self-revelation of the creator God. It is through Christ that one finds the divinity, and John equates the discovery of God in Jesus with the finding of "eternal life" (cf. Jn. 1; 17:13).

John presents man's search for a knowledge of God as an act of choosing (Jn. 3) that may force the one who first meets Christ to some reaction. It is therefore clear that a desire for God, or even the simple living of a Christian lifestyle, can force one to *think*, in the same terms that the primal experience forced Old Testament man to think.

b) The Journey from the "Sign" to the Reality

What most distinguished the Gospel of John is the clear distinction between *works* (that is, the Christ-event as perceived) and *signs* (the way the individual interprets this). Historically, a limited number of people experienced the works, and not all of those came to find God through them. Yet Jesus, who performed them, tends to be the one who calls them "works," for that is all they are to him: simply, God's acts presented in Christ. The "signs," however, are the way the "works"—even at second hand, by recitation or recounting—are viewed and accepted by the audience. In the first place, those who hear of (or, of course, experience) a "sign" accept it *as having a value* of demonstration. To such, they are no less than theophanies in effect. They demonstrate the reality of a relationship between Jesus and God that starts one thinking (Jn. 7:31).[34]

One of the best examples of this to be found in the Johannine synthesis is the key "sign" of John 6:66ff: "We believed" is one thing, but the sequel that "we came to *know*" is another, and shows a leap of perception from experience to discovery that marks the Fourth Gospel. More obvious, perhaps, is the episode recounted in John 8:13–20 that views Jesus as "light of the world." Why "light"? one asks; in what way is this an adequate sign? Well, taking this text in the whole perspective of the Gospel one recalls:

1. The situation of mankind is one of "darkness" (1:5ff);
2. To know the *facts about Jesus* is simply a matter of history, open to many (what Paul in *Romans* might call "natural" knowledge);
3. But to have "faith-knowledge"—that is, in John's perspective, to see these experiences from the point of view of God's eternal nature[35]—is in fact to enter the sphere of Jesus' own knowledge;
4. So Jesus throws light upon the event/sign, making it meaningful.

In its own way the miracle of John 9 stands as a paradigm of the value of "sign" as witness to God. First comes, quite simply, the experience of God's intervention (vv. 1–7). Then follows the human reaction, as reason (or skepticism) grapples with reality (vv. 8–12) and the witnesses refuse the total implications of what they have seen. When this is pretty much confirmed, they accept (to a greater or lesser degree, it is true) the *historical* evidence but refuse to accept its moral implications (vv. 13–34)—and it is no surprise that this section is formally the most imposing of the pericope. For everyone who approaches the *event* at second hand is left asking questions. Logic alone, it is clear, cannot bridge the gap (except for the blind man, perhaps) between "event" and "discovery" of God behind that event. The imponderables that enter at this secondary level are: first, the moral quality of the hearer (one sees a progression from Pharisees in v. 13 to parents in v. 18 to the primary recipient of the "sign" in v. 35); second, the action of God, the interpretative word of which John 6:44 is so classic an example; and finally, the gift of the Spirit.

The most psychologically significant text of John that deals with the human side of the search for God is 20:6ff, where the author sets out a deliberate contrast in terms of two parallel reactions to the same experience of divine intervention: "Simon Peter came, following him [John] . . . and saw," whereas John "saw and believed." The psychological depth of this statement is noteworthy.

In fact John, with his theological interest in the relationship between Christ and the Father, has a very marked conception of God, and a concern for growth in knowledge of him (14:9; 1:18; 1 Jn. 4:12), and there is a perceptible sequence of thought that follows from the Synoptic tradition

1. Jesus is the supreme revelation of God;
2. and God is essentially a father who initiates salvation;
3. to him all things tend (17:3; 20:17);
4. and he draws the believer towards Christ (6:43–45);
5. thus Christ's humanity becomes the arena of discovery,
6. and man's humanity leads to a discovery of God.

John speaks of "knowing" God through knowledge of the Son. Certainly, this fact of intimate relationship between the two has to be, for the reader, more than a subjective perception of God as a "meaningful religious sentiment." There is something onthological in question, as indeed is stressed by John's use of the formula "I am" in Greek in the texts where Jesus speaks of himself (such as 4:26; 6:35; 8:11, 23; 10:7–11; 11:25; 14:6; 15:1; 18:5).[36] To some extent this called forth the enmity of the leaders of the people, but it no less called forth a decisive declaration on the part of would-be believers (1:38; 9:35). It is clear, then, that Jesus was "son"—whatever that relationship *meant to him*; and indeed this is the context of the supreme statement of recognition that is found elsewhere in the Gospel tradition in Matthew 16:16— "who do *you* say I am?"

John's is a Gospel of signs, and the value of "sign" as the fourth Evangelist uses it is quite important for his readers. Without ever having met the historical Jesus, by being presented with a "sign"—a "testimony value" that an event had for first-level disciples—the second-level disciple (the reader of the Gospel and the Epistles) can be led to *enter into* the value of the event itself. At least it interests, perhaps even convinces, him; as event it may be presented as a personal motivation; and it may evoke a personal response.

Of course, it can be rejected at the personal level—event as "sign" is always an option; but it is likely that if the event is presented sharply to a reader it will leave some trace behind, even if only an uncomfortable feeling that one is missing out on something (Jn. 3). The text shows that many Jews *saw* the signs they asked for and never passed on to real discovery; many Christians of John's community never saw a sign, but the narration affected their lives. The implications of the post-Resurrection episode of John 20:24–29 are of particular interest here.[37]

In his Epistles John seems to make a comprehensive statement (1 Jn. 4:7; 4:8): whoever *loves*, evolves to a state where he is *born of* (i.e. baptism) and *knows* God. As John sees it, only the Christian can so know God, for to discover him fully one needs first to be born of his grace. And one cannot help being struck by the fact that John, through his pervasive use of the term "to know," sees the discovery of God as something experiential and affective rather than as pure intellectual perception. But this grows intellectually in the Christian as he pursues this intimacy from primary gift to experience perceived to a cultivated growth.

The New Testament Way to Discovery

Jesus, as Christ-event, is the mid-point of time, the bridge between the Scriptures and the eschatological now of the community. To recognize him it is essential to trace the process from Calvary to Apostolic Church; that is, to trace the progress of the growing self-awareness of the first disciples, which was an evolving consciousness of the implications of the Christ-event. From that point it is necessary to look again at, and appreciate with hindsight, the historical person of Jesus and his mission. One thus arrives at a recognition of the mystery of God. For the central dynamic of the New Testament is the fact that human existence has been radically transformed by encounter with the Christ-event. This happens, historically, on two levels: encounter with Christ directly (the experience of the disciples) and encounter with the community as mediator of the event. This was perceived by the early church precisely as "gospel"—glad news, joy-bringing news (cf. Gal.

5:22); a message of freedom and liberation. The central point of tension is the fact that the "news" *is a person*—God himself. And the discovery of God has come full circle, from promise to Abraham that "I shall be with you" to the fact of Christ—God who *is* with us in our nature and our form (Phil. 2:6ff).

The revelation of God in the New Testament is no longer through or in the history of one people, but is universal.[38] It is based on the nature of man himself, and this is seen in the way Christ, at least to a remarkable degree, based his ethical teaching on the Old Testament *tôrôt* of entry[39] (such as Ps. 15 and Ps. 24, esp. vv. 3–6), where the emphasis is less on ethics as observance of an external code than on morality as the articulation of one's interiority as a human being. Thus God can be discovered by each generation—in its own humanity and in his fatherhood. God is father; that determines man's true nature. God is discovered in the human, as man achieves his full human dignity by coming to him who is that to which humanity aspires.

Practically, for the post/Ascension community the discovery of God must in some way be coterminous with the reality of Christ. That is, in Christ we have the self-revelation of God addressed to all. Therefore we must find the "language" of discovery in the experience of the Christ-event.

The discovery of God always begins on the level of life as experienced. This is evidenced by the "vocation" texts of the Gospels, as one sees the development of discipleship in which "fishermen," by means of encounter, become "fishers of men" through a process of deepening awareness that leads to faith. It is essential to New Testament catechesis that in the "good news" we are not presented with a *doctrine of God*, but with a person; so discovery is in fact a process of plumbing the depths of a personality—it is very intimate for each individual and very experiential. The New Testament offers no thesis on God, but presents a person who becomes an arena of encounter in which each individual may experience some aspect of him that can focus personal commitment.

The human environment is offered as a sacrament of Christ in the writings of the New Testament, where the emphasis is probably more anthropological than messianic.[40] Faced with Christ and humanity as reality, a choice must be made, even forced. Since the quest ends in the discovery that God is "father," the choice must be at the level of the discovery of fatherhood in God, and the exclusive role of sonship in the disciple. In effect, biblical "catechesis" thrusts the recipient into a situation where a choice becomes real.

General Conclusion

A voyage of discovery begins with experience, with the "I." One interrogates one's own perceptions of self and of environment, and if it is self-sufficient, if there are no questions, then probably the first spark that lights the fuse has not been given. One has not been granted the primary gift of divine discontent.

The Old Testament sets the stage for this interrogation by means of its double dynamic: the tension inherent in a history that is geared to fulfillment, and the repeated revelations about God, man, and the world that activate man's thinking. This was the role of religious education as the Bible saw it—*creating a space,* showing one's limits and needs, establishing an arena where encounter becomes possible. One discovers oneself, and one discovers God at the same time, though it is not always the fact of *Christ* that one perceives. Yet the discovery of God in the history of his self-revelation (e.g. Wis. 13:1–5 and Rom. 1:18ff) leads to liberation, as one becomes more human, more naturally geared to a created world that one has not created oneself and that thus presses on one as alien, unless integration is achieved by finding the creator. Only in Christ can one achieve full integration, because only thus does one become fully human, and Christ is the answer to human needs and human aspirations.

Man's search for God in the Bible is in fact not the starting point, but the consequence of the fact that God, the transcendent, is the environment in which we breathe. Catechesis is successful because God seeks us more than we seek him; he is neither outside us nor inside us for us to seek—he is our natural ambient all at once. That was the prophetic insight; it remains the intuition of all on the way to discovery. Historically (in Judaism and Christianity) the discovery of a personal God is due to an individual experience of an outside intervention.

Those who discover him—those whom in reality he has "discovered"—will always remain a "remnant" in their own society, for ultimately it is only those whom God chooses who find him. The gift is given only to some, and to Christ this remains part of the "mystery of

God" (see Mt. 20:16 and 22:14 par.). In the last analysis it is God's gift to man, and not all are called to that intimacy that is discovery.

Notes

1. J. Coppens, "La Notion vétérotestamentaire de Dieu. Position du problème," in *La Notion Biblique de Dieu* (Leuven: University Press, 1976), p. 63.
2. See for example G. von Rad, *Genesis*, OTL (London: S.C.M., 2nd ed. 1963), pp. 154ff. In his commentary E. A. Speiser, *Genesis*, AB (New York: Doubleday, 1964), spoke of the human detail of Abraham's obedience and his acceptance of the changed form of the name.
3. See H. Ringgren, *Israelite Religion* (Philadelphia: Fortress Press, 1966), pp. 66ff.
4. G. E. Wright, *God Who Acts. Biblical Theology as Recital* (London: S.C.M., 1966), pp. 20ff.
5. J. Marsh, *Saint John* (Harmondsworth: Pelican Gospel Commentaries, 1968), p. 98.
6. See Wright, *God Who Acts*, pp. 33ff.
7. A. Soggin, *Joshua*, OTL (London: S.C.M., 1972), p. 230.
8. Wright, *God Who Acts*, pp. 59ff.
9. This idea reaches its climax in 1 Cor. 12:3: "No one can discover Jesus to be Lord except by the Holy Spirit."
10. H. Cazelles, "Le Dieu du Yahviste et de l'Elohiste," in *Notion Biblique de Dieu*, pp. 81ff.
11. For the whole of this section of Ex. 3, a useful background can be found in G. Childs, *Exodus*, OTL (London: S.C.M., 1974), pp. 71ff.
12. Coppens, in *Notion Biblique de Dieu*, pp. 66ff.
13. See A. Gelin, *Key Concepts of the Old Testament* (Glen Rock, N.J.: Paulist, 1963), pp. 15ff.
14. See Coppens, "La Notion vétérotestamentaire," pp. 66ff.
15. This idea is developed in J. L. Mays, *Hosea*, OTL (London: S.C.M., 1969).
16. An intuitive treatment of this whole idea is presented by A. J. Heschel, *The Prophets*, II (New York: Harper & Row, 1962), pp. 1ff.
17. In the Hebrew canon of the Old Testament this comprises Job, Psalms, Proverbs, Qoheleth and Song of Songs. Added to this one can include Wisdom and Sirach. A good introduction can be found in B. W. Anderson, *Understanding the Old Testament* (Englewood Cliffs, N.J.: Prentice Hall, 3rd ed. 1975), pp. 502–562.
18. The dialogue develops through a conflict of orthodoxy and heresy, as Job responds to the arguments of the three friends: 4–5 vs. 6–7; 8 vs. 9–10; 11 vs. 12–14; 15 vs. 16–17; 18 vs. 19; 20 vs. 21; 22 vs. 23–24; 25 vs. 26–27.

19. R. A. F. MacKenzie, "The Purpose of the Yahweh Speeches in the Book of Job," in *Bib* 40(1959), pp. 432–445.

20. D. Cox, *Proverbs, With an Introduction to Sapiential Literature*, (Wilmington, N.J.: Michael Glazier, 1982), chapter 3 passim.

21. P. Drijvers, *The Psalms. Their Structure and Meaning* (New York: Herder, 1965), pp. 104ff.

22. See the essay in G. E. Wright and R. Fuller, *The Book of the Acts of God* (Harmondsworth: Penguin, 1957), pp. 26ff.

23. For a more complete treatment of the concept of re-presentation, see R. Clements, *God's Chosen People. A Theological Interpretation of the Book of Deuteronomy* (London: S.C.M., 1968).

24. W. Eichrodt, *Theology of the Old Testament*, II (London: S.C.M., 1967), pp. 268ff.

25. See Wright, *God Who Acts*, pp. 46ff.

26. Gelin, *Key Concepts*, p. 14.

27. See Wright, *God Who Acts*, p. 59f.

28. See E. Viau, "'Connaître Dieu', une expression johannique," in *VieSpir* 77 (1947), pp. 324–333; and J. Gaffney, "Believing and Knowing in the Fourth Gospel," in *TS* 26 (1965), pp. 215–241.

29. See J. Giblet, "La Révélation de Dieu dans le Nouveau Testament," in *Notion Biblique*, pp. 233f.

30. J. Jeremias, *New Testament Theology, I, The Proclamation of Jesus* (London: S.C.M., 1971), pp. 61ff.

31. Ibid., pp. 152ff. See also C. Westermann, *Praise and Lament in the Psalms* (Edinburgh: T. & T. Clark, 1982).

32. Giblet, "La Révélation de Dieu," p. 239.

33. An idea that is not too far removed from the sapiential idea of Wisdom personified.

34. See R. E. Brown, *The Gospel According to John*, AB, I (New York: Doubleday, 1966), pp. 315ff, and J. Marsh, *Saint John* (Harmondsworth: Pelican Gospel Commentaries, 1968), pp. 335ff.

35. Marsh, *Saint John*, p. 355.

36. Ibid., passim.

37. Ibid., pp. 644ff.

38. Giblet, "La Révélation de Dieu," p. 231.

39. Jeremias, *New Testament Theology*, pp. 154f.

40. Giblet, "La Révélation de Dieu," p. 232.

CHAPTER 4

Faith

David Whitten Smith

A recent article in the press carried the headline, "United States, Eire lead world in faith." The article reported on an international survey. In the United States, 95 percent stated that they believe in God and 48 percent rated God's importance as number ten on a scale of one to ten. In Europe, belief in God was only 75 percent overall.[1]

Would the United States still have been first if the questions posed had been those suggested by James Fowler in *Stages of Faith?*

— What are you spending and being spent for? What commands and receives your best time, your best energy?
— What causes, dreams, goals or institutions are you pouring out your life for?
— As you live your life, what power or powers do you fear or dread? What power or powers do you rely on and trust?
— To what or to whom are you committed in life? In death?
— With whom or what group do you share your most sacred and private hopes for your life and for the lives of those you love?
— What *are* those most sacred hopes, those most compelling goals and purposes in your life?[2]

The contrast between the view of faith underlying the newspaper article and the view underlying Fowler's study is important for religious educators. Many in our culture take for granted an abstract faith that has little relation to their lives. This is not biblical faith, as we will see.

Other topics of special interest to religious educators will be treated as the chapter proceeds. The material will be arranged according to the major sections of the Bible which relate extensively to faith. Here are some of the topics which will be treated in more detail and where their treatment is found:

The relationship between faith and healing will be discussed in the section on the synoptic Gospels. Some Christians claim that God is always ready to heal. If someone with whom a Christian prays for healing continues to be sick, they say, it must be because that person does not have faith.

The relationship between miracles (spectacular signs) and faith will be discussed in the section on John. There I will accept the reality of God's power in our own time. But I will also suggest that the anxiety to identify particular actions as miracles can be an effort to force faith on unbelievers.

The question of justification by faith will be treated in the section on Paul. The relation between Paul and James will be faced there, and some reference to Roman Catholic and Lutheran traditions offered.

Some Christians identify faith with commitment to precise statements inherited from the past. While I respect tradition highly, I will point out in several places how often biblical trust in God involves the risk of a certain ambiguity. We must accept God's new action which cannot be adequately understood simply by accepting all that we have learned from our elders. Spiritual discernment is an essential part of faith.

Of all these questions, the one most crucial for an understanding of faith in the Bible is the contrast between a mainly intellectual faith— belief in certain propositions—and a radical faith of self-surrender and trust. To this question we turn first.

Fowler's questions are helpful for several reasons. They move us beyond an abstract faith into the roots of our being. They help us see that we all have faith in something: The crucial question is *what* we put our faith in.[3]

The true object of our faith is revealed most clearly in times of crisis when we are forced to make painful choices. But even in less stressful times, when our deepest roots may remain invisible even to ourselves, we operate daily on the basis of certain beliefs about the nature of this mysterious experience we call life or creation. We put our trust in someone, something, or some combination of elements. We follow the direction in our lives implied by the choices we have made. Ultimately, we entrust ourselves, our hopes and dreams, our very life and future to these decisions and to the objects of our faith. If these choices lead us to invest faith in an unworthy object, it will let us down in time of crisis. We will be "put to shame" for having trusted in it.

We recognize easily that our commitments and actions are affected by our faith. If we place ultimate faith in money, in success, in clever tricks, in the influence of powerful friends, in our own strength or intelligence, we will make certain kinds of commitments and choose certain actions. But the opposite is also true: Our faith is affected by the commitments and actions we choose. Our very vision of reality and understanding of value are influenced by the choices we have made. If our choices are in accord with reality and true value, we will see things that others do not see or understand. We choose on the basis of what we see, but we also see on the basis of what we choose.

Our blindness resulting from wrong choices is the reason God speaks so often in paradox and parable. He is trying to break open our closed minds so that a glimmer of new vision may lead us to take new actions, resulting in progressively clearer vision. But the beginnings of this process may seem to move us from clarity to ambiguity. Clarity based on false vision is of no value. But the acceptance of ambiguity as a necessary step along the way takes courage. Spiritual discernment, growing from a trusting and living relationship with God, can help us through this painful process.

Biblical Faith

Like Fowler's questions, biblical faith looks beyond cognitive questions to consider how we express our convictions in actual practice. It does not simply ask, "Does God exist," nor even, "How important is God?" Rather it considers alternative objects of faith, especially in time of crisis, and asserts that they are inadequate. Some examples of these alternatives are military might and alliances:

> Woe to those who go down to Egypt for help,
>   who depend upon horses;
> Who put their trust in chariots because of their number,
>   and in horsemen because of their combined power,
> But look not to the Holy One of Israel
>   nor seek the LORD! (Is. 31:1).[4]

city defenses:

> But if you do not hearken to the voice of the LORD, your God . . . [your enemy] will besiege you in each of your communities, until the great, unscalable walls you trust in come tumbling down all over your land (Dt. 28:15 and 52).

family, relatives, friends:

> Even my friend who had my trust
>   and partook of my bread, has raised his heel against me.
> But you, O LORD, have pity on me, and raise me up (Ps. 41:10–11a). [5]

one's own riches or intelligence:

> Why should I fear in evil days
>   when my wicked ensnarers ring me round?
> They trust in their wealth;
>   the abundance of their riches is their boast.
> Yet in no way can a man redeem himself,
>   or pay his own ransom to God;
> Too high is the price to redeem one's life; he would never have enough
>   to remain alive always and not see destruction.
> For he can see that wise men die,
>   and likewise the senseless and the stupid pass away,
>   leaving to others their wealth (Ps. 49:6–11).

evil plots, extortion, what is crooked and devious:

> Therefore, thus says the Holy One of Israel:
>   Because you reject this word,
> And put your trust in what is crooked and devious,
>   and depend on it,
> This guilt of yours shall be
>   like a descending rift
> Bulging out in a high wall
>   whose crash comes suddenly, in an instant (Is. 30:12–13). [6]

idols, other gods:

> They shall be turned back in utter shame
>   who trust in idols;
> Who say to molten images,
>   "You are our gods" (Is. 42:17). [7]

and even elements of "true faith" itself, but improperly understood, insincerely practiced, or in isolation from a life of justice:

> Thus says the Lord of hosts, the God of Israel: Reform your ways and your deeds, so that I may remain with you in this place. Put not your trust in the deceitful words: "This is the temple of the LORD! The temple of the

LORD! The temple of the LORD!" Only if you thoroughly reform your ways and your deeds; if each of you deals justly with his neighbor; if you no longer oppress . . . will I remain with you in this place, in the land which I gave your fathers long ago and forever. . . . Because you have committed all these misdeeds, says the LORD, . . . I will do to this house named after me, in which you trust, and to this place which I gave to you and your fathers, just as I did to Shiloh. I will cast you away from me (Jer. 7:3–7 and 13–15).

Let us suppose you bear the name of "Jew" and rely firmly on the law and pride yourself on God. Instructed by the law, you know his will and are able to make sound judgments on disputed points. . . . You who pride yourself on the law, do you dishonor God by breaking the law? . . . Circumcision, to be sure, has value if you observe the law, but if you break it you might as well be uncircumcised! (Rom. 2:17–18, 23, 25).

None of those who cry out, "Lord, Lord," will enter the kingdom of God but only the one who does the will of my Father in heaven. When that day comes, many will plead with me, "Lord, Lord, have we not prophesied in your name? Have we not exorcised demons by its power? Did we not do many miracles in your name as well?" Then I will declare to them solemnly, "I never knew you. Out of my sight, you evildoers!" (Mt. 7:21–23).

"You are the Messiah," Simon Peter answered, "the Son of the living God!" Jesus replied, "Blest are you, Simon son of John! . . ."

From then on Jesus [the Messiah] started to indicate to his disciples that he must go to Jerusalem and suffer greatly there. . . . At this, Peter took him aside and began to remonstrate with him. . . . Jesus turned on Peter and said, "Get out of my sight, you satan!" (Mt. 16:16 and 21–23).

From the examples given, we see the adequate object of biblical faith, its characteristics, and its relational quality. The object is principally God, secondarily humans or institutions insofar as God is working in and through them. The characteristics include belief, trust, obedience to direction, and self-surrender. The relational quality is based on the fact that our faith is a response to God's self-revelation. He invites us to enter into communion with himself. That call-response in the Old Testament is centered on the covenant. In the New Testament it is centered on Jesus Christ and his self-sacrifice on the cross. Through him and his sacrifice God reveals himself to us and invites us into communion with himself and with each other.

In recent Roman Catholic tradition, these points are well expressed in the document on revelation from the Second Vatican Council. For example:

In his goodness and wisdom God chose to reveal himself and to make known to us the hidden purpose of his will (see Eph. 1:9) by which through Christ, the Word made flesh, man might in the Holy Spirit have access to the Father and come to share in the divine nature (see Eph. 2:18; 2 Pt. 1:4). . . .

"The obedience of faith" (Rom. 16:26; see 1:5; 2 Cor. 10:5–6) "is to be given to God who reveals, an obedience by which man commits his whole self freely to God, offering the full submission of intellect and will to God who reveals," and freely assenting to the truth revealed by him.[8]

Old Testament

In the Old Testament, the concept of faith is widespread. It is especially frequent in contexts of beginnings, of severe threat, and of expression of piety. Thus we find the concept important in the traditions about Adam, about Abraham, in the exodus-desert-conquest traditions, in the Assyrian and Babylonian threats culminating in the exile, in Job, and in the Psalms.

Several Hebrew words are frequently used. The box shows the basic meaning of the most common verbs. They are often used in parallel verses or passages as nearly equivalent.

		either absolutely:	to be full of confidence, unsuspecting
bātah	to *feel safe*, to *trust*	or with an express object:	to trust in someone or something
hāsăh	to *seek refuge* in something or someone		
he'emîn	to *be sure in the mind* about something or someone, and so as a result to *trust* in it or them		

The verb *he'emin* is related linguistically to the verb *ne'eman*:

ne'emān	to prove oneself reliable or "faithful"
	to have stability, to remain

The range of meanings of *he'emin* is perhaps closest to the English word "faith" (balanced between belief and trust), that of *bātah* closest to the English word "trust."

He'emin and *ne'eman*, related in origin, are also related in meaning. We want the objects we believe in and put our faith in (*he'emin*) to be truly solid and reliable (*ne'eman*). We don't want them to let us down. Both these verbs are related linguistically to the exclamation *'amēn*, one of the few Hebrew words all Christians know. *Amen* expresses the confidence a person has (*he'emin*) in something he or she judges to be solid and reliable (*ne'eman*).

Other words important for the concept of faith include the verbs "wait for," "hear," "fear the Lord," and "not be put to shame."[9]

The precise sense of a given word in a particular passage depends more on context than on the dictionary. For example, the verb *he'emin* is thought by some to stand for the most authentic Hebrew faith. Yet the word can also be used of an object of faith which is not religious and not worthy of confident belief. In First Samuel 27:12 the Philistine chief Achish trusted (*he'emin*) David to stay on his side and fight for him, but his trust was based on David's lies. Hebrew and Christian belief takes its certainty not from the dictionary meaning of the word used but from the facts of the case.

Not all passages important for our study of faith use these words. One can talk about faith, especially in narrative, without using any words for it at all.

Beginnings 1: Adam

All sin and all misery flow from a radical original act of broken faith. As Genesis visualizes this primal event (chapters 3–11), Adam and Eve's refusal to believe, trust, and obey God breaks all faithful relationships—our relationship with God and our relationships with each other. Suspicion and self-seeking enter the world.

All the rest of Scripture chronicles the divine-human adventure seeking to undo that primal revolt. Radical sin requires radical healing.

Beginnings 2: Abraham

The traditions about Abraham show the foundational importance of faith. Abraham was invited to entrust his life and future to this "strange god" who called (Gn. 12:1–4), to respond to that call by leaving home and family, to believe that God's promise of offspring could be trusted (15:6), and to trust that promise even when he was called to sacrifice his only son Isaac—a demand which seemed to make mockery of the promise (ch. 22).

The risk Abraham took was to believe that this "new god" was honest, knew what he was talking about, and had the power to make it work. Thus he trusted enough to risk his whole future to this God rather than to his family, friends, city of origin, and habitual life. He lived out that belief and trust by following God's directions and abandoning all those other things which might have given meaning to his life. This faith was tested day by day as actual events did not seem to fulfill the promise. God kept promising a more complete fulfillment in the future. Finally, toward the end of his long life, Abraham could actually see the beginning of that fulfillment in his son Isaac. At that point the ultimate test asked him to sacrifice that one concrete realization of the promise which he could see, and believe that God could fulfill the promise and give meaning to Abraham's life despite the seeming collapse of all grounds for hope. With this background in mind, the story of the sacrifice of Isaac (Gn. 22) has a powerful impact.

Abraham's faith was essential for the foundation of the promised nation. Both Paul and James return to his example when they discuss faith.

Notice the importance of spiritual discernment in Abraham's case. His faith could not be confident acceptance of his pagan tradition. As we proceed we will see the importance of discernment in other cases where its necessity may not be so clear—where the tradition is in fact authentic. Authentic tradition may not be authentically understood. And even authentic tradition may not prepare us completely for what God will do in a new situation. The Pharisees and Sadducees were traditionalists, but they missed what God was doing in Jesus. Faith is not just an acceptance of what we were taught in the past. Our faith is in God, but we must discern what is of God.[10]

Beginnings 3: Exodus, Desert, Conquest

The next major step in God's call of his people was the exodus from Egypt, the Sinai covenant, and the entry into the Promised Land. Moses was afraid the people would not believe that the Lord had sent him, so God gave him several signs. When the people saw the signs, they believed. When they heard what God intended to do for them, they bowed and worshiped (Gn. 4).

This initial faith in the reality of God's revelation and the trust-worthiness of his promise had to be translated into action. The people had to consent to leave Egypt and to follow Moses' leadership. Again and again as they wandered in the desert they lost confidence and withdrew their obedience despite the signs of God's presence and power. As we will see again in the Gospels, God's "signs" are adequate for the well-disposed, but not compelling.

> And the LORD said to Moses, "How long will this people spurn me? How long will they refuse to believe in me, despite all the signs I have performed among them?" (Nm. 14:11).
> The whole community broke out with loud cries, and even in the night the people wailed. All the Israelites grumbled against Moses and Aaron, the whole community saying to them, "Would that we had died in the land of Egypt, or that here in the desert we were dead! Why is the LORD bringing us into this land only to have us fall by the sword? Our wives and little ones will be taken as booty. Would it not be better for us to return to Egypt?" So they said to one another, "Let us appoint a leader and go back to Egypt" (Nm. 14:1–4). [11]

At Sinai the Israelites committed themselves to God in a community act of faith (Ex. 24:6–8). But the covenant which promised a special relationship with God also warned of disaster if they refused to respond in faith. The Lord is a jealous God. If his people prefer to trust something or someone else, he will let them depend on what they wish—to their shame. The covenant curses warned:

> "If you do not hearken to the voice of the LORD, your God, and are not careful to observe all his commandments which I enjoin on you today, all these curses shall come upon you and overwhelm you. . . . The LORD will raise up against you a nation from afar. . . . They will besiege you in each of your communities, until the great, unscalabel walls you trust in come tumbling down all over your land" (Dt. 28:15, 49, 52).

And in the Song of Moses from Deuteronomy we read:

God will say, "Where are their gods
 whom they relied on as their 'rock'?
Let those who ate the fat of your sacrifices
 and drank the wine of your libations
Rise up now and help you!
 Let them be your protection!" (Dt. 32:37–38).

In this period of national beginnings, the crucial element is the communal faith which puts the whole people into a special relationship with God. This special relationship is freely offered by God. The people have done nothing to earn or deserve it. But it can only be maintained if they respond in faith, obedience, and trust. This pattern of undeserved rescue received in a surrender of faith is experienced more deeply still in the sacrifice of Jesus for our salvation, and is the basis of Paul's concept of justification by faith.

National Threat: Assyria, Babylonia, and Exile

The faith by which an individual or a community lives becomes clearest in situations of crisis. We find frequent references to faith when the nation's very existence is threatened by Assyria and Babylonia, the time when so much of the prophetic literature arose.

The prophets frequently call the people to trust in the Lord rather than in alliances and military defenses.

Woe to the rebellious children,
    says the LORD,
Who carry out plans that are not mine,
    who weave webs that are not inspired by me,
    adding sin upon sin.
They go down to Egypt,
    but my counsel they do not seek.
They find their strength in Pharaoh's protection
    and take refuge in Egypt's shadow;
Pharaoh's protection shall be your shame,
    and refuge in Egypt's shadow your disgrace (Is. 30:1–3).[12]

The necessity of trust is the main point of the famous Emmanuel passage in Isaiah chapter 7. King Ahaz' neighbors are threatening to depose him and substitute a king of their own choice. He plans in fear to appeal to Assyria for protection. Isaiah confronts Ahaz, warning him not to appeal to Assyria. Isaiah prophesies in the name of the Lord that, despite fearsome appearances, Ahaz will be succeeded by his own son ("The virgin shall be with child, and bear a son." 7:14) and his enemies will be destroyed ("Before the child learns to reject the bad and choose the good, the land of those two kings whom you dread shall be deserted." 7:16). All this is guaranteed because the Lord is with his people ("[The virgin] shall name him Immanuel [with-us-is-God]." 7:14).

Typically, Isaiah can offer no proof aside from his claim that it is the Lord's word he is speaking. All political indications point the other way. Faith here depends not just on trust that God is honest and able to bring about what he promises, but also on the discernment that what Isaiah says is indeed the word of the Lord. One who is accustomed to trust the Lord rather than political and military strength is disposed to discern the prophetic word correctly. Isaiah warns:

> Unless your faith is firm [he'emin]
>   you shall not be firm [ne'eman]! (Is. 7:9).

Note how risky is the act of faith that Isaiah is urging. Ahaz chooses not to take the risk.

About two decades later Ahaz' decision brings disaster for his successors. Assyria did respond to his appeal and destroy his enemies. But now Assyria has turned on Judah and Jerusalem. Jerusalem is under siege. Representatives of the Assyrian king urge the city to surrender, arguing that it is too risky to trust in the Lord, as Ahaz himself had earlier decided:

> "On what do you base this confidence of yours? Do you think mere words substitute for strategy and might in war? On whom, then, do you rely, that you rebel against me? This Egypt, the staff on which you rely, is in fact a broken reed which pierces the hand of anyone who leans on it. That is what Pharaoh, king of Egypt, is to all who rely on him. But if you say to me, We rely on the LORD, our God, is not he the one whose high places and altars Hezekiah has removed, commanding Judah and Jerusalem to worship before this altar in Jerusalem? . . .
> "Do not listen to Hezekiah when he would seduce you by saying, the LORD will rescue us. Has any of the gods of the nations ever rescued his land from the hand of the kin of Assyria? Where are the gods of Hamath and Arpad? . . . Where are the gods of the land of Samaria?" (2 Kgs. 18:19–22 and 32–34).

Yet Isaiah expresses trust in the Lord by referring to God's promise to protect the temple, the king, and the holy city Zion:

> Therefore, thus says the LORD GOD:
>   See, I am laying a stone in Zion,
>   a stone that has been tested,
> A precious cornerstone as a sure foundation;
>   he who puts his faith in it shall not be shaken (Is. 28:16).

Therefore, thus says the LORD concerning the king of Assyria: He shall not reach this city, nor shoot an arrow at it, nor come before it with a shield, nor cast up siegeworks against it. He shall return by the same way he came, without entering the city, says the LORD. I will shield and save this city for my own sake, and for the sake of my servant David (Is. 37:33–35).

This time king and people take the risk to trust Isaiah's prophetic message. And Isaiah's confidence is proven to be well-founded—in his day. Yet this was a prophetic promise for that particular situation, not a universal promise the people could presumptuously depend on in a very different situation. A century and a half later, Jeremiah had to pass on another prophetic word which seemed on the surface to conflict with Isaiah's:

> Put not your trust in the deceitful words: "This is the temple of the LORD! The temple of the LORD! The temple of the LORD!" Only if you thoroughly reform your ways and your deeds . . . will I remain with you in this place, in the land which I gave your fathers long ago and forever (Jer. 7:4–5, 7).

In Jeremiah's case, king and people fail to discern God speaking in his oracles. They prefer to trust Isaiah's earlier prophecy which all acknowledge to be authentic, applying it mechanically to their very different situation. The result is disaster, as Jeremiah had correctly predicted. This example shows how inadequate to true faith is a merely intellectual assent to a proposition that does not penetrate to the heart of the matter. Even true words of God cannot be used mechanically to understand a current situation. Only the person who is in touch with the reality behind the words can understand them correctly. Sometimes religion itself is a barrier to faith.

This problem of discernment at the base of faith is powerfully illustrated again when Jeremiah confronts the prophets Hananiah and Shemaiah. Jeremiah has been prophesying after the first exile of 597 that the Lord wants his people to submit to Babylon. Hananiah confronts Jeremiah directly, claiming that the Lord is about to break the yoke of Babylon and set free those who are in captivity. Jeremiah can only refer to the experience of the past, that prophets have usually prophesied disaster. Prophecies of peace are a risky business. Soon after, Jeremiah sends a letter to the exiles in Babylon, proclaiming that the Lord wants them to settle down and prepare for a long stay. Shemaiah, a prophet in exile, writes back to the priests in Jerusalem urging them to arrest and punish Jeremiah. Other prophets in Babylon are prophesying against Jeremiah's message, too. Jeremiah prophesies punishment against these various prophets, but to the people of the time the task of discerning true prophecy from false must have been very difficult:

> Hear this, Hananiah! The LORD has not sent you, and you have raised false confidence in this people (Jer. 28:15).
>
> Thus says the LORD of hosts, the God of Israel: Do not let yourselves be deceived by the prophets and diviners who are among you. . . . For they prophesy lies to you in my name; I did not send them, says the Lord (Jer. 29:8–9).
>
> Because Shemaiah prophesies to you without a mission from me, and raises false confidence, says the LORD, I will therefore punish Shemaiah, the Nehelamite, and his offspring (Jer. 29:31–32).

Second Isaiah, during the exile in Babylon, begins a development which will be helpful for discernment and will be greatly expanded in the New Testament. This is the concept of the Suffering Servant. Much false discernment is based on the presumption that God wants us to prosper in all situations without the necessity of suffering. In contrast, the Suffering Servant carries out his task before God in humility, poverty, weakness, and suffering. He is willing to walk in darkness, trusting the Lord when all visible indications deny the Lord's providence.

> Who among you fears the LORD,
>   heeds his servant's voice,
> And walks in darkness
>   without any light,
> Trusting in the name of the LORD
>   and relying on his God? (Is. 50:10).
>
> Who would believe what we have heard?
>   To whom has the arm of the LORD been revealed?
> He grew up like a sapling before him. . . .
> He was spurned and avoided by men,
>   a man of suffering, accustomed to infirmity
>
> While we thought of him as one stricken,
>   as one smitten by God and afflicted.
> But he was pierced for our offenses,
>   crushed for our sins.
>   .   .   .   .
> Through his suffering, my servant shall justify many,
>   and their guilt he shall bear.
> Therefore I will give him his portion among the great (Is. 53 *passim*).

Here we see faith going deeper than a mere belief of a particular statement or trust in a particular situation. There is no bargaining here. No part of life is left out of the surrender of faith. The Servant is so transformed by faith that he surrenders his whole life and future into the hands of the Lord. It is a depth of surrender like that of Abraham called to sacrifice Isaac, the one thing that gives meaning to his whole life. In the other direction, we discern the shadow of Jesus, who will do only what the Father calls him to do and will submit to the degradation and torture of the cross.

Wisdom Literature: Job

The book of Job is a fictional account of extreme crisis, the depths of despair. Job's friends emphasize that one cannot trust worldly goods, but their assurances are formalistic and irrelevant to Job's true situation. Job despairs of support from his friends and sees no promise of results from trust in God.

The resolution is unexpected. God does not answer Job's problems and questions. Rather he reveals *himself* to Job. This self-revelation in vision does not answer Job's questions; it changes his whole way of seeing the problem. As a result, Job ceases to demand answers. Instead he surrenders himself freely and totally to the God who has appeared to him.

> I know that you can do all things,
>   and that no purpose of yours can be hindered.
> I have dealt with great things that I do not understand;
>   things too wonderful for me, which I cannot know.
> I had heard of you by word of mouth,
>   but now my eye has seen you.
> Therefore I disown what I have said,
>   and repent in dust and ashes (Jb. 42:2–6).

The Swiss psychotherapist Paul Tournier shows how insoluble dilemmas can be moments of grace leading us deeper. They force us to let go of our own analysis of the problem, to let go of our own control and stop trying to force God to answer the problem as we have posed it:

> There are, then, two distinct levels: the level of logic and reason, of dilemma, of all our insoluble questions and problems. Then there is the deeper level of the personal, of life, of a living and personal encounter with

God and with men. The solution of our problems is to be found always on
the deeper level.[13]

We must leave the level of conflicts and dilemmas to the level of self-
examination under the searching light of God. We then can understand
that a dilemma is a sign; it is a sign that there are deeper discoveries to be
made, a new order to perceive which will transform the whole nature of the
problem.[14]

A contemporary example of crisis leading to new or deepened faith
is the twelve-step program of Alcoholics Anonymous. Those who have
passed through the purifying crisis of alcoholism frequently show an
exceptional faith. The first step involves a turning away from false
gods, especially alcohol and the illusion of self-control. The second
step is a rejection of despair, and the third an initial surrender of self to
an adequate object of ultimate faith:

1. We admitted we were powerless over alcohol—that our lives had become unmanageable.
2. Came to believe that a Power greater than ourselves could restore us to
   sanity.
3. Made a decision to turn our will and our lives over to the care of God *as
   we understood Him*.[15]

Another moving example of faith purified through deep crisis is the
story of Fr. Walter Ciszek, an American Jesuit priest who spent twenty
years under arrest in Russia. After two severe crises under interrogation, in which he nearly killed himself to avoid the strain, he suddenly
came to understand that:

God's will was not hidden somewhere "out there" in the situations in
which I found myself; the situations themselves *were* his will for me. What
he wanted was for me to accept these situations as from his hands, to let go
of the reins and place myself entirely at his disposal. He was asking of me
an act of total trust, allowing for no interference or restless striving on my
part, no reservations, no exceptions, no areas where I could set conditions
or seem to hesitate. He was asking a complete gift of self, nothing held
back. It demanded absolute faith: faith in God's existence, in his providence, in his concern for the minutest detail, in his power to sustain me,
and in his love protecting me. It meant losing the last hidden doubt, the
ultimate fear that God will not be there to bear you up. It was something
like the awful eternity between anxiety and belief when a child first leans
back and lets go of all support whatever—only to find that the water truly
holds him up and he can float motionless and totally relaxed.[16]

Expressions of Piety: The Psalms

Faith in the Lord is at the heart of the Psalms. They express in prayer and liturgy the people's individual and community experiences of God's power and protection, and their hope for continuing protection. The risk involved in faith is expressed in the frequent reference to being put to shame. One who invests her faith in an inadequate or unworthy object will be let down in time of need, she will be put to shame for having trusted herself to it. A few examples from the many possible will illustrate the points:

> In you I trust; let me not be put to shame,
>   let not my enemies exult over me.
> No one who waits for you shall be put to shame;
>   those shall be put to shame who heedlessly break faith (25:2–3f).

> But they sinned yet more against him,
>   rebelling against the Most High in the wasteland,
>
> . . . .
>
> Then the LORD heard and was enraged
>
> . . . .
>
> Because they *believed* not God [*he'emin*]
>   nor *trusted* in his help [*batah*] (78:17, 21–22)

> You who dwell in the shelter of the Most High,
>   who abide in the shadow of the Almighty,
> Say to the LORD, "My refuge and my fortress,
>   my God, in whom I *trust*" [*batah*].
> For he will rescue you from the snare of the fowler,
>   from the destroying pestilence.

> With his pinions he will cover you,
>   and under his wings you shall *take refuge* [*hasah*];
>   his faithfulness is a buckler and a shield (Ps. 91).

New Testament

The first box shows the meaning of the most common Greek verbs relating to faith. The second box shows the correspondence between the Hebrew of the Old Testament and the Greek of the New.

English raises a special problem in translation. English has no convenient verb relating adequately to the noun "faith." We have the verb "to believe" for the noun "belief," the verb "to trust" for the noun "trust." But there is no verb "to faith" for the noun "faith." Translators

$pisteu\bar{o}$ <	to *believe* a person or thing.
	to *trust* or *rely on* a person or thing, to *obey*.

(*peithō* to persuade or convince)	
pepoitha (perfect tense of *peithō*)	To *be persuaded, have confidence,* trust in, put one's confidence in, obey.

elpizō to *hope,* expect, fear; to put one's hope in, *trust.*

USUAL CORRESPONDENCE IN TRANSLATION from the Hebrew to the Septuagint Greek.

batah	peithō
hasah	elpizō
he'emin ⟶	pisteuō

frequently render the Greek verb *pisteuō* by the English verb "to believe." Unfortunately our English "to believe" emphasizes the intellectual aspect of the concept much more than the Greek *pisteuō* does, tempting us to overlook the aspects of trust, self-commitment, and obedience. It would be better often to paraphrase, using an expression like "to put your faith in" or "to have faith."

With a few exceptions the Scripture quotations in this chapter are from the New American Bible. I have not changed its use of the verb "to believe." Keep in mind that it most frequently renders *pisteuō* with the wider connotations indicated here.

We find reflections of Old Testament usage in the New Testament, but we also find a new element—emphasis on faith in Jesus. It will be important to see the implications of such faith in Jesus. They go far beyond mere intellectual assent.[17]

The Synoptic Gospels

Old Testament faith in the God of Israel is presupposed in such passages as Jesus' story about the lilies of the field and the birds of the air: "If God can clothe in such splendor the grass of the field . . . will he not provide much more for you, O weak in faith!" (Mt. 6:30).

Jesus did not merely preach such confidence; he lived it. Especially in his passion and death, he entrusted himself totally to God in weakness and darkness. There was tremendous risk involved. If his vision of God were wrong, his whole life and ministry would be proven worthless. The Pharisees and chief priests understood this and made a point of it in their taunts: "He relied on God; let God rescue him now if he wants to. After all, he claimed, 'I am God's son'" (Mt. 27:43).

Jesus challenged his followers to act the same way in their lives. One of the central emphases of Mark's Gospel is this call to Christians to take up their own crosses, follow the path of weakness and obscurity, be servants rather than masters, and lose their lives in order to save them.

We see these points powerfully made in the responses to each of Jesus' three passion predictions (Mk. 8:31; 9:31; 10:32–34). Mark heightens the challenge of the call by following each prediction with an incident revealing that the disciples do not understand. For example, Peter argues with Jesus when he predicts his passion (Mk. 8:32–33). The disciples argue over who is the most important (Mk. 9:33–34). James and John ask for the two most important seats (Mk. 10:35–40). After each of these misunderstandings, Jesus explains what true discipleship means (Mk. 8:34–38; 9:35–37; 10:41–45). Faith in Jesus includes faith in his passion and death, both for Jesus and for us.[18]

No one has a complete New Testament faith in Jesus unless he or she is living this call to suffering and self-surrender in some real way. A merely intellectual assent to truths is an inadequate faith.

The distinctly new element in New Testament faith is the call to faith in Jesus himself. In the Synoptic Gospels, this faith is frequently associated with Jesus' healings and other acts of power. Frequently Jesus demands faith as a presupposition to healing. "Do you believe that I can do this?" is asking in part about faith in his power to heal. But it is more than a mere inner assurance which a person might try to work up within himself. Jesus was seen as highly controversial and even dangerous. In that concrete circumstance, faith in Jesus includes a willingness to ask, a willingness to face the criticism of associating with one so despised by the important people of the day. How many today are afraid to get involved in something untested and new, something demanding a public step?

We see this relationship between faith and a willingness to stand out in a public association with Jesus in Luke's account of the penitent woman who washed Jesus' feet with her tears and perfumed them in the house of the inhospitable Pharisee (Lk. 7:36–50). The Pharisee has insulted Jesus by failing to provide the normal marks of respect due an invited guest. In this atmosphere of hostility the sinful woman shows public respect for the shamed guest. She is thus subject in the eyes of the Pharisee to double criticism: for her own notorious sin and for her mark of respect toward Jesus. The scene closes with Jesus' words to the woman, "Your faith has been your salvation. Now go in peace."[19]

From indications in the Synoptic Gospels, some Christians claim that believers can have whatever they ask for, provided they believe firmly enough that the answer will be "yes." Support for this view is seen negatively in Mark's scene of Jesus at Nazareth:

> And he could do no mighty work there, except that he laid his hands upon a few sick people and healed them. And he marveled because of their unbelief (Mk. 6:5 RSV).[20]

And positively in Jesus' reply to the disciples after the fig tree he cursed withered:

> '"Put your trust in God. I solemnly assure you, whoever says to this mountain, 'Be lifted up and thrown into the sea,' and has no inner doubts but believes that what he says will happen, shall have it done for him. I give you my word, if you are ready to believe that you will receive whatever you ask for in prayer, it shall be done for you" (Mk. 11:22–24).

There is truth in this claim, but it needs to be seen in context. Many Christians do not expect God to work in power. Their timidity and failure to ask in prayer cripples what God is ready to do.[21] At the same time, Christian prayer is not a technique by which we can make God do *our* will, it is a living conversation with our Lord by which we discern and cooperate with *his* will.

The passage just quoted above gives a clue as to the wider context. It begins "Put your trust [*pistis*] in God." In this relationship of self-surrendered faith we are so conformed to God's vision and will that we do not ask for anything other than what God wants to do. God always answers prayers that are in conformity with his will, not because of the force with which they are asked (based on inner assurance) but because they are in cooperation with what he is doing. The sense is close to Augustine's famous saying, "Love God and do what you want"—a saying that is also often abused.

We should be careful, then, not to press "inner assurance" faith as if it were a magic technique. Jesus did heal the son of the man who exclaimed, "I believe; help my unbelief!" (Mk. 9:24 RSV). We should also beware of acting like Job's friends by charging that those who are not healed by prayer lack faith. In this same story, Matthew emphasizes not the weakness of the father's faith, but that of the disciples (Mt. 17:19f).

God always wills healing, but he does not always will to start with the symptom that most distresses us. That symptom is often the key to a deeper problem that needs to be dealt with first. Recall the quotations from Paul Tournier in the discussion of Job above. Why should God remove the distressing symptom, only to leave us with the deadly hidden cancer?[22]

The Gospel According to John

In the Synoptic Gospels one must have faith first, before a healing can occur. John in contrast sometimes suggests that the "signs" can lead to faith: "Jesus performed this first of his signs at Cana in Galilee. Thus did he reveal his glory, and his disciples believed in him" (Jn. 2:11).

In his commentary on John, Raymond Brown points out that the matter is complex.[23] Jesus' "signs" can be related to faith in four ways. First, the signs can simply be rejected: "Despite his many signs performed in their presence, they refused to believe in him" (Jn. 12:37).

Next, the signs can lead to a certain faith, but an inadequate one that will not stand up under pressure:

> While he was in Jerusalem during the Passover festival, many believed in his name, for they could see the signs he was performing. For his part, Jesus would not trust himself to them because he knew them all. He needed no one to give him testimony about human nature. He was well aware of what was in man's heart (Jn. 2:23–25).

Third, the signs can lead to true faith, as we saw in the case of the disciples at Cana. But in this case more than just the sign is at work. The person who is led to true faith has to make a risky commitment. There is also a mystery of God's grace involved. Both elements are illustrated at the end of John chapter 6. The crowds who followed Jesus after he multiplied the loaves are beginning to leave him because they cannot accept what he says about being himself the bread of life. The twelve take the risk of staying, even though they understand no better than the others what he is talking about:

> "This is why I have told you
> that no one can come to me
> unless it is granted him by the Father."

> From this time on, many of his disciples broke away and would not remain in his company any longer. Jesus then said to the Twelve, "Do you want to leave me too?" Simon Peter answered him, "Lord, to whom shall we go? You have the words of eternal life. We have come to believe; we are convinced that you are God's holy one" (Jn. 6:65–69).

Fourth, one can have true faith without seeing a powerful sign. This is the point of Jesus' comment to Thomas after the resurrection: "You became a believer because you saw me. Blest are they who have not seen and have believed" (Jn. 20:29).

Signs and Faith

The relation between signs of power and the commitment of faith is an important question. As a participant in the charismatic renewal and an active user of healing prayer in my counseling and ministry, I have seen surprising and powerful acts of God. I have seen beautiful moments of grace for people already committed to God in faith, and challenges to nonbelievers to reexamine their convictions. But I have seen no signs that could drag a nonbeliever to faith by undeniable force of evidence. I have sensed a desire for such a sign in some people, but this desire asks the signs to carry a weight they were not designed to carry. We find a similar desire among some in the Gospels, but it is a desire which Jesus repudiates. For him, it indicates a lack of faith:

> The Pharisees came forward and began to argue with him. They were looking for some heavenly sign from him as a test. With a sigh from the depths of his spirit he said, "Why does this age seek a sign? I assure you, no such sign will be given it!" (Mk. 8:11–12).[24]

Such desire is also a vain hope because any action is capable of more than one interpretation. In the exorcism of the blind and mute man, the crowds ask, "Might this not be David's son?" But the Pharisees say, "This man can expel demons only with the help of Beelzebul, the

prince of demons" (Mt. 12:23–24). Jesus calls their judgment a sin against
the Holy Spirit (vv. 31f). To attribute to Satan what is really the act of
God is to make oneself unable to see anything correctly. As long as one
persists in that mistaken judgment, one's state is truly hopeless.

The search for a compelling sign also misunderstands the nature of
sign. At the Last Supper:

> Judas (not Judas Iscariot) said to him, "Lord, why is it that you will reveal
> yourself to us and not to the world?" Jesus answered
>
> "Anyone who loves me
> will be true to my word,
> and my Father will love him;
> we will come to him
> and make our dwelling place with him.
> He who does not love me does not keep my words.
>
> . . . .
>
> the Paraclete, the Holy Spirit
> whom the Father will send in my name,
> will instruct you in everything,
> and remind you of all that I told you" (Jn. 14:22–24, 26).

At first sight, Jesus seems not to answer the question. But in fact the
answer is that Jesus can be seen clearly only by those who love him.
The usual way of "seeing" him is through his indwelling and the
indwelling of the Holy Spirit who makes him present in his risen state.
Even external visions, like Paul's vision on the road to Damascus, can
be properly interpreted only with the help of some sort of inner presence or revelation. Paul's companions experienced something, but
they could not discern what it was (Acts 9:7; 22:9).

Most Christians come to experience Jesus in an internal and intuitive but powerful way through his risen presence within them. This
presence in the well-disposed enables them to interpret correctly whatever external signs of God's presence and power they experience. They
sometimes wonder how unbelievers can observe the same marvels of
creation and grace that they do and still deny God. The reason is that
the unbelievers do not "see" what they see.

There is another factor in the reciprocal relation between faith and
signs. Because a correct faith includes not only a correct vision but also
an appropriate self-commitment and trust, inappropriate commitments can be positive barriers to faith. One who is committed ulti-

mately or deeply to objects incompatible with God or extraneous to God finds true vision difficult or impossible. Then even the signs are misunderstood. We might guess, for example, that those Pharisees who opposed Jesus were committed to their own vision of righteousness, to their earned status in the community, to their own expectations and understanding. With those commitments, they couldn't even see the new thing God was doing. They were pressed to find some other explanation for this Jesus who so threatened everything they had trusted themselves to. (See Mt. 21:23–27.) We are inclined to say that seeing is believing. It is also true that believing is seeing, when believing includes the actions that flow from faith. [25]

Look again at John's judgment on those who see the signs and still refuse to believe. He quotes from Isaiah chapter 6 to illustrate the point:

> Despite his many signs performed in their presence, they refused to believe in him. . . . The reason they could not believe was that, as Isaiah says elsewhere:
> "He has blinded their eyes,
> and numbed their hearts,
> lest they see
> or comprehend,
> or have a change of heart—
> and I should heal them" (Jn. 12:37, 39–40).

This same passage from Isaiah is quoted in the Synoptic Gospels to illustrate the stubbornness of those who cannot see even with the help of parables (Mt. 13:13–15). It is quoted again at the end of Acts to illustrate the stubbornness of the Roman Jews who refused to put their faith in Jesus despite the evidence of prophecies fulfilled (Ac. 28:25–28). Prophecies fulfilled, signs of God's power, parables—all three are able to jar a mind which has been blinded by wrong presuppositions and open it to see. But not even all three together can force the mind which is too firmly committed to what is not of God. When the new vision which God is offering threatens the very purpose to which we have committed our lives, only those can see who are willing to die to what has been most meaningful and important to them. Perhaps this step is easiest for those who have seen little meaning in their lives in any case: the sinners, the poor, the outcast. Easier also for those who have "hit bottom" and lost whatever meaning they once saw: Job on his dungheap, Walter Ciszek in his Russian prison, or the alcoholic who has lost job, family, and fortune. Jesus was received most readily by such people: the rich young man walked away (Mk. 10:17–27). God is God of the poor partly because the rich have other gods, much as they may think otherwise.

Paul

Paul's letters provide well-known formulas which are easy to take in a superficial sense. We need to consider the context in which they were written to understand the full depth and demand of his statements. For example, we see in Romans:

> If you confess with your lips that Jesus is Lord, and believe in your heart that God raised him from the dead, you will be saved. Faith in the heart leads to justification, confession on the lips to salvation. Scripture says, "No one who believes in him will be put to shame" (Rom. 10:9–11).

We saw the phrase to be "put to shame" in our study of the Psalms. It reminds us that faith is not just an intellectual statement but a commitment involving risk. If the commitment is wrong intellectually, it will have disastrous practical results: we will trust in something that lets us down, and our enemies will taunt us.

Faith "in the heart" is not merely "a hidden interior belief." In the Bible, the heart is the human core or center of each person, what is of ultimate significance, the source of our decisions, thoughts, and actions. The sense then is, "If you are committed at the very center of your being to the mystery that God raised Jesus from the dead—that God brings life out of defeat and that Jesus is risen and active—you will be brought into right relation with God by the power of that death and resurrection, you will be justified."

Finally, "confession on the lips" also has practical consequences. In the mid first century when Paul was writing, Jewish leaders were putting pressure on the Christian movement. Christian Jews were tempted to remain secret believers. To "confess with the lips" meant to make a public declaration that left one open to persecution. It meant to commit oneself and identify oneself publicly with an executed criminal and a small group of people popularly seen as fanatics or worse.

Earlier in Romans Paul offers another formula whose meaning goes deeper than may first appear. Paul describes Abraham's faith as a willingness to follow God's directions despite the seeming impossibility of their fulfillment. Then he suggests that we respond in the same way:

> [Abraham] never questioned or doubted God's promise; rather, he was strengthened in faith and gave glory to God, fully persuaded that God could do whatever he had promised. Thus his faith was credited to him as justice.
> The words, "It was credited to him," were not written with him alone in view; they were intended for us too. For our faith will be credited to us also if we believe in him who raised Jesus our Lord from the dead, the Jesus who was handed over to death for our sins and raised up for our justification (Rom. 4:20–25).

This act of faith means more than to believe that God exists, more than to believe that God historically raised Jesus from the dead. It means also that we trust ourselves in faith to the God who acts this way, even to our own personal death in similar circumstances.

These passages from Romans raise two points that deserve fuller treatment. The first is the question of justification by faith. The second is the claim that Paul calls us to trust God in circumstances similar to those of Jesus, that he calls us to die together with Christ in weakness in the face of evil. We will begin with the first and then proceed to the second.

Justification by Faith

Paul treats justification by faith especially in Galatians 2:15–3:9; Romans 3:19–31 and 7:14–25; and Philippians 2:12–13.

Paul uses two different Greek terms that are sometimes confused in popular translation and use. One (*dikaiosyne*) is translated "justification" or "righteousness." The other (*sōteria*) is translated "salvation" or "deliverance." Justification happens at the *beginning* of a Christian's conversion; salvation is not complete until the *end*. Popular reference to "salvation by faith" corresponds to what Paul normally called "justification by faith."

In secular Greek, to be justified is to be declared innocent by a judge. Transferred to religious use, it refers to our standing before God. Corresponding to its use in the law courts, people without much experience of God or awareness of their inner selves often suppose that we can be justified before God by pointing out to him that we have always kept the law or our own conscience. But Paul insists that this is impossible. In fact it is too late: All have already broken that relationship.

The next step for many, when they realize that the relationship has been broken, is to hope that God will overlook the past if they live now the life that God calls them to. But when they try to do so, if they try seriously and have the courage to know themselves, they find that it doesn't work. Something has gone dead in us, and on our own we cannot bring it back to life. Sin has so infected our deep heart that, even in our best efforts, an inner cancer derails and distorts what we are really trying and yearning to do. The person who has enough self-knowledge to recognize this fact is led to the despair expressed in Romans 7:14–25. The person who does not have self-knowledge is led instead to self-delusion, self-righteousness, and arrogance as described in Romans 2:17–29. By centering attention on the sins and faults of others, such a person tries to divert attention from self.

Note that Paul was in self-delusion rather than in despair before his conversion, despite his use of the first person in Romans 7. It was only after his conversion, looking back on what he had been, that he was able to write Romans 7 and to understand "What a wretched man I am" (7:24). The French writer André Frossard describes a similar experience in his own life. Raised as a Communist, he was converted by a vision as spectacular as Paul's. Commenting on that vision, he says

> This surging, overwhelming invasion brought with it a sense of joy comparable to that of a drowning man who is rescued at the last moment, but with this difference that it was at the moment in which I was being hauled to safety that I became aware of the mud in which, without noticing it, I had till then been stuck; and now I wondered how I had ever been able to breathe and to live in it. [26]

So Paul's description in Romans 7 does not refer solely to those acts that we recognize at the time as sin. Much of our anguish comes when we realize that it is especially those actions which we thought were our best that have been twisted by the inner cancer to cause evil. Paul was motivated by what he thought were noble purposes when he set out for Damascus to arrest Christians. But when God intervened and Paul saw Jesus, he could finally see events in their true light. Paul had thought that he was upholding God's own law by suppressing the Christian movement. Now he could see that his very zeal was opposing God's plan in Jesus Christ:

> [Paul's] belief in the existence of demonic powers behind the law owed a very great deal to his own religious experience. For Paul had been an enthusiastic devotee of the Torah, determined to establish his own righteousness by obedience to its commands. . . . His zeal for the law had led him to repudiate Jesus as a blasphemer who had died under the curse of the law. It had led him to persecute the church, whose existence seemed to him to be an affront to God's honor. Then in a flash of illumination he had seen the glory of God in the face of Jesus Christ, and in the light of that experience he saw his past life exposed in all its contradiction. He who had thought to possess in the law the complete and final revelation of God had failed to recognize God in the person of his Son. In defending the honor of God's law he had become the enemy of God. . . .
>
> But how did the law, holy, just, and good as it was, produce such terrifying results? Paul's treatment of the law bears at every point the indelible mark of that moment in his own spiritual history when he had realized that everything he had regarded as highest and best had combined to put Christ on the Cross. His doctrine of principalities and powers provided him with an answer to this intensely personal problem. All power and authority belongs to God, and evil can exist as a force in the world only because it is able to take the powers and authorities of God and to transform them into world-rulers of this darkness. So it had come about that Israel and Rome, the highest religion and the best government that the world had seen, had conspired to crucify the Lord of Glory.[27]

This new valuation of what had seemed noble is illustrated in Aleksandr Solzhenitsyn's experience, not on the basis of a sudden vision but of years of purification in Soviet prison camps:

> Looking back, I saw that for my whole conscious life I had not understood either myself or my strivings. What had seemed for so long to be beneficial now turned out in actuality to be fatal, and I had been striving to go in the opposite direction to that which was truly necessary to me. But just as the waves of the sea knock the inexperienced swimmer off his feet and keep tossing him back onto the shore, so also was I painfully tossed back on dry land by the blows of misfortune. And it was only because of this that I was able to travel the path which I had always really wanted to travel. . . .
>
> In the intoxication of youthful successes I had felt myself to be infallible, and I was therefore cruel. In the surfeit of power I was a murderer, and an oppressor. In my most evil moments I was convinced that I was doing good, and as I was well supplied with systematic arguments. And it was only when I lay there on rotting prison straw that I sensed within myself the

first stirrings of good. Gradually it was disclosed to me that the line separating good and evil passes not through states, nor between classes, nor between political parties either—but right through every human heart.[28]

This ability of evil to twist even our noblest strivings, especially our zeal to uphold God's honor and true religion, is a sobering thought to serious Christians. It is not enough to hold tenaciously to traditional formulations of faith, not even when these are authentic. We must be open to what God is doing in our own day, even when we could not anticipate his new action on the basis of the old tradition:

> The charismatic is essentially new and always surprising. Of course it also stands in the inner though hidden continuity with what came earlier in the church and fits in with its spirit and with its institutional framework. Yet it is new and incalculable, and it is not immediately evident at first sight that everything is as it was in the enduring totality of the church. For often it is only through what is new that it is realized that the range of the church was greater from the outset than had previously been supposed. . . . [The charismatic feature] can be mistaken for facile enthusiasm, a hankering after change, attempted subversion, lack of feeling for tradition and the well-tried experience of the past. And precisely those who are firmly rooted in the old, who have preserved a living Christianity as a sacred inheritance from the past, are tempted to extinguish the new spirit, which does not always fix on what is most tried and tested, and yet may be a holy spirit for all that, and to oppose it in the name of the church's Holy Spirit, although it is a spiritual gift of that Spirit.[29]

In the study just quoted, Karl Rahner suggests a middle path between arrogant self-assurance and timid or irresponsible inaction. His comments are based on the principle that the Holy Spirit directs the church by simultaneously and variously inspiring leaders, movements, and individual faithful, giving no single person the whole vision or all the gifts. Thus we are forced to trust and cooperate with one another if we are to fulfill God's plan:

> Ultimately only one thing can give unity in the church on the human level: the love which allows another to be different, even when it does not understand him. . . . One alone has always been completely right, the one Lord of the church who, one in himself, has willed the many opposing tendencies in the church.
> What has been said would be quite misunderstood if anyone drew the conclusion that everything in the church must be left to go its way, that no

one may have the courage to offer opposition to another trend in the church, to utter warnings against it, to challenge it to real and serious combat. . . . One must have this courage, even if one must tell oneself, knowing the limits of one's own judgment, that probably the further history of the church will show that one was not entirely right, that one was only one servant among many of the one Lord of the church, and not the only one to represent him, in fact, that the Lord was also acting in that other person whom one had the task of putting in his place, and convincing of his limitations. [30]

If God had not acted in power our relation with him would still be trapped either at the level of despair or at the level of self-delusion and arrogance. We could have gone no further by ourselves. But Paul rejoices in the fact that God did act in unexpected and mysterious power, freely and without any merits on our own part, through the historical act of the life, death, and resurrection of Jesus.

We take part in justification, our renewed relation with the Father, by uniting ourselves with Jesus through faith. The faith by which we accept his act of justification is that total surrender of self that includes belief, trust, and obedience. We surrender ourselves in a personal relation with Jesus that gradually conforms us to him not only in what we think of as his virtues (love, peace, patience, etc.) but also in the pattern of his self-sacrificing love which leads to persecution, misunderstanding, suffering, and death. We abandon ourselves to him beyond calculation, with no external proofs of his love which could convince a nonbeliever that our actions are rational and sensible. Yet, by grace, God gives us signs and indications which are adequate to move us to the act of faith.

Christians dispute what relation our good acts have to this faith and justification. The acts are best seen not as an added factor, but rather as our response to what God has done, as the concrete acts produced by our self-abandonment in faith. They are themselves a gift from God, part of the total gift of faith which he gives us through the sacrifice of Jesus. Because of what God has done in Jesus, when we turn to Jesus in faith, give him our lives, and receive baptism, he sends the Holy Spirit to transform us and produce in us "good deeds."

The relationship between our actions and God's is mysterious, paradoxical, and one of the most difficult questions of theology. God and humanity are not equal partners. Any deeds we perform related to our salvation flow out of our faith in response to God's saving act.

Note that Paul speaks of our working for salvation, earning a reward, and being judged according to our works:

> God will repay every man for what he has done: eternal life to those who strive for glory, honor, and immortality by patiently doing right; wrath and fury to those who selfishly disobey the truth and obey wickedness (Rom. 2:6–8).[31]

Recall that for Paul justification is at the beginning of the new Christian life. Salvation is at the end, not yet fully present, something accepted in hope and trust but which we cannot claim from God as an absolute possession. See for example the following passages:

> It is now the hour for you to wake from sleep, for our salvation is closer than when we first accepted the faith (Rom. 13:11).
>
> What I do is discipline my own body and master it, for fear that after having preached to others I myself should be rejected (1 Cor. 9:27).
>
> Let anyone who thinks he is standing upright watch out lest he fall (1 Cor. 10:12).
>
> It matters little to me whether you or any human court pass judgment on me. I do not even pass judgment on myself. Mind you, I have nothing on my conscience. But that does not mean that I am declaring myself innocent. The Lord is the one to judge me, so stop passing judgment before the time of his return. He will bring to light what is hidden in darkness and manifest the intentions of hearts. At that time, everyone will receive his praise from God (1 Cor. 4:3–5).

These passages can all be understood as I suggested above: After we have given ourselves in faith to Jesus he transforms us through the Holy Spirit, giving us the power and the guidance to participate in the process of our salvation. The balance is expressed neatly in Philippians:

> So then, my dearly beloved, obedient as always to my urging, work with anxious concern to achieve your salvation, not only when I happen to be with you but all the more now that I am absent. It is God who, in his good will toward you, begets in you any measure of desire or achievement (Phil. 2:12f).

In other words, cooperate in the process leading to your final salvation. But even as you do so, realize that you wouldn't even want to do so unless God had given you the desire as a free gift, and you wouldn't be able to carry out the desire unless he had given you the ability to do so as a free gift.

With this background, we can consider the passage in James which is sometimes thought to contradict Paul:

> My brothers, what good is it to profess faith without practicing it? Such faith has no power to save one, has it? If a brother or sister has nothing to wear and no food for the day, and you say to them, "Good-bye and good luck! Keep warm and well fed," but do not meet their bodily needs, what good is that? So it is with the faith that does nothing in practice. It is thoroughly lifeless. . . .
>
> Show me your faith without works, and I will show you the faith that underlies my works! Do you believe that God is one? You are quite right. The demons believe that, and shudder (Jas. 2:14–19).

James goes on to give us examples of what he means by works underlain by faith: Abraham's sacrifice of his son Isaac and Rahab's harboring of the Israelite spies.

In comparing James with Paul, note first of all that Paul expects the Christian to live a life informed by saving faith. This life includes particular ways of acting which Paul does not hesitate to recommend throughout his letters. He also expects the Christian to be judged on the basis of these actions. But the surrender of faith is the starting point.

James also believes that faith is the starting point. He speaks of the faith that underlies his works, of practicing faith. He does not say that faith without works is inadequate, but rather that it is lifeless or dead. Dead faith cannot be saving faith. Since faith normally gives rise to new life, if a Christian shows no good works one is justified in questioning whether that Christian has really made the surrender of faith.

This understanding is confirmed when we examine the examples that James gives. We see that James' opponents present a merely intellectual faith: they believe that "God is one." This is not James' view of faith, but theirs, as we see by looking at James' examples. The "good works" of his examples are killing one's own son in sacrifice, and betraying one's own city by harboring enemy spies. Apart from the relationship with God implied, these don't look like "good works." It is what they reveal about Abraham and Rahab's relation with the God of Israel that makes them works that faith underlies.

We have already studied Abraham's faith in our consideration of the

Old Testament. We saw that his willingness to kill Isaac in sacrifice to God was an act of total self-surrender without calculation: He was risking everything he was, all his hopes for purpose in life and a meaningful future.

Rahab too was risking her life and future when she chose the God of Israel. Seeing the conflict looming between her city and the Israelites, between her ancestral gods and their God, she placed her hope on the unknown God of the strangers despite the apparent strength of her city, its defenses and defenders. She had a lot to lose if her gamble proved ill-founded. Her actions make sense only in the context of radical trust in the God of Israel: Her actions are based on her faith.

Even the deeds which James urges in verses 15 and 16—meeting the bodily needs of the naked and hungry—are based on trusting faith in God. Much of our hesitation to share what others need is based on a fear that we may not have enough left for ourselves. We want the security of a little extra. We do not trust God to meet our needs if we meet those of our neighbor.

The actions of faith which James urges are far removed from the purely ceremonial observances which Paul's opponents urge, and which Paul denounces when he says that "a man is justified by faith apart from observance of the law" (Rom. 3:28). The differences of emphasis between Paul and James come from the different opponents they are combatting.[32]

Roman Catholic and Lutheran traditions are closer on this question than most Catholics and Lutherans realize. For example, Thomas Aquinas, a major representative of Roman Catholic tradition, commenting on the passage from Philippians that we considered above (2:12f), insists that our initial justification does not come from merit in any way:

> Then when he says, *for God is at work in you, both to will and to work*, he strengthens their confidence, and he excludes four false opinions: the first is the opinion of those who believe that man can be saved by his own free will without God's help. Against this he says: *for God is at work in you, both to will and to work*: "The Father who dwells in me does his works" (Jn. 14:10); "Apart from me you can do nothing" (Jn. 15:5). . . . The fourth is the opinion that God accomplishes every good in us and does this through our merits. He excludes this when he says [*according to*] *for his good pleasure*, and not our merits, because before we get God's grace there is no good merit in us: "Do good to Zion in thy good pleasure" (Ps. 51:18, emphasis added).[33]

On the other side, Luther complains that some take license from his preaching of justification by faith, and he insists that faith includes a response:

> The flesh simply does not understand the teaching of grace, namely, that we are not justified by works but by faith alone, and that the Law has no jurisdiction over us. Therefore when it hears this teaching, it transforms it into licentiousness and immediately draws the inference: "If we are without the Law, then let us live as we please. Let us not do good, let us not give to the needy; much less do we have to endure anything evil. For there is no Law to compel or bind us."
>
> Thus there is a danger on both sides, although the one is more tolerable than the other. If grace or faith is not preached, no one is saved; for faith alone justifies and saves. On the other hand, if faith is preached, as it must be preached, the majority of men understand the teaching about faith in a fleshly way and transform the freedom of the spirit into the freedom of the flesh. This can be discerned today in all classes of society, both high and low. They all boast of being evangelicals and boast of Christian freedom. Meanwhile, however, they give in to their desires and turn to greed, sexual desire, pride, envy, etc. No one performs his duty faithfully; no one serves another by love. This misbehavior often makes me so impatient that I would want such "swine that trample pearls underfoot" (Mt. 7:6) still to be under the tyranny of the people.[34]

Trust Despite Weakness, After Pattern of Jesus

It is fascinating to follow Paul's career from his initial misguided Jewish zeal, through the shock of his encounter with the risen Lord Jesus, gradually into a new, redirected but still immature zeal, through the ambiguities and pain of his ministry spotted with frustrations like Galatia, near disasters like Corinth (reflected in Second Corinthians) and life-threatening persecutions. We begin to understand the concrete reality behind statements like the following which are scattered throughout his writings:

> Brothers, we do not wish to leave you in the dark about the trouble we had in Asia; we were crushed beyond our strength, even to the point of despairing of life. We were left to feel like men condemned to death so that we might trust, not in ourselves, but in God who raises the dead (2 Cor. 1:8–9).
>
> When I arrived in Macedonia I was restless and exhausted. I was under all kinds of stress—quarrels with others and fears within myself. But God,

who gives heart to those who are low in spirit, gave me strength with the arrival of Titus (2 Cor. 7:5–6).

I was given a thorn in the flesh, an angel of Satan to beat me and keep me from getting proud. Three times I begged the Lord that this might leave me. He said to me, "My grace is enough for you, for in weakness power reaches perfection." And so I willingly boast of my weaknesses instead, that the power of Christ may rest upon me (2 Cor. 12:7–9).

I have full confidence that now as always Christ will be exalted through me, whether I live or die (Phil. 1:20).

Even now I find my joy in the suffering I endure for you. In my own flesh I fill up what is lacking in the sufferings of Christ for the sake of his body, the church (Col. 1:24).[35]

But these experiences are not reserved for Paul alone. He reminds us in numerous places that we ourselves are called to experience a similar identification with the dying and rising Christ:

It is your special privilege to take Christ's part—not only to believe in him but also to suffer for him. Yours is the same struggle as mine, the one in which you formerly saw me engaged and now hear that I am caught up [in prison in danger of death] (Phil. 1:29–30).

We sent [Timothy] to strengthen and encourage you in regard to your faith lest any of you be shaken by these trials. You know well enough that such trials are our common lot. When we were still with you, we used to warn you that we would undergo trial; now it has happened, and you know what we meant (1 Thes. 3:2–4).[36]

Both for Jesus and for us, the call to die in darkness trusting the Father is no arbitrary demand. It is integrally related to the primal act of faithlessness that brought sin and misery into the world. Paul develops the theme of Jesus as the Second Adam (Rom. 5:12–21). Jesus' act of trusting faith, flowing from a self-sacrificing love without calculation of reward, radically heals the results of Adam's faithless act of self-seeking. The contrasts between faith and mistrust, between selflessness and self-seeking, stand at the center of the human tragedy. We allow ourselves to be incorporated into Jesus' dying and rising because a life of total trust in God is what we were created for. Through this mystery of suffering in faith, we are restored to the original right relation with God and with each other. The communal effects of this restoration are expressed especially well by L. John Topel:

From the time of Adam his selfishness provoked a reaction of selfishness in another, until self-seeking became a way of life, and so death-dealing was a contagion over the whole world. When Christ entered the world, however, as the one who would not succumb to this contagion, who refused to do evil for evil, but would rather lay down his life than reject the truth of his Father's vision for humankind, then another contagion came into the world. Those who take the risk of faith in that style of life, who enter through faith and the Spirit into identification with that Light which is Life, are freed from sin and death. As they themselves exercise that freedom of the Servant's way of life, with their selfishness healed by love, they foster and promote that contagion of goodness in the world that overcomes the contagion of sin still remaining from Adam. [37]

We surrender in faith to God and to his plan of redemptive love in our lives, including weakness and suffering. The joy that results is expressed especially well in Philippians and in Romans chapter 8:

> Rejoice in the Lord always! . . . Dismiss all anxiety from your minds. Present your needs to God in every form of prayer and in petitions full of gratitude. Then God's own peace, which is beyond all understanding, will stand guard over your hearts and minds, in Christ Jesus (Phil. 4:4, 6–7).

> We know that God makes all things work together for the good of those who have been called according to his decree. . . . Who will separate us from the love of Christ? Trial, or distress, or persecution, or hunger, or nakedness, or danger, or the sword? . . . For I am certain that neither death nor life, neither angels nor principalities, neither the present nor the future, nor powers, neither height nor depth nor any other creature, will be able to separate us from the love of God that comes to us in Christ Jesus, our Lord (Rom. 8:28, 35, 38–39).

These statements come easily to mind. But it is another question whether we truly believe them in the depths of our being. Perhaps we will not know until we ourselves are faced with the collapse of our other supports and objects of trust, as Jesus and Paul were. In any case, it is important to reflect that it is of trust in such depth that biblical faith speaks. We are far removed from the merely intellectual response to an impersonal survey with which this chapter began.

Hebrews, Revelation

Lack of space prevents detail, but we should at least mention two other New Testament books. Chapter 12 of Hebrews has a long treatment on faith, with numerous examples from the Old Testament. The sense of faith reflected there is close to what we have already seen in the Old Testament, although it is presented to urge faith in Jesus despite persecution:

> Let us keep our eyes fixed on Jesus, who inspires and perfects our faith. For the sake of the joy which lay before him he endured the cross, heedless of its shame. He has taken his seat at the right of the throne of God. Remember how he endured the opposition of sinners; hence do not grow despondent or abandon the struggle (Heb. 12:2–3).

The Book of Revelation urges Christians to maintain their faith commitment to Jesus despite persecution to the point of death. The main purpose of the book is to encourage such perseverance by revealing how the situation looks from the standpoint of heaven.

Conclusion

The core of biblical faith and of the Christian faith it reflects is a trusting self-surrender to the God who reveals himself in Jesus of Nazareth. It is he whom we trust, beyond the clarity of our concepts, beyond the assurance we can feel. He is greater than our flawed accomplishments and virtues, greater than our weakness, greater even than our sin. Resting confidently in his love and forgiveness, we can bear deadly persecutions by unbelievers, accept confusion and uncertainty within ourselves, tolerate conflicts among believers and varied expressions of faith among those who love him authentically. Aware that we have nothing quite pure to offer God, nothing with which to bargain, aware of the evil parasite distorting even the best within us, yet responding to the Spirit to the best of our ability, we let go of all security in anything but the promise of his love and forgiveness and cry out with Paul:

> Who can free me from this body under the power of death? All praise to God, through Jesus Christ our Lord! (Rom. 7:24).

Notes

1. From NC news service. Seen in *The Advocate:* The newspaper of the Roman Catholic Archdiocese of Newark, New Jersey, Wednesday, June 9, 1982 (31:23), p. 1.
2. James W. Fowler, *Stages of Faith: The Psychology of Human Development and the Quest for Meaning* (San Francisco: Harper & Row, 1981), p. 3.
3. The main purpose of Fowler's book (n. 2 above) is to study *how* people put their faith in whatever it is they commit themselves to. That is also a very interesting and fruitful question, but it is not our main concern here.

4. See also Is. 30:15f.

5. See also Jer. 9:3f; Mi. 7:5f.

6. See also Prv. 14:32.

7. See also Hab. 2:18.

8. *Dogmatic Constitution on Divine Revelation* of the Second Vatical Council, solemnly promulgated by His Holiness, Pope Paul VI on November 18, 1965. Also known under the titles *Dei Verbum* and *De Divina Revelatione*. Available in various editions and translations. The paragraph numberings are common to all editions. These quotations are from paragraphs 2 and 5 in the N.C.W.C. translation.

9. For theological or linguistic studies of the various terms for faith in the Old Testament, see the relevant sections of standard Bible dictionaries, for example *The Interpreter's Dictionary of the Bible: An Illustrated Encyclopedia* (Nashville, Tenn.: Abingdon, 1962), vol. 2, pp. 222–228; supplementary volume (1976) pp. 329–332; *Theological Dictionary of the New Testament*, ed. Gerhard Friedrich, tr. and ed. Geoffrey W. Bromiley, Vol. VI (Grand Rapids, Mich.: Eerdmans, 1968), pp. 174–202; *A Theological Word Book of the Bible*, ed. Alan Richardson (New York: Macmillan, 1950), pp. 75f.

10. On discernment, there is considerable literature growing out of the rules for discernment given in the *Spiritual Exercises of St. Ignatius* paragraphs 313–336 (available in numerous editions). St. Ignatius warns that his second set of rules (parr. 328–336) cannot be understood properly until a person is at a certain level of spiritual growth (see par. 9). Another approach to discernment, growing from the theories of Jung, is represented among Christian writers by, for example, Morton Kelsey, *Discernment: A Study in Ecstasy and Evil* (New York: Paulist, 1978).

11. See also Dt. 1:32–36.

12. See also Is. 30:12–16.

13. Paul Tournier, *To Resist or To Surrender?* tr. John S. Gilmour (Atlanta: John Knox Press, 1964), p. 60 (paperback edition).

14. Ibid., p. 62.

15. *Alcoholics Anonymous*, 3d edition (New York City: Alcoholics Anonymous World Services, Inc., 1976), p. 59.

16. Walter J. Ciszek, S.J. with Daniel L. Flaherty, S.J., *He Leadeth Me* (Garden City, N.Y.: Images Books, 1975), pp. 88–89. Other examples useful for religious educators include Aleksandr I. Solzhenitsyn, *The Gulag Archipelago 1918–1956: An Experiment in Literary Investigation*, especially Vol. 1 (first two Russian volumes in one English volume), tr. Thomas P. Whitney (New York: Harper & Row, 1973, 1974) 130–131 and vol. 2 (Russian 3–4), same translator (1975), pp. 597–617; and Richard Wurmbrand, *Tortured for Christ* (Glendale, Cal.: Diane Books, 1969).

17. For more detailed treatments, see the relevant sections of the works listed in note 9: *Interpreter's Dictionary of the Bible*, Vol. 2, pp. 229–234, supplement, pp. 332–335; *Theological Dictionary of the New Testament*, Vol. 6, pp. 203–228; *A Theological Word-Book of the Bible*, pp. 75f.

18. This example is worked out in more detail by Ludger Schenke, *Glory and*

the Way of the Cross: The Gospel of Mark (Herald Biblical Booklets), tr. Robin Scroggs (Chicago: Franciscan Herald Press, 1972).

19. The interpretation suggested here is more fully explained by Kenneth E. Bailey, *Through Peasant Eyes: More Lucan Parables, Their Culture and Style* (Grand Rapids, Mich.: Eerdmans, 1980), pp. 1–21.

20. I use the Revised Standard Version here because the New American Bible translation of this passage is very free and misleading.

21. My experience in physical and emotional healing and my ideas on the subject follow the general direction of books like Agnes Sanford, *The Healing Light* (St. Paul: Macalester Park Publishing Co., 1947 revised 1972); Morton T. Kelsey, *Healing and Christianity In Ancient Thought and Modern Times* (New York: Harper & Row, 1973); Francis MacNutt, *Healing* (Notre Dame, Ind.: Ave Maria Press, 1974) and *The Power to Heal* (Notre Dame, Ind.: Ave Maria Press, 1977); Dennis and Matthew Linn, *Healing Life's Hurts: Healing Memories through Five Stages of Forgiveness* (New York: Paulist, 1978); and Frank Lake, *Clinical Theology: A Theological and Psychiatric Basis to Clinical Pastoral Care* (London: Darton Longman & Todd, 1966) and *Tight Corners in Pastoral Counselling* (London: Darton, Longman and Todd, 1981).

22. A useful book for this question is Carmen Benson, *What About Us Who Are Not Healed?* (Plainfield, N.J.: Logos International, 1975).

23. "Appendix III: Signs and Works," in Raymond E. Brown, The Gospel According to John (i–xiii), The Anchor Bible, Vol. 29 (Garden City, N.Y.: Doubleday, 1966), pp. 525–532.

24. There is a helpful discussion on the role of contemporary healings and the difficulties of "proving" a miracle in "Chapter 5: Healings" of René Laurentin, *Catholic Pentecostalism*, tr. Matthew J. O'Connell (Garden City, N.Y.: Image Books, 1978), pp. 115–149. Laurentin uses the medical commission at Lourdes as a case study, comparing it with the practice in charismatic prayer groups. For an example of excessive demand for "proof," see Louis Rose, *Faith Healing* (H armondsworth, Middlesex, England: Penguin Books, 1968, 1971), esp. pp. 156–177.

25. There is a good discussion of this reciprocal relationship between faith/commitment and vision/understanding in Bruce C. Birch and Larry L. Rasmussen, *Bible and Ethics in the Christian Life* (Minneapolis: Augsburg, 1976), esp. pp. 86–92. See also Bernard J. F. Lonergan, *Method in Theology* (A Crossroad Book; New York: Seabury, 1979), pp. 115–124. Lonergan defines faith as "the knowledge born of religious love" (p. 115).

26. André Frossard, *I Have Met Him: God Exists*, to Marjorie Villiers (New York: Herder and Herder, 1970), p. 119. The full description of his vision is deeply moving.

27. G. B. Caird, *Principalities and Powers: A Study in Pauline Theology* (The Chancellor's Lectures for 1954 at Queens University, Kingston, Ontario; Oxford: at the Clarendon Press, 1956), pp. 52f.

28. Aleksandr I. Solzhenitsyn, *The Gulag Archipelago 1918–1956: An Experiment in Literary Investigation*, tr. Thomas P. Whitney, Vol. 2 (New York: Harper & Row, 1975), p. 615.

29. Karl Rahner, "The Charismatic Element in the Church" in *The Spirit in*

the Church (A Crossroad Book; New York: Seabury, 1979), p. 73. The same article is also printed in Karl Rahner, *The Dynamic Element in the Church* (Quaestiones Disputatae) (New York: Herder and Herder, 1964) (quote there from p. 83). Note that in the former, the "not" has been omitted from the third sentence quoted.

30. Ibid., pp. 65–68 (74–77) *passim*. Rahner speaks of "inevitable disagreement in the Church," pp. 64–68 (73–77), "The burden of a charisma," pp. 68–72 (77–82), and "The courage to receive new gifts," pp. 72–73 (82–83).

31. See also 1 Cor. 3:8 and 9:27; 2 Cor. 5:10 and 11:15; and (from a letter many scholars believe to be written by a follower of Paul rather than by Paul himself) Eph. 6:8.

32. A similar relationship between faith and works is evident in 1 John, for example 1:6; 2:4–6; 4:20 and especially 3:17.

33. Thomas Aquinas, *Commentary on Saint Paul's First Letter to the Thessalonians and the Letter to the Philippians*, tr. F. R. Larcher and Michael Duffy (Albany: Magi Books, 1969), pp. 87f.

34. Martin Luther's comment on Gal. 5:13, quoted from *Luther's Works*, Volume 27: *Lectures on Galatians 1535 Chapters 5–6 and Lectures on Galatians 1519 Chapters 1–6*, ed. Jaroslav Pelikan and Walter A. Hansen (St. Louis: Concordia Publishing House, 1964), p. 48. The same passage is available in *The Writings of St. Paul: A Norton Critical Edition*, ed. Wayne A. Meeks (New York: W. W. Norton & Company, Inc., 1972), p. 249. For a recent, very detailed story of justification by faith in the New Testament, coming out of the Lutheran-Catholic Dialogue, see John Reumann, *"Righteousness" in the New Testament: "Justification" in the United States Lutheran-Catholic Dialogue*, with responses by Joseph A. Fitzmyer and Jerome D. Quinn (New York: Paulist Press and Philadelphia: Fortress Press, 1982).

35. Note that some scholars think Colossians was written by a follower of Paul, not by Paul himself.

36. See also 1 Pet. 2:19–21. Our identification with Christ in suffering is further developed by David M. Stanley, "'Become Imitators of Me': Apostolic Tradition in Paul" in A *Companion to Paul: Readings in Pauline Theology*, ed. Michael J. Taylor (New York: Alba House, 1975), pp. 197–211; and by Victor Paul Furnish, *Theology and Ethics in Paul* (Nashville & New York: Abingdon, 1968), pp. 216–224. Most of Paul's "imitate me" passages refer to imitating his sufferings under persecution. See also G. B. Caird, *Principalities and Powers* (note 27), esp. pp. 88–101.

37. L. John Topel. *The Way to Peace: Liberation Through the Bible* (Maryknoll, N.Y.: Orbis Books, 1979), p. 112. This book is intended to give the scriptural basis for a course on liberation theology. While this is not true of all liberation theologians, Topel is committed to an active but nonviolent response to oppression. I recommend the book highly. For those who may feel that active nonviolence is impractical, I recommend Gene Sharp, *The Politics of Nonviolent Action* (Boston: Porter Sargent Publisher, 1973). Sharp is much less theological than Topel, and his analysis covers a much broader range of ethical vision, but he provides an encyclopedic array of historical examples.

CHAPTER 5

Commitment and Discipleship in the New Testament

Ugo Vanni

1. Commitment and Discipleship: a Problem

The discourse of Jesus on discipleship within the New Testament never ceases to surprise the reader. Surprise is felt when Jesus pronounces the sharp command: "Follow me!" (cf. Mk. 2:14; 10:21, etc.).

The meaning of Jesus' request comes out clearly from the various contexts in which it is made. It is always a question of a basic choice, of a turning point in life. Jesus presents himself as an absolute value, to which it is necessary to subordinate everything else, radically and with no exceptions. The episode of the "rich young man" (cf. Lk. 18:18–23) tells us so in a special way. This is an exceptional man: He has kept all the commandments of the Old Testament since his youth; he is endowed with a sincere goodwill which at once attracts Jesus to him. Jesus, acknowledging the moral commitment of the young man as well as his availability, suggests that he should leave all his riches and follow him. One is astonished indeed; a question spontaneously arises: How can Jesus, in such a natural manner, pronounce a command that is so demanding? How can he request such a radical change in values? Why does he do it?

To the astonishment caused by Jesus' command another reason for surprise is added: The command is immediately obeyed (cf. Mt. 9:9; Mk. 2:14, etc.). Levi goes as far as celebrating. On the other hand, the rich young man who, faced with Jesus', "Follow me" is at first hesitant and then withdraws, far from being happy at the thought that he will be able to enjoy his wealth, becomes very"melancholy," according to

Translated by Gianna Vaudano

Luke's precise expression (Lk. 18:23). One asks: How is it that Jesus succeeds in eliciting this turning point of discipleship in people's lives? Is it because of his charm, or, is it a question of liking or affinity, or perhaps of fanaticism, as has happened more than once in history and in a variety of fields, ranging from the religious to the political?

Why do the disciples follow Jesus? What are they looking for? What do they find?

The aim of this essay is to respond to these questions. Consequently, its development will be as follows: The first part focuses attention on Jesus who commands his disciples to follow him; in the second part we will study the attitude of the disciples, from the first "yes" to the maturity of discipleship. We will then be able—and this will be our conclusion—to see what significance the discourse of Jesus' discipleship has for all of us, today, and what its prospects are.

2. Jesus, the Protagonist of Discipleship

A look at the Gospels shows us Jesus' constant attitude of availability to the Father. At twelve years of age, in contact with the Temple, the "Father's House" (cf. Lk. 2:49), he feels that his role is precisely to occupy himself with the things of his Father, to live always in his house. All the rest—the affection and care of Mary and Joseph and their anxiety—almost surprises him (cf. Lk. 2:49).

The baptism by John, which marks the opening of the public life of Jesus and stresses his choice to serve people, is explicitly and solemnly approved by the Heavenly Father. This approval will be the incentive, the secret urge of Jesus' entire life. He will declare this openly and repeatedly. When—in John 4:31–34—the disciples offer him something to eat, Jesus speaks of a mysterious food, arousing their astonishment. He then explains: "Doing the will of my Father, who has sent me, and bringing his work to completion is my food." In fact, in all his activity he continually refers to the will of the Father: "It is not to do my will that I have come down from Heaven, but to do the will of him who sent me" (Jn. 6:38; cf. also 4:34). It is a desire that Jesus loves and appreciates and for which he is longing with enthusiasm and passion: "I always do what pleases him" (Jn. 8:29).

When it is a matter of facing "his hour," the sacrifice of himself in the supreme gift of his life, Jesus feels the need to manifest his interior availability openly: "But the world must know that I love the Father and do as the Father has commanded me. Come, then! Let us be on our way" (Jn. 14:31). His passion will follow. To sum it up: Jesus is the first to practice the discipleship which he then demands. All his life is oriented to do the will of his Father. Without an appreciation of this total availability to do the Father's will, the life and figure of Jesus would be incomprehensible.

3. To Follow Jesus Is Like Following Yahweh

Having discovered and practiced the meaning of his life in an uninterrupted dedication to the Father, Jesus proposes the same way of life to his disciples. But, since he himself is the interpreter of the Father ("Whoever has seen me has seen the Father," Jn. 14:9), the availability to the Father will have to pass through him. In order to please the Father the disciple will necessarily have *to follow* Jesus.

The term, "to follow," requires an explanation. It seems to have been chosen—among other comparable terms, such as, "to imitate," "to obey," "to dedicate oneself," etc.—for reasons of continuity. In the Old Testament, at the time of the desert the people of God had "to follow" Yahweh. The sign of Yahweh—the cloud during the day and the column of fire during the night—determined the movement of the people in an exclusive, assertive sense. Only when the people were really open to this sign, and only in the measure in which they were so, could they advance in the desert toward the Promised Land. "To follow Yahweh" was the cause of the very life of the people.

When Jesus addresses to his future disciples the peremptory invitation to follow him, this Old Testament context is recalled. Jesus is to be followed as Yahweh was followed.

This radical requirement to relativize everything in light of the person of Jesus and of his invitation to follow can then be understood. The person and the invitation of Jesus have the same absolute character that God himself possesses. When this absolute character is perceived, discipleship becomes spontaneous, at least—as we will see—in its initial step. On the other hand, when this absolute character of Jesus and his equivalency with God are not clearly perceived, his request to leave everything and follow him appears excessive and discouraging. In all probability this is the reaction of the rich young man: While addressing Jesus as "good" teacher (cf. Lk. 18:18), he has not yet perceived that in the goodness of Jesus the very same goodness of God is hidden.

4. The Discipleship of Jesus: the First Step

Being available to Jesus as his disciple, which means being available to God, cannot have reservations or conditions, just as the need of the people of God in the desert "to go after Yahweh" did not admit of reservations or conditions. Any hesitation would have demonstrated a lack of faith and would have even have implied the abandonment of Yahweh or making a foolish substitution, as the episode of the golden calf shows us (cf. Ex. 32:1–24).

Similarly, the discipleship of Jesus cannot be weakened. If its level decreases, discipleship degenerates. Either it is absolute, or it is no longer a discipleship. We see this in a Gospel passage, expressed in difficult, but effective, symbolic language.

A disciple has detected something of the absolute character of discipleship. He therefore expresses himself in these words: "I will be your follower wherever you go" (Lk. 9:57). Jesus' reply accepts the unconditional availability. "The foxes have lairs, the birds of the sky have nests, but the Son of Man has nowhere to lay his head" (Lk. 9:58). Discipleship will require promptness, spiritual agility, and an availability without reservations and without pauses.

Another disciple accepts Jesus' command, but presents a request that expresses in symbolic language a reasonable condition from the human perspective: "I will follow you, but let me bury my father first" (Lk. 9:59). Yet, this "reasonable" condition lowers the transcendent, absolute level of discipleship. We understand, then, Jesus' disconcerting answer: "Let the dead bury their dead" (Lk. 9:60). The language is symbolic. The dead, as such, cannot bury! But this does not make Jesus' words less demanding. Whoever follows Jesus "shall never walk in darkness; he shall possess the light of life" (Jn. 8:12). Nondiscipleship, precisely in contrast with the light of life, evokes an area of darkness, an absence of life and moral death. Closing oneself to the discipleship of Jesus, one remains in a system of interhuman relationships which only in appearance are relationships of life. In reality, it is as if dead people were the protagonists of this illusory life: they serve, help, and bury one another, but do all this under the ominous sign of a lack of vitality. It is the world as it would be without Christ.

A third disciple manifests a desire that—even in its metaphorical terms—expresses a humanly reasonable request: "First let me take leave of my people at home" (Lk. 9:61). No less than in the previous case, we find here the attempt to fit the transcendence of discipleship into a plan of human convenience. Discipleship would undoubtedly appear easier, but it would run the risk of becoming weaker, with the danger, then, of failing completely.

The answer of Jesus brings discipleship back to the track of the absolute: "Whoever puts his hand to the plow but keeps looking back is unfit for the reign of God" (Lk. 9:62). The following of Jesus, as the following of Yahweh in the Old Testament, admits of no interferences and much less of any nostalgic look to the past. The people of God will have to overcome their homesickness for Egypt and look only forward, toward the Promised Land. The same is true for the Christian.

5. The First Development of Discipleship: The Galilean Phase

The texts from Luke that have been quoted show us discipleship still at the starting point. Following Jesus must be understood, precisely in the light of the following of Yahweh in the Old Testament. It is a matter of desiring to follow and then of finally choosing to do so.

Once the first step has been definitely taken, what happens to the disciples? What does the fact of having chosen Jesus and of following him imply, and what change does it cause in their life?

There is, first of all, a relationship of special intimacy and familiarity with Jesus. This intimate relationship, with all the manifold enrichment derived from those small elements of living together in daily life, gradually mold the disciples. Jesus preaches, and his preaching is addressed to the crowds, but always in the presence of the disciples (cf. Mt. 5:1). His teaching takes shape in the disciples: They learn to think as he does and to evaluate people and things as he does. With his turning to parables, his teaching will become more demanding; it will be necessary for those who are listening to "have ears" in order to understand the parables (cf. Mk. 4:9 and Synoptics). That is, it will be necessary to apply one's mental resources actively to the deciphering of the metaphorical language typical of the parables. Jesus helps the disciples to do this work of interpretation. They will have to know, closely and deeply, "the mysteries of the Kingdom of God" (Mk. 4:11).

Besides teaching, Jesus cares for the persons: He takes interest in them, cures them of their illnesses; he even forgives their sins. It is sufficient to read some chapters from Mark—for instance, 1:21–39 and 5:21–43—to relive the way Jesus was with the people. The disciples are with him; they participate and are involved. The feelings, the kindness, and the reproaches of Jesus have a repercussion on them, move them to react, and mold them from the inside.

Discipleship, as it is presented to us in the Gospels, is never an individual adventure. Jesus is to be followed together, in a group. It is exactly in the group of disciples that tensions and even conflicts often arise—as happens in any group living certain values together and trying to deepen them. The most noticeable conflict is one of disconcerting realism: The disciples, who have admired and experienced the attitude of Jesus who came "not to be served but to serve" (Mk. 10:45), fall to a level of petty competition. They excitedly and repeatedly discuss who will be the greatest. The mother of James and John intervenes too, asking for her two sons the first places in the Kingdom of God. The two do not even grow discouraged at Jesus' sharp reply: "You do not know what you are asking" (Mk. 10:38). Jesus is fully aware that the disciples, though they have left everything to follow him and have really taken him as an absolute, need to grow, and such growth is slow. The first step is an important beginning, but persons still remain basically as they used to be. Jesus knows how to take his disciples at the point where they really are. He does not expect them to be immediately perfect, but he educates them toward maturity. In this incident of rivalry he taught them that true Christian greatness consists in the willingness to serve (cf. Mk. 9:33–37). But there may have been many such cases, and Jesus surely took care of each of them.

Jesus, though spending most of his time with the disciples, goes aside once in a while and passes long periods of time—occasionally entire nights—absorbed in prayer. The disciples realize this: They are aware that in Jesus who prays there is something new. They ask Jesus to teach them how to pray. Jesus teaches them the Our Father, which will become the Christian prayer par excellence. But it is not a matter of a simple formula, detached and deteachable from life. All of life, lived as Jesus lives it, is a continuous prayer; it is the bright background which also enhances prayer as a formula.

We have seen some examples of what following Jesus meant to the disciples. These examples have only an indicative value, not simply because there were certainly others besides them which went by unobserved in the tradition and the drawing-up of the Gospels, but also, and above all, because of another factor. Discipleship pervades the whole personality of the disciples, involving a desire to assimilate values which are present and recognizable in the personality of Jesus. A process of this kind is global of its very nature; it cannot be measured and cannot be quantified. The examples presented are like a revealing evidence, a symptom of something more that is happening in the soul of the disciples and that little by little transforms them. To them, to follow is to imitate. But to what point does this daily growth reach in the assimilation of the values of Jesus?

6. The Decisive Phase: Discipleship to Jerusalem

The level of discipleship is reflected in the depth of the knowledge of Jesus that the disciples succeed in reaching. An episode that is rightly considered central in the three Synoptics is very enlightening.

Jesus is in the northernmost part of Galilee, at Caesarea Philippi. It is an out-of-the-way place. There is not a crowd that wants him at all costs, as was often the case in Capharnaum and surroundings. This is a moment of special intimacy between Jesus and the disciples. Jesus asks them a crucial question about his identity: "Who do people say that I am?" (Mk. 8:27–30 and parallels). Vague as it is in its formulation, the answer is interesting: Jesus is thought to be John the Baptizer, Elijah, or one of the great prophets; according to the people, Jesus still has a place, a particularly relevant one maybe, in the sphere of the Old Testament. Jesus insists, asking the disciples the same question in a direct way, and Peter answers on behalf of them all: "You are the Messiah." Jesus approves of and praises this affirmation on Peter's part. He is really the Messiah, surely outside and above the Old Testament, even if seen in the most representative figures. This recognition of Jesus by the disciples is the most beautiful fruit of their discipleship: staying with him, differently from the people who have had only sporadic contacts, they have assimilated his personality and values and have understood him. But—and this is the question we were asking ourselves above—to what level of depth have they been able to do so?

The text that immediately follows is truly disappointing with regard to the level of discipleship reached by the disciples. It shows us how the following of Jesus, precisely because Jesus is an absolute and not merely a great human figure of teacher and prophet, always contains surprises and is and must remain open to something more, something better, and something unforeseen. If it is considered to be complete, it ceases to be discipleship.

But let us examine the text more closely. Building on the understanding that the discipleship practiced so far has created in the disciples, Jesus wants to bring them to greater depth. They have recognized him as the Messiah, but do they know exactly what this means in the vision of Jesus? "Jesus then," Mark tells us in 8:31–37, "began to teach them that the Son of Man had to suffer much, be rejected by the chief priests and the scribes, be put to death, and rise three days later." It is the clear picture of his Messiahship, as he perceives it and intends it. The first reaction of the disciples is not only one of astonishment—this would be understandable—but one of rejection. Peter, shortly before the authoritative and approved spokesman of the disciples concerning the identity of Jesus, with an unprecedented gesture "took Jesus aside and began to remonstrate with him." It is the reversal of discipleship: Peter feels that he himself is the determinant element of the life of Jesus. It is this abnormal reversal that triggers the very hard reaction from Jesus: "Get out of my sight, you satan! You are not judging by God's standards, but by man's." On Peter's side, discipleship has not been denied, but it has come, as it were, to a deadpoint. The attitude of Jesus explains the situation to us. In fact, after rebuking Peter for his absurd position, Jesus goes to the roots. His talk widens in perspective and addresses not only Peter and the disciples, but also the crowd that Jesus has explicitly summoned. The talk dwells precisely on discipleship: "Having called the crowd with the disciples, he said to them: 'If a man wishes to come after me, he must deny his very self, take up his cross, and follow in my steps'" (Mk. 8:34).

These are strong words, which leave an impression upon the listeners. Discipleship on the part of Peter, the disciples, and even our own discipleship, will come out of the quicksand of dilettantism and will grow in proportion to the extent that we have the courage to accept the logic of the gift proper to the Paschal Mystery. Jesus does not ask of others anything regarding discipleship that he will not himself do first; i.e., being totally available to the will of the Father. Going to Jerusalem, Jesus will fulfill his fundamental choice of being obedient "accepting even death, death on a cross" (Phil. 2:8). To follow Jesus means, then, to go with him to Jerusalem, with the prospect of sharing in his Paschal Mystery. The words he speaks thus acquire a more precise meaning, no less demanding, but more encouraging. To follow him implies "to deny oneself." Yet, it is not a matter of depersonalization, of a stifling of one's tendencies and aspirations, which after all would be neurotic behavior. Much more deeply and simply, it is a matter of denying one's selfishness and of not accepting the inclination to make of oneself, of one's small or big daily interests, the determinant factor, the idol of life. It is a matter of placing the very center of oneself, of one's personality, out of self, into the love for others, to the point of sacrificing and giving one's life for them. It is the basic choice of discipleship that becomes operative and concrete in the gift of self to others.

In light of this overcoming of our egoism, of this inversion of the tendency that makes us look out for ourselves rather than for others, the other expression, no less impressive and harsh than the previous one, receives emphasis, too: "Let him take up his cross and follow me." Let us clarify immediately: it is not a question of a fanatical and neurotic search of sacrifice for sacrifice's sake. The cross to be taken up is the cross of Jesus, which, becoming our own, allows a complete fulfillment of discipleship. This is to say that, taking up his cross, Jesus offers himself and dedicates all his life to others in the supreme sacrifice. If and in the measure in which this attitude becomes ours, his cross becomes our own. Carrying it with him, behind him, we fully achieve our discipleship. There is not, then, a complete discipleship without the cross, understood in the sense we are examining: the sincere, but still unshaped discipleship reached by Peter and the other disciples before Caesarea Philippi. Neither can we speak of the cross of Christ, the one that we are invited to take up and carry, out of the context of discipleship: If we reduced the "cross" to be taken up and carried day by day simply to the sufferings of daily life, isolating them from the perspective of the gift of self to others which is proper of discipleship, we would have a reductive interpretation of Jesus' words.

Jesus himself explains: "In fact, whoever would preserve his life, will lose it, but whoever loses his life for my sake and the Gospel's, will preserve it." It is really a matter of a decisively important choice: A mistake would be fatal.

Whoever chooses himself, his own egotism, as the reference point of his life, will lose his life. Whoever does not have the courage to deny himself in the sense we have specified above will not fulfill himself. On the contrary, whoever makes a gift of his life, giving it up in following Christ, will arrive, as Christ did, to the optimal fullness of himself. We are given a glimpse of the luminous goal of that fullness of life and vitality which is achieved in the resurrection. The cross of

Christ, that has become our own, makes it feasible for us to share also in the resurrection.

At this point, we may ask ourselves whether it is possible for us, by human resources, even with all our goodwill, to achieve the total giving of ourselves for others, as Jesus has done. He invites us to follow him to Jerusalem, but where will we find the strength to undertake and bring to full completion a walk of this kind?

The question is pertinent, and the passage we have examined gives a hint at the answer. Jesus goes to Jerusalem to live the Paschal Mystery, and he will do it for us. Precisely in order to carry out, without limitations of time and space, this corroborating action of his with regard to us, the day before his passion he instituted the Eucharist. The Paschal Mystery of Christ, his will to be for others and his availability to the Father, aims, through the Eucharist, at being assimilated by the church and at transforming it. The secret of a fulfilled discipleship consists in this ecclesial assimilation of the Paschal Mystery—the acceptance of Jesus' forgiveness, the participation in the Eucharist, and so on.

We observe this in the person of Peter. Jesus' harsh reproach surely impressed him, but did not convince him at once. At the beginning of the passion, we find Peter moved by the best goodwill; he will protest—and will do so sincerely—that he wants to give his own life for Jesus. It is an honest goodwill of dsicipleship. But when he finds himself faced with the event, he will first try to resist even by the use of force; then, he will not stand by Jesus when he is arrested and, reaching the depth of his weakness, he will deny him. In Peter who denies Jesus, the very same Peter remonstrating with Jesus at Caesarea Philippi reemerges. Afterward, there will be the liberating forgiveness of Jesus; there will be the death of Jesus with all its strengthening efficacy, and there will be the prolonged and deepened practice of ecclesial life. At this point we find a different Peter, finally able to commit himself to total discipleship.

The so-called appendix to the Gospel of John, chapter 21, tells us about him: The figure of Peter gains a really special emphasis; Jesus bestows on him the responsibility for all the new people of God: "Feed my lambs, feed my sheep" (Jn. 21:16–17), but he does so explicitly requesting of Peter, three times, a profession of love. The denial, the antidiscipleship attitude of Peter, is thus overcome in terms of love. Truly loving Jesus with the logic of the heart that is typical of love,

Peter will now be able to comprehend, to feel discipleship in all its radicality. No longer does he presume to rely on himself. He well knows that the strength to follow Jesus comes only from Jesus and from love, matured in suffering and in the acceptance of forgiveness. His following this time will be really complete: "I tell you solemnly: as a young man you fastened your belt and went about as you pleased; but when you are older you will stretch out your hands, and another will tie you fast and carry you off against your will" (Jn. 21:18). The allusion to Peter's death is clear, and John makes it explicit: "What he said indicated the sort of death by which Peter was to glorify God" (Jn. 21:19). But—and this is the topic with which we are dealing—the gift of life that Peter will offer for Jesus and the Church dying as a martyr is framed in the context of discipleship, of which it represents the climax. "When he had finished speaking he said to him, 'Follow me!'" (Jn. 21:19).

7. The Route of Discipleship

Having reached this point of our study, we can glance over the road we have taken for the purpose of grasping the essential traits of discipleship as they appear in the Gospels and, then, bringing them into the practice of our life.

Discipleship begins with Jesus' invitation. Jesus takes the initiative and presents himself to the person as the absolute value that gives full meaning to life. This absolute characteristic of discipleship makes it objectively necessary. To follow Jesus or not, is not an extra, a luxury for man: Man will not be able to fulfill himself fully apart from the discipleship of Jesus.

This objective necessity does not deprive man of the responsibility of a choice. Discipleship may be accepted or refused. This is shown in all clarity by the episode of the rich young man who does not feel like relativizing everything in face of the absolute value of Jesus and goes away very "melancholy." The acceptance of discipleship is thus a binding decision; we can even say the most important decision in life. The insistence, therefore, on the radicality that it demands since the beginning should not surprise us.

Once the first step has been taken, discipleship goes through a phase of almost imperceptible growth. It is a matter of learning from Jesus, observing his behavior, listening to his doctrine, and reacting while staying with him. Thus, gradually, a first image of Jesus, with the corresponding desire to imitate him, is formed in the disciple. It is the Galilean stage of discipleship and comes to its conclusion at Caesarea Philippi.

The first idea, the first image of Jesus, and the first attempts at imitation demand, then, a decisive deepening: Jesus is the Christ, who gives up himself, dies, and rises again for man; the disciples will have to gradually assimilate this aspect, comprehend it, and make it their own. It is the discipleship to Jerusalem. It will require the will of offering up themselves as gift, the will of coming to a total renunciation, typical of Christ, in order to participate in and also communicate the vitality of the resurrection. Both the first stage of discipleship, which we have called Galilean, and the second, the one of Jerusalem, are reachable, thanks to the active influence of Christ, developed within the ecclesial life, where he relives for us his Paschal Mystery.

8. Concluding Reflections: Education to the Discipleship of Jesus

What is the position of the Christian educator vis à vis the theological-biblical aspect of discipleship? Both the analysis of texts that we have made and the final synthesis contain hints which are interesting at the educational level; if they are adequately detected by the educator, they can and must be translated into practical suggestions.

Let us make some suggestions along this line, without any presumption of being able to exhaust them all.

First of all, discipleship, also when viewed from a pedagogical point of view, must be understood in the light of the full development of the person. To follow Jesus, to be his disciples, does not mean a precarious subordination, a reductive humiliation of one's personality. The contrary is exactly true: Peter, as we have seen, finds in discipleship the best self-fulfillment. Discipleship makes of him the Peter we know. Otherwise, he would have remained an unknown fisherman from Capharnaum, all absorbed in his little world. The rich young man, when he refuses to follow Jesus, goes away very "melancholy," and we lose sight of him. Had he accepted the invitation of Jesus, he would have found the optimal self-fulfillment that could have made of him a great apostle. Therefore, to educate to discipleship, to the following of Jesus, adequately understanding the two, means to thrust the person toward the development of the best of himself, of his most authentic values. Discipleship is entirely to the advantage of man.

Here is another observation: The Galilean phase of discipleship shows us two elements, each of them having a great educational importance. To follow Jesus, to become his disciples, means to live with him in everyday life. It is through the sum of what Jesus does, says, teaches, and of how he behaves that his figure emerges and leaves an impression on the disciples. Sharing Jesus' life, they learn to know Jesus in a very real way. It is the same today. To educate to the discipleship of Jesus does not mean to copy, materially and anachronistically, some details of his life; rather, it means to teach how to lead others to know, love, and appreciate Jesus as a person, in those living values that, then, can be manifested and expressed in the details of daily life.

The Galilean phase suggests another element: gradualness. Discipleship requires at the beginning a fundamental choice, a decisive and uncompromising one. After this, its growth is slow. In fact, it is a matter of values which must be assimilated and personalized and which little by little shape a way of looking at things and a mentality that will guide and direct in life's choices. All this cannot be improvised, except to the risk, equally insidious, of either superficiality or fanaticism.

There is, finally, the following to Jerusalem. It is there that, in the fulfilled will of giving himself completely, Jesus achieves the maximum of personal discipleship. He invites the disciples to do the same. To educate to discipleship, therefore, means to inculcate, continually, on every occasion, "every day," the thought that there are opportunities to give oneself to others and that life should be committed to this. The cross to be taken up every day must be presented not as the search for an extra suffering, but as heartfelt attention to others who should be helped; to do this, it is necessary to come out of the circle of one's selfishness.

In conclusion: the church, its liturgy, and the intersubjectivity that takes place in it are—as we have noticed more than once—the indispensable environment in which, since the beginning, discipleship has become real. It will be as such also today, no less than at the beginning. Jesus is to be followed together, in the joyful reciprocity of our being church. Any education toward living as church is education to discipleship.

CHAPTER 6

Prayer

Carroll Stuhlmueller

Prayer is as essential to Bible-based religious education as eating and heartbeat are to the human body. Without faith and a spirit of prayer, the Bible becomes a dead letter and religious education easily turns into an autopsy of a corpse. Students and teachers are no longer in contact with a living person. The autopsy consists of intellectual exercises about the content of faith, but the person in whom one believes and about whom one studies seems lifeless. Religious education loses its sense of wonder over a personal God far beyond our intellectual reach.

Bereft of prayer, biblical investigation is restricted to archaeological sites and ancient manuscripts; it deals with cultural habits, even with religious norms, yet as these are rolled flat into a book, not as heard from a living person. Without prayer the Bible remains what this word means in its ancient Greek origin, *biblia* or "books," which can be put back on the shelf when one becomes tired of the message. Prayer transforms the book into a living person who cannot be shelved but continually attracts us into the mystery of our own human dignity as God converses with us.

As we will see in the development of this chapter, prayer enables the Bible to become a conversation between the living God and ourselves in the reality of our human existence. While prayer begins and remains within the realm of earthly reality, it plunges us into the mystery at the heart of this reality where God and ourselves are intimately yet invisibly united.

In dealing with this paradox, and approaching an invisible mystery within a visible world, the pure and all-holy within a sinful and imperfect situation, prayer follows a pattern obvious even to first readers of the Bible. The Bible, in fact, will seem too human to be a divine word, as when the patriarch Abraham declares his wife to be only his sister, indeed three times, as though once were not too often (Gen. 12:10–20; ch. 20; 26:6–11), or when Paul refers to "certain false claimants to the title of brother [who] wormed their way into the group to spy on the freedom we enjoy in Christ Jesus" to ascertain if Titus is circumcised or not (Gal. 2:4). At other times the Bible overwhelms us with the supernatural, and "a great awe" overcomes us as it did the first disciples, when Jesus calmed the storm at sea and the disciples "kept saying to one another, 'Who can this be that the wind and the sea obey him?'" (Mk. 4:41).

This combination of the human and the divine, which prayer respects in reading or studying the Bible, appears in a striking way in the Book of Sirach, also called Ecclesiasticus because of its being the most quoted Old Testament book after Psalms in early church liturgy. Sirach may even seem to go to extremes in stressing the need of human endeavor and "good works." He reverses the sequence of biblical events in the life of Abraham. While Genesis *first* presents God's blessing and promises (Gen. 12:1–3) and *then* Abraham's good works in circumcision and the willingness to sacrifice Isaac (Gen. 17 and 22), Sirach transposes the order: *first* Abraham "observed the precepts of the Most High . . . incised the ordinance in his own flesh and when tested was found loyal" (Sir. 44:20), and *then* came the blessing: "For this reason, God promised him with an oath that in his descendants the nations would be blessed" (Sir. 44:21).

Sirach emphasized the need of "study for a long time" according to the Foreword composed by his grandson, in order to deal with "the law of the Most High" (Sir. 39:1). Nonetheless, his primary "care is to seek the Lord, his Maker . . . and to open his lips in prayer [that he may] be filled with the spirit of understanding" (Sir. 39:6). The first edition of his work, moreover, concludes:

> More than this we need not add;
>   let the last word be, God is all in all!
> Let us praise him the more, since we cannot fathom him,
>   for greater is he than all his works. . . .
> Extol him with renewed strength,
>   and weary not, though you cannot reach the end:
> For who can see him and describe him?
>   or who can praise him as he is? (Sir. 43:28–33).

Prayer enabled the sage to be inspired and guided by the *mystery* of

God while seeking a clear, nonmysterious answer in the *human* study of the Bible. The Bible never advises short-circuiting the human endeavor and going immediately to God in prayer. Like Sirach's grandson who devoted "many sleepless hours of close application . . . to finishing the book for publication," again we are quoting from the Foreword, religious educators must not neglect any pedagogical or academic means of learning more about the Bible, but through prayer their final word must be, "God is all in all! Let us praise him the more, since we cannot fathom him." Principally—perhaps we should write "only"—through prayer do we realize that God is beyond our study and cannot be fathomed by human effort alone.

As we explore the role of prayer in religious education with the Bible, a preliminary definition of prayer may be helpful. Prayer is understood as the attitude of faith and the silent composure of one's spirit as we listen to God, personally speaking the words of the Bible to ourselves today. The principal sections of this chapter will turn to the Bible in order to appreciate the major sections of this definition: 1) God's speaking the Scriptures; 2) to ourselves today; 3) within the liturgy and the canonical arrangement of the Bible; as well as 4) within the lonely stretches of divine silence.

I

Prayer: Listening as God Speaks the Words of Scripture

If we scan the overall structure of the Book of Exodus, the Bible will appear not only as the Word of God but also as the Word being spoken by God. In many ways the Book of Exodus places us at the heart of the Torah and therefore at the central point of Old Testament religion. Here Moses receives the Law and the covenant promise from the Lord. Chapters 1 to 18 bring the Israelites out of Egypt to the base of Mount Sinai. Within chapters 19–21 Moses climbs Mount Sinai and enters within the cloud, where thunder and lightning, trumpet blasts and smoke accompanied the Word of God. God spoke face to face with Moses in giving him the Decalogue. Chapters 21–23 record the covenant laws and chapter 24 recounts the sealing of the covenant by means of sacrifice and a sacred meal. Chapter 24 concludes:

> After Moses had gone up, a cloud covered the mountain. The glory of the
> Lord settled upon Mount Sinai. . . . Moses passed into the midst of the
> cloud as he went up on the mountain; and there he stayed for forty days
> and forty nights.

The entire momentum of Exodus, chapters 1–24, therefore, is symbolized in a journey, that of the Israelites to Mount Sinai and the
journey of Moses to the top of Mount Sinai where God came down to
speak with him. The Torah is Yahweh's personal gift to Moses.

The next series of chapters, 25 to 31, describe the tabernacle, its
furnishings, the consecration of priests and other ritual details. These
are presented in the context of Moses' long forty day retreat with
Yahweh on Mount Sinai. Chapter 31 concludes with the statement:

> When the Lord had finished speaking to Moses on Mount Sinai, he gave
> him the two tablets of the commandments, the stone tablets inscribed by
> God's own finger (Ex. 31:18).

The following section, chapters 32–34, offer a theological commentary upon the covenant and its laws which Moses had just received
from the Lord. This commentary combines a moral sense of sin and its
atonement along with exalted reaches of mystical theology. From a
literary viewpoint the chapters form a compact unit. Brevard S. Childs
writes:

> . . . Chs. 32–34 were structured into a compositional unit in one of the
> final stages of the development of the book of Exodus. First of all, the
> chapters have been placed within an obvious theological framework of sin
> and forgiveness. Chapter 32 recounts the breaking of the covenant; ch. 34
> relates its restoration. Moreover, these chapters arc held together by a series
> of motifs which are skillfully woven into a unifying pattern. The tablets [of
> the law] are received, smashed in ch. 32, recut, and restored in ch. 34.
> Moses' intercession for Israel begins in ch. 32, continues in ch. 33, and
> comes to a climax in ch. 34. The theme of the presence of God which is
> the central theme in ch. 33 joins, on the one hand, to the prior theme of
> disobedience in ch. 32, and on the other hand, to the assurance of forgive-
> ness in ch. 34 (*The Book of Exodus*, Philadelphia: 1974, pgs. 557–8).

Beginning with the incident of the golden calf in chapter 32, we are
caught within a dramatic story of contrasts. While the mystic Moses is
conversing with God on Mount Sinai during a forty-day retreat, the
frivolous people and the weakhearted Aaron are swept into lascivious

feasting at the base of the mountain. The chapter, moreover, is still more seriously trenchant as a warning to the church and to religious educators. Again to quote from Brevard S. Childs:

> What gives the story such a cutting edge is its penetrating insight that religion itself can be a means to disobedience (pg. 580).

Rather than deal with a distant God and a mystical Moses, Aaron decides to give the people a god made by human hands. In religious education we are always in danger of doing the same thing. Our golden calf can be our way of reducing Bible study simply to an academic pursuit, an exclusively human endeavor, albeit in the name of scientific critical investigation. The golden calf, a visible pedestal for God's invisible presence, becomes more important than God, the rational pursuit more important than the arational goal, the impersonal investigation about God more important than the personal God.

We now come to the gem of the Torah, perhaps of the entire Hebrew Bible. It is not surprising that the text is complex, even contradictory; mystic phenomena can never be clearly explained and remain true to what is happening. Ecstasy reaches beyond rational discourse. In chapter 33 we are told that "the Lord used to speak to Moses face to face" (33:11). Yet a little later, when Moses begs of God, "Do let me see your glory," Yahweh replies, "My face you cannot see, for no one sees me and still lives." This contradiction is the fate of every mystic. Absorbed into the immediate presence of God, a person is wrapped in light so bright and intense, beyond that even of the sun, that the mystic is blinded and feels lost in total darkness. When God is closest, he will always seem farthest away. Only the memory survives—as God says to Moses:

> When my glory passes I will set you in the hollow of the rock and will cover you with my hand until I have passed by. Then I will remove my hand, so that you may see my back, but my face is not to be seen (Ex. 33:22–23).

While chapter 32 records the excesses and misdirection of religion, chapter 33 prepares us for the correct way to receive the word of God. The solemn moment of interpreting the Torah as truly the Word of God comes in chapter 34. Moses stands at the peak of Mount Sinai with the two tablets of the law in his arms. God passes by to explain how this word is to be received. No explanation can take the place of the biblical word at this point:

Moses then cut two stone tablets like the former [which he had smashed to pieces in chapter 32], and early the next morning he went up Mount Sinai as the Lord had commanded him, taking along the two stone tablets.

Having come down in a cloud, the Lord stood with him there and proclaimed his name, "Lord." Thus the Lord passed before him and cried out, "The Lord, the Lord, a merciful and gracious God, slow to anger and rich in kindness and fidelity, continuing his kindness for a thousand generations, and forgiving wickedness and crime and sin. . . ." Moses at once bowed down to the ground in worship (Ex. 24:4–8).

After this theophany of wondrous compassion and after a few additional laws, we are told that "Moses stayed there with the Lord for forty days and forty nights, without eating any food or drinking any water" (Ex. 34:28). When Moses came down, his face thereafter became so radiant with light that the people were fearful to look at him. Thereafter he always wore a veil over his face, except when he "entered the presence of the Lord [in the meeting tent] to converse with him" (Ex. 34:34).

In the arrangement of material in the book of Exodus, a new series of chapters, 35 to 39, provide further laws and regulations for the ritual. The book concludes, in chapter 40, with the erection of the sanctuary or dwelling of the Lord, also called the Meeting Tent. In one of the final verses we are told:

The cloud covered the meeting tent, and the glory of the Lord filled the Dwelling (Ex. 40:34).

Again we are faced with textual difficulties. It is said that "Moses could not enter the meeting tent, because the cloud settled down upon it and the glory of the Lord filled the Dwelling." Previously, Moses did approach the Lord amidst the cloud of glory. An element of mystery and darkness surrounds our final verses. God elusively slips beyond the grasp of the biblical text and even Moses, its originator.

This brief analysis of the canonical arrangement of the Book of Exodus insists upon prayer, even upon ecstatic contemplation, to reach the proper attitude for interpreting the Torah. There is probably no more glorious scene in the entire Old Testament than the portrayal of Moses on Mount Sinai, majestically holding the two tables of the Law and hearing the thunderous sound of the Lord, passing by, proclaiming "The Lord, the Lord, a merciful and gracious God, slow to anger and rich in kindness and fidelity." Law was to be interpreted as spoken by such a merciful, compassionate God.

Moses could never have arrived at such a moment without a long boot camp of training in forgiveness toward others, in compassion and understanding toward the weakness and faults of others. The wonder of God had bowed the head of Moses and had steeped his heart in humility.

Moses' prayer was accompanied with fasting and personal penance. Here was another way by which the great saint felt himself absorbed within the ranks of the poor and needy. Fasting weakened him; it also sharpened his desire for God.

This combination of prayer and law, within a biblical text that is marred with inconsistency and even with contradiction, shows that God's message can not be attained simply by studying the text. One must be able to read between the lines and words. Here we begin to realize that contemplation and the blinding light of God's holy presence always leave us a bit confused, beyond the purely rational approach, absorbed within the holiness of the all holy God. Only when prayer trains our instincts in the way of a compassionate, merciful and faithful God can we land with our two feet on a solid base of peace and understanding.

Even though none of us will see God immediately—for that would destroy our eyesight more quickly than direct exposure to sunlight— still we must be attracted towards this vision of the Lord. We need to be drawn toward the blinding light of the Lord's glory. Even though the voice still resounds from a distant place, we must climb Mount Sinai and listen for the Lord, speaking the words of the Bible to us.

Chapter 32 also warns us that religion can become a trap, even a source of trouble and sin. If *too much* attention is given to the human side, whether this be ritual or reasoning, we can be accused of building our golden calf to worship. Prayer, linked with regard for the poor, can be our surest and sturdiest defense against this degeneration. Prayer keeps us attuned to a *personal* God who will not allow his servant to be overly absorbed in externals and formalities. Bonding with the poor prevents the waste of time and resources in formalistic ritual; it also induces a healthy common sense. The poor, who often have little or no time for the intricacies of law and even less concern for stern rubrics, help religious educators to read and interpret biblical law as spoken by a God, "slow to anger and rich in kindness and fidelity."

Prayer then enables the religious educator to acquire a posture of *listening* in ever closer union with God, as *God speaks* the words of Scripture.

II

Prayer: Listening as God Speaks the Words of Scripture to Us Today

The insistence upon long, contemplative prayer in the first section of this chapter may seem to undercut our contact with reality. However, a second, closer reading of the same material will spot a secondary theme: humble regard for the poor, even for sinners who deliberately harm us. This latter concern will quickly shatter our blind, silent contemplation with the crashing sound of reality. Even if Moses twice remained forty days and forty nights on Mount Sinai, according to the Book of Exodus, nonetheless, he did return to the plain where the rest of the people were encamped. Here, we are told,

> Moses' wrath flared up, so that he threw down the tablets [inscribed by God's own finger—Ex. 31:18] and broke them on the base of the mountain. Taking the calf they had made, he fused it in the fire and then ground it down to powder, which he scattered on the water and made the Israelites drink (Ex. 32:19–20).

Moses the mystic was also a fiery flesh-and-blood Moses! His prayer maintained a touch of earthiness, as his body and mind were absorbed in God!

One of the essential elements for genuine biblical prayer is derived from our contemporary world and from our own personality and temperament. We can perceive this characteristic of prayer more clearly, if we look at several places where the Bible quotes the Bible, not in any literal way but with notable adaptation. Because God speaks within the reality of our life, a reality that changes and evolves in sometimes delicate and sometimes revolutionary ways, the biblical word takes on a new kind of message, even when the words remain the same or else are adapted only slightly. A few examples may ease the flow of our discussion.

The first example is not an instance of the Bible quoting the Bible but of the Bible undergoing official translation into another language, in this case the Greek language spoken in Egypt after the conquest of Alexander the Great and the Aramaic language spoken in postexilic Israel. We quote in English from the Hebrew, Greek, and Aramaic of Isaiah 19:24–25, one of the most gracious, universal statements in the

entire Old Testament. We give v. 24 for the setting; then we provide
the three renditions of v. 25.

> v. 24. On that day Israel shall be a third party
> with Egypt and Assyria, a blessing in the
> midst of land, when the Lord of hosts blesses
> it:

v. 25 *Hebrew*	v. 25 *Greek*	v. 25 *Aramaic*
Blessed be my people Egypt, and the work of my hands Assyria, and my inheritance, Israel.	Blessed be my people *who are in* Egypt and *who are in* Assyria and my heritage Israel.	Blessed be my people *whom I brought forth out of* Egypt. *Because they sinned before me, I carried them into exile to* Assyria, but now that they have repented, they shall be called my people, and my inheritance Israel.

As mentioned already, the Hebrew signals one of those rare moments
of universal salvation in the Old Testament. In fact, such a hated
enemy as the Assyrian, known for calculated cruelty to discourage
revolt and to maintain obedient servitude, seems on a par with Israel
and to receive equal blessings. Egypt too is no longer the land out of
which God brings his people; Egypt, equally with Israel, is "my
people."

Whatever the reasons, a later scribe could not accept this universal
salvation; it must have seemed too easy an ecumenism which lost
rather than contributed its richness. Or perhaps the fear and hatred of
the Egyptians, after one of the pogroms against the Israelites, made it
pastorally impossible for Isaiah's text to be acceptable. The translator
felt that Isaiah would have said it differently, had he lived in this later
age and different place.

The Aramaic translation, part of which is called the *Targum*, was
used in the land of Israel after the people returned from exile. Hebrew
was no longer their everyday means of communication. During this
later period the people tended to live almost a ghetto existence, confined to a small territory around Jerusalem. They became more and
more closed in upon themselves, fearful and antagonistic towards foreigners. This was a period of maintaining their small sacred territory,
of collating and preserving their sacred tradition, and of dreaming of

the eschatological future when God would intervene in world politics in their favor and set up the Kingdom of God. Some of their dreams are expressed in Psalms like Psalms 96–99.

It is interesting to compare part of one of these Psalms with its source or parent, Psalm 29. Again we place the relevant passages in parallel columns:

Psalm 29:1–3
Give to the Lord, *you sons of gods,*
  give to the Lord glory and praise,
Give to the Lord the glory due his name;
  adore the Lord in holy attire.
The voice of the Lord is over the waters,
  the God of glory thunders,
  the Lord, over vast waters.

Psalm 96:7–10
Give to the Lord, *you families of nations,*
  give to the Lord glory and praise,
give to the Lord the glory due his name!
Bring gifts, and enter his courts;
worship the Lord in holy attire.
  Tremble before him, all the earth;
say among the nations: The Lord is King.

(Note: the Psalms are listed according to their numbering and versification in the *New American Bible.*)

Psalm 96 is clearly quoting from Psalm 29, one of the earliest hymns of praise in the Psalter. The latter, in fact, may have been composed by a Canaanite. With only slight retouching, principally the substitution of the name Yahweh for Baal, the Psalm was ready for use in Israelite sanctuaries. At this time, the theological eye or conscience of the Israelite priest or levite was not sharpened or refined in regard to monotheism. Somehow or other mammoth powers in the cosmos were seen to possess "divine" or superhuman qualities. They were servants of Yahweh and gave him glory within his holy temple. Yet, there they were, secondary or tutelary gods. (Compare the somewhat blatant polytheism even in Deut. 4:19; 29:25; 32:8–9.)

At a later period after the return from exile, even such incidental expressions of polytheism could no longer be tolerated. What in the earlier, preexilic times enabled Israel to live with an overwhelming sense of mystery and to see God majestically enthroned amid such wonders, was now looked upon as one of the sources or causes of Israel's collapse into various forms of sinfulness. Postexilic Israel could never again permit any soft tolerance toward foreign gods or toward any rival gods even in the throne room of Yahweh.

A number of other examples of adaptation of God's inspired word to later circumstances can be spotted in the Hebrew Scriptures: for instance, an almost identical passage is quoted three times, each time with a slightly different nuance and meaning. In Amos 1:2, the liturgical refrain is directed against the [now defunct] northern kingdom of Israel; in Joel 4(3):16 it is clearly in favor of God's people against the Gentiles; and in Jeremiah 25:30 it condemns the Gentiles along with the Israelites.

The Bible, therefore, was not quickly, nor simplistically, quoted as the final, clear, and absolutely unchanging word of God. It was indeed the word of God. Otherwise, why quote from it as an authority in religious questions, particularly in moments of worship. Yet, just as the original biblical word was heard from God within a human setting, likewise the same word at a later time would absorb the new human setting as an integral part of its message. It was not a matter, therefore, of quoting the Bible and closing the case—at least on most occasions. The following diagram may help to explain the case:

W O R D

of

PEOPLE of G O D 's   RELIGIOUS LEADERS

's

W O R L D

In this diagram God is at the center of four interactions. Naturally, the sacred text is accepted as the WORD OF GOD, authoritative, normative, inspired, the quintessence of the best that has come from earlier traditions and religious instructions among the assembly of Israel. Another part of the diagram is devoted to the PEOPLE OF GOD. Israel had been chosen as "my special possession, dearer to me than all other people . . . a kingdom of priests, a holy nation" (Ex. 19:5–6). The third area is allocated to Israel's RELIGIOUS LEADERS, chosen and anointed by God, entrusted with the Ark of the Covenant and the sacred traditions, as these were preserved in such shrines as Shiloh and later at Jerusalem. Of one of these groups of leaders, the elders, we read in the Book of Numbers:

> Taking some of the spirit that was on Moses, the Lord bestowed it on the seventy elders; and as the spirit came to rest on them, they prophesied (Num. 11:25).

The fourth part of our outline is assigned to GOD'S WORLD, created carefully by God and declared by God in each of its parts to be "good." Repeatedly the refrain rings out in the story of creation: "And God saw that it was good . . . indeed very good" (Gen. 1:3, 12, 18, 21, 25, 31).

No single element of the fourfold group in our outline can be appreciated independent of the other. We need to preserve the unity of God and the diversity of God's goodness as it was diffused through the sacred traditions, the people Israel, their religious leaders and the world at large. The world of any "today" raises questions which were never clearly faced before this time: it may have been royalty in the time of Samuel or nuclear bombs in the twentieth century. The people of God have good instincts. Yet they also need the guidance of religious leaders, trained in the knowledge of the Bible and in the sacred traditions of worship, stories of the saints and earlier moral decisions. Religious leaders hopefully clarify the issue, point out the relevant biblical texts and the spirit behind these texts.

Religious educators, therefore, interpret the Bible against this larger context. To do this, they must arrive at a peaceful unity and strength in their own character. They realize the place of one and the same God in themselves, in their religious community or church, in their world, and of course in the Bible. They must become ever more God-conscious across the entire spectrum of their existence. They cannot autocratically enforce the word of God as simplistically the final authority. It is essential to hear the word of God in a *symphony of voices* where God is speaking: among the people, among nonbelievers and members of other churches across the world, among religious leaders from their own church and other churches. At times in the human situation there are discordant sounds; it may be difficult to distinguish them from the genuine "word of God" within the symphony. We recognize the need of attentive study and dialogue, wisdom and experience, a swiveling back and forth with the Bible and church tradition to check out the voices, a humble realization that some cacophonous sounds may disturb even one's own "word of God."

Religious leaders need to study and to discern. Here, however, we are insisting on the necessity of prayer, prolonged prayer that enables a person to evolve into a "God-conscious" being. Always and everywhere, a religious educator must grow in awareness that God is present. At times this theophany of God comes like a whirlwind, as in the final chapters of Job, where God is seen entering the sources of the sea and walking about in the depths of the abyss, begetting the drops of dew and giving hoarfrost its birth in the skies, sending forth the lightning so that they say, "Here we are!" (Jb. 38:16, 28, 29, 35). Prayer forms that God-minded attitude, enabling the person to hear a sound of truth and goodness in every human voice, actually the sound of God within the speech of man and woman. St. Paul instructs us in attuning ourselves to the ubiquitous voice of God:

> Finally, my brothers and sisters, your thoughts should be wholly directed to *all* that is true, *all* that deserves respect, *all* that is honest, pure, admirable, decent, virtuous, or worthy of praise (Phil. 4:8).

Only by living long in God's presence through contemplative prayer can religious educators attune themselves to this delicately fine awareness of God's presence and word in *all* that is true, honest, pure, admirable, decent, virtuous, or worthy of praise.

In this second major section of our study, prayer is proposed as the enabling agent by which we listen to God speak the words of Scripture *to us today*. To hear this voice of God, we need to be conscious of *God's personal presence, teeming all about us.* Everywhere and always, as the prophet Isaiah advises us:

> By waiting and by calm you shall be saved,
>   in quiet and in trust your strength lies. . . .
> Yes the Lord is waiting to show you favor,
>   and he rises to pity you;
> For the Lord is a God of justice;
>   blessed are all who wait for him (Is. 30:15, 18).

In this calm attitude of waiting upon the Lord, moment by moment, we can interpret the ancient word as God's word today. Prayer cultivates the composure, physically and mentally to wait and listen; prayer intensifies our faith that we wait and listen *to God*. All the while God's word, like ourselves, absorbs elements of our contemporary world.

III

Prayer: Listening as God Speaks the Scriptures to Us Today in the Canonical Arrangement of the Bible and in the Liturgy

Our discussion of the role of prayer in religious education inches forward. We first delayed over the biblical posture of *listening* to the word of God as *personally spoken by God*. After that we moved from the more passive stance of listening to the more active way of relating the Scriptures to our own contemporary world. This latter investigation enabled us to look upon the Bible as the word of God spoken *to us in our contemporary world*. Both of these sections dealt with an attitude which can be properly called "prayer." Listening always positions us in the Lord's presence; listening within the context of our contemporary world means that we possess a strong, active attitude of recollection and of God-mindedness throughout our day.

Another form of prayer comes from our bond of worship within the church. Here we view the prayerful approach toward the Bible, first as a "canonical" book, compiled in its present form by Israel and the church, and second, as a liturgical text particularly in the celebration of Mass. In each case the religious leaders within Israel or the Church have drawn upon preexisting sacred literature and traditions and after serious study and reflection have arranged the material precisely to communicate an important message or at least to draw us into prayerful meditation.

The relation of the new section with the preceding two sections can also be viewed in this way. Prayer, as we have seen already, is a reflective time in God's presence. It can be induced and sustained by slowly reading a single passage of Scripture and listening to it as spoken *personally by God* and also as spoken *to ourselves today*. It can also result from the *arrangement* of biblical passages either in the Scriptures or else in the liturgy. The flow of one passage after another possesses a unique capacity to stir us into serious thought. In this juxtaposition of passages God is speaking to us a new message.

The canonical shape of our Bible—the Bible as it has been transmitted to us as a sacred book or collection—did not happen by chance. The raison d'être of an ancient scribe in placing passages side by side may not always be apparent to our modern eyes. Yet we must always presume that an intelligent, well-meaning person accomplished this task. There was a good purpose of promoting strong faith as well as an authentic insight into the mystery of God our Savior.

We will work with the example of chapter 1 of Isaiah; the material here is sizable and manageable.

I

¹The VISION which Isaiah . . .   *The word VISION, the first word*
experienced concerning Judah and   *in Isaiah's prophecy, signals myste-*
Jerusalem. . . .   *ry and divine communication to*
                                         follow.

II

²Hear, O heavens, and listen, O earth,
FOR THE LORD SPEAKS:
CHILDREN have I raised and reared,
but they have disowned me!
³An ox knows its owner,
and an ass, its master's manger;

But Israel does not know,
my people has not understood.

III

⁴Ah! sinful nation, people laden
with wickedness,
evil race, corrupt CHILDREN!
They have forsaken the Lord,
spurned the Holy One of Israel,
apostasized. . . .
⁷Your country is waste
⁵Where would you yet be
struck. . . .
The whole head is sick
the whole heart faint.
⁶From the sole of the foot to the head
there is no sound spot. . . .
⁷Your country is waste,
your cities burnt with fire. . . .
⁹Unless the Lord of hosts
had left us a scanty remnant,
We had become as SODOM,
we should be like
GOMORRAH.

IV

¹⁰Hear the word of the Lord,
princes of SODOM!
Listen to the instruction of our God,
people of GOMORRAH!

¹¹What care I for the number of your
sacrifices?
says the Lord. . . .

Vv. 2–3 summon the culprit. The key phrase, FOR THE LORD SPEAKS corresponds with the final line (v. 20) in this "judgment speech." CHILDREN in v. 2 links vv. 2–3 with vv. 4–9 which were inserted here towards the end of Isaiah's career. Notice too the contrast between CHILDREN and the ox and the ass.

Vv. 4–9 were added to the earlier judgment speech (vv. 2 3 + 10–20). While the latter provided for a second chance (see v. 16), vv. 4–9 come after the second chance had been gambled away and the land almost totally destroyed. The word CHILDREN is used to stitch this section into the preceding one, see CHILDREN in v. 2.

The words SODOM and GOMORRAH join the closing line of this later insertion (vv. 4–9) with the continuation of the "judgment speech" in v. 10 where the words are repeated.

Once again, as in vv. 2–3, the defendant is summoned before the court.

Vv. 11–15d record the questioning of the culprit and the listing of crimes.

¹⁴Your new moons and festivals I
detest;
  they weigh me down, I tire of
the
    load. . . .
¹⁵Your hands are full of blood!
¹⁶Wash yourselves clean!
  Put away your misdeeds from
before
  my eyes;
cease doing evil; ¹⁷learn to do
good.
Make justice your aim; redress the
    wronged,
  hear the orphan's plea, defend
the
    widow. . . .
¹⁹If you are willing, and obey,
  you shall EAT the good things
of
    the land;
But if you refuse and resist,
    the sword shall EAT you:
    for THE MOUTH OF THE
LORD SPEAKS

*This final line of V. 15 gives the
verdict of "GUILTY!"*
*Vv. 16–20 offer probation instead
of punishment to the culprit; not
to comply, however, means serious
reprisals.*

*The word EAT links the final
verses together: either you will eat
good things or else the sword will
eat you.*

*The final phrase repeats one of the
opening words (v. 2) and indicates
the end of the trial.*

                    V
²¹How has she turned adulteress,
    THE FAITHFUL CITY, so
upright!
JUSTICE used to lodge with her,
    but now, murderers. . . .
²³The ORPHAN they defend not,
    and the WIDOW'S plea does
not
    reach them.
²⁶I will restore your judges as
        at first,
    and your counselors as in the
        beginning;
After that you shall be called
    CITY OF JUSTICE, FAITH-
FUL CITY
                    VI
²⁷Zion shall be redeemed by
judgment,

*This new section (vv. 21–26) or
major speech of Isaiah begins and
ends with FAITHFUL CITY*

*V. 23 ORPHAN AND WIDOW
link this section with the preceding
judgment scene (v. 17).*

*CITY OF JUSTICE & FAITH-
FUL CITY not only forms an "inclusion," with the opening verse of
this section (v. 21) but also forms
a link with the section to follow in*

and her repentant ones by
JUSTICE
28Rebels and sinners TO-
GETHER shall
be crushed,
those who desert the Lord shall be
EATEN UP.
29You shall be ashamed of the
OAK TREES
which you prized, . . .
30You shall become like a TREE
with
falling leaves. . . .
31The strong man shall turn to
tow,
and his work shall become a
spark;
Both shall burn TOGETHER,
and there shall be none to
quench the flames.

*v. 27. Verses 27–28, 29, 30, 31
constitute an appendix of four, independent "one-liners." Notice
how they are interconnected Vv.
27–28 and v. 31 (first and last of
the four "one-liners") include the
word TOGETHER. The two middle "one-liners" each have a word
for TREE.*

Chapter 1 of Isaiah offers a typical example of how the Bible was
edited. In fact, this chapter was probably added very late to the ensem-
ble of the prophecy because chapter 2 has all the signs of another
introduction: 2:1, similar to 1:1, the naming of the prophet; 2:2–5, a
vision that provides insight into the final goals and hopes of Isaiah, a
magnificent overture to the collection of speeches and reflections that
follow.

Returning to chapter 1 and viewing it within our theme of the
religious educator and prayer, we observe several striking invitations to
stop and reflect: the juxtaposition of major parts; repetition of key
words and their intriguing interrelation. But first, however, it may be
useful to delay momentarily over the literary form of this opening
chapter of a major prophetic collection.

This chapter consists of three principal speeches or sermons:

1) 1:2–3, 10–20, a judgment speech is modeled upon legal proceedings from the summoning of the defendant (vv. 2–3, 10), to questioning (vv. 11–12), evidence of misdeeds (vv. 13–15d), verdict (v. 15e)
and sentencing, or in this case probation and instructions (vv. 16 +
19–20). This judgment speech begins and ends with the identical
phrase (a technique called "inclusion"), "The Lord speaks" and "The
mouth of the Lord speaks." This speech was given early in the career of

the prophet. It consists more of a warning and threat than of condemnation and punishment.

2) Vv. 4–9, a "woe discourse." Its opening word in the Hebrew is *hoy* or woe! (see Amos 4:18; 6:1). Probably one of the final speeches of the prophet, it sees the entire land devastated by the Assyrians after the invasion of 701 B.C., an event described in Isaiah 36–37. Because Judah did not listen to God's warning through the prophet, punishment swept through the land. Even so, there is hope for "the remnant," a favorite word of Isaiah and the name of his elder son (7:3; 10:19–22).

3) Vv. 21–26 combine a funeral lament to prophetic reproach and like vv. 2–3, 10–20 probably dates from an early period of the prophet's career. Again we notice the inclusion achieved by the key word, "faithful city" in vv. 21 and 26.

4) Vv. 27–31 consist of four "one-liners," each an undeveloped saying that circulated independently and added within this appendix. Such a practice is seen at the end of the major collection of Isaiah's speeches (chapters 36–39) and elsewhere in the Bible (i.e., 2 Sam. 21–24, which interrupt the sequence of events from 2 Sam. 20 to 1 Kgs. 1).

This bird's-eye view, the canonical form of chapter 1, shows a very serious, reflective person at work. This individual, a disciple of a later generation (cf., 8:16, "the sealed instruction kept among my disciples"), must have known the master's words by heart, that he or she could swivel among the collected or remembered words this easily. We have already referred to a prayerful person as "God-minded"; we can also describe such a one as "Bible-minded"! Touching this easily upon the large repertoire of Isaiah's preaching, this person quickly recalled the appropriate passage that would enlighten or challenge, comfort or threaten, as the Spirit would want.

As we apply this "editing process" to ourselves, we take note that we need *all* the Scriptures and traditions. We cannot anticipate the crises which will upset our normal equilibrium and leave us in danger of foolish, abrupt responses or of squandering opportunities for grace or of falling apart and destroying the important relationships of our life: our marriage and home, our vocation and employment. If we have learned well, even memorized the wide expanse of biblical literature, if we have experienced the important ways by which these statements have come to our rescue, then when serious dangers erupt, God's word will immediately speak a message of salvation:

> If you are willing and obey,
> you shall eat the good things of the land (1:19).

Another preparation for prayer is provided by the relation of several sermons in chapter 1. When vv. 4–9 are seen within the larger judgment speech (vv. 2–3 + 10–20), the prophet's steady hand is supporting us at times of failure. We had truly been warned—"put away your misdeeds . . . learn to do good" (v. 16)—but we were not willing to obey. See v. 19, quoted just above. The punishment fell heavily upon us: "From the sole of the foot to the head there is no sound spot" (v. 6). Yet God is providing a second chance even at the end of our life: "The Lord of hosts had left behind a scanty remnant" (v. 9). Scanty, yes! but at the end of our lives we survive by clutching on to frail expressions of life, faint memories that hold enormous hopes. For us this life extends into our future generations on earth and into our final reunion in heaven. Further study of the canonical arrangement of Isaiah's preaching in chapter 1 would lead to other promises of forgiveness and hope, words of crucial importance at the end of our life on earth.

The canonical shape of the Bible also comes to our assistance at times of prayer by the use of key words. At times these show up by way of contrast, at still other times they reenforce each other. During meditation it can be helpful to reread the entire chapter with one or two of these words in mind, so that each new line of the prophet enables us to see the key word or idea in a new light. Or we can delve into the profound consequences by joining the words.

We give this example. The people of Israel are truly God's CHILDREN, vv. 2 and 4, raised and reared with love as the Lord shared the secrets of his heart in the sacred Scriptures. Yet, oxen and asses respond towards their master with a better sense of loyalty and gratitude. How unnatural can Israel be, violating the deepest human responses of blood and life! Israel, therefore, is SODOM and GOMORRAH, cities which have gone down in Israel's history for their unnatural sins of ingratitude (Gen. 13:10–13; 14:2, 17–24; 18:20–33; ch. 19). We who have experienced still more tender and gracious touches of God's goodness can be still worse in our sins that violate justice and harm the defenseless people of our society, the orphans and the widows. Yet, there is hope; God leaves behind a "remnant" that will see us into the future.

Another meditative response consists in rereading chapter 1 and focusing the light of any one of the key words upon each line of the chapter. We take the example of "justice" which shows up very conspicuously in the second part of the chapter, vv. 21–31. Within Semitic culture and therefore within the thought patterns of the Bible, this word appears as a life-giving force. It reaches far beyond the narrow parameter of what is due a person for their good or evil actions. Within the Bible "justice" is observed and publicly acknowledged when family and community bonds of life bring nourishment, protection, and purification in almost the same way as blood contributes to the health of the body. As we reread chapter 1 with this understanding of "justice," we begin to realize how justice reaches into the strength of family life, to care for the orphan and widow as though for one's own body, to the enduring power of life like a tree's roots which hold promise of producing a fresh new sprout. In this last case compare vv. 29 and 30 with 11:1 of Isaiah. These conclusions are not seen quickly; their implications require a meditative space of time.

Just as we have reached new insights by the canonical arrangement of material in the Bible—our study of chapter one of Isaiah is just one example of what is possible—we can also be drawn into meditative prayer by the liturgical arrangement of biblical passages. When the church juxtaposes the first and second reading in the lectionary, and for Sundays the three readings from the Old Testament, the Epistles, and the Gospel, one passage throws light upon another. Sometimes we can see a key word or major theme, threading its way through all the readings, uniting the selections drawn from various parts of the Bible and enabling us to arrive at a new and enriched theology of that word or theme.

We work with the example of Tuesday, the second of Lent. The first reading is taken from chapter 1 of Isaiah, which we have already discussed from its canonical form. The lectionary drops vv. 11–15 which recount the charges against Israel and the fearsome verdict of "Guilty! Your hands are full of blood!" It includes the strong entreaty, the demand made upon guilty Israel in its period of probation: "Hear the orphan's plea, defend the widow." God then reasons with his people: "Come now, let us set things right. Though your sins be like scarlet, they may become white as snow" (Is. 1:18ab). The Gospel selection for this day is taken from Matthew 23:1–12, in which people in authority are condemned for the heavy loads that they inflict upon others "while they themselves will not lift a finger to budge them." Furthermore, these same high-ranking people "are fond of places of honor at banquets and the front seats [in religious assemblies], of marks of respect in public" and of honorary titles. Jesus concludes against this scramble for power and repute by advising: "The greatest among you will be the one who serves the rest."

Combining the intimate, blood bond at the basis of justice in the first reading with the expectations in the Gospel for an honest, exterior manifestation of who we are as family and community, our meditation leads to important insights. In declaring us purified and just—"though your sins be like scarlet, they may become white as snow"—God does not simply cover up our guilt and hide it beneath dignified titles of rabbi or teacher, father or mother. Nor can we disguise our sinfulness and masquerade as a saint by taking places of honor at banquets and front seats in synagogue or church, or by widening our phylacteries and wearing huge tassels—in our language, dangling an ever larger rosary and wearing an extra medallion of the saints or on Ash Wednesday carefully keeping, perhaps extending the smudge of ashes on the forehead. God will not tolerate this fake form of holiness that violates bonds of family and community love and yet shows up in sanctimonious poses. God will declare: "Guilty! Your hands are full of blood!" God will also shout at us with fearsome indignation: "Come now, let us set things right!"

When we rely upon the canonical form of biblical readings or upon the liturgical combination of passages, it is necessary to spend more time in prayer and reflection. We are not simply drawing a conclusion from a single biblical text. Rather, we are relating one set of words or ideas with the larger passage; we are looking for new insights into the ancient well-known texts. This procedure necessarily requires time; it presumes quiet and even leisure so that the insights can emerge from the hiding place between the lines and words, or within the relation of one passage with another.

Scripture then leads to a spirit of prayer, first when we listen to the biblical words as spoken by God, second when we listen from our setting in life today, and third when we ponder the arrangement within a chapter or section of the Bible or within the lectionary. We now proceed to a fourth and final way of praying with the Bible.

IV

Prayer: Listening to an Absent and Silent God in the Words of Scripture

Samuel Terrien wrote a book entitled *The Elusive Presence* (Harper & Row, 1978). He describes the leitmotiv in this way:

> In biblical faith, human beings discern that presence is a surging which soon vanishes and leaves in its disappearance an absence that has been overcome. . . . It is when [divine] presence escapes man's [and woman's] grasp that it surges, survives, or returns. . . . In biblical faith, presence eludes but does not delude" (pg. 476).

While reviewing this book for *Horizons*, the journal of the College Theology Society (Spring, 1980), I admitted that Samuel Terrien "makes a notable contribution to our appreciation of biblical mysticism." But I considered the book "seriously flawed in what it leaves underdeveloped or denied." Terrien overlooks the power of the liturgy in leading a person into deep moments of prayer, even into mystical prayer. One example among many where formal liturgy leads to informal prayer can be seen in Psalms 42–43.

This Psalm, given two numbers (Pss. 42–43) yet consisting of a single poem through structural unity, careful development of images, and a thrice repeated refrain, belongs to the first series of "Psalms of Korah" (Pss. 42–49). Another series of "Psalms of Korah" is found later in the Psalter, Psalms 84–85, 87–88. Each series is introduced by a lament; both Psalms 42–43 and Psalm 84 bemoan the psalmist's absence from the sanctuary. It is possible that the psalmist belongs to a group of levites, "Sons of Korah," not only persecuted by foreigners in the far northern reach of the land of Israel, but also demoted by fellow levites from their former prominent place in temple services and now reduced to the "charge of preparing the flat cakes" for the liturgy (1 Chr. 9:31) and to the "assigned task [of] guarding the entrance" (1 Chr. 9:19).

The poem is taut with a series of contrasts: God is distant yet intimately present; water is food but also destructive; a person is downcast yet found in a posture of worship; the psalmist is roaming the dry wilderness and then is hearing the roaring sound of cataracts whose breakers and billows pass over the person. Whenever a person is caught between such extremes, there is no clear answer, no sound theological position, only the bewildering and anxious desire for God. And according to mystical theology in its most accurate expression, God is never more present than when God seems surrounded by a total blackout or absence! When our longing is intense and our anguish overwhelming, no presence of God as perceived by intellect and explained by theology can adequately express the object of our desires. God is so divinely present that no human endeavor can measure up to the experience. Love draws us beyond the powers of the intellect and we can speak only of longing and desire. In Psalms 42–43 liturgical phrases and actions that normally symbolize the presence of God are turned into the language of divine absence.

Some of these liturgical phrases and actions can be mentioned:

"When shall I go and behold the face of God," a technical expression for journeying to the sanctuary. While it is generally agreed that this translation represents the original phrase of the psalmist, nonetheless the Hebrew text made a theological correction and read the statement in a passive form, "that I may be seen [in] the presence of God." According to our earlier discussion of Exodus chapters 32–34, "No one sees me," God declared, "and still lives." Deuteronomy 31:11 recalls the original form, "when all Israel comes to appear before the face of the Lord your God at the place which he will choose."

"My tears are my food day and night," transfers the sorrows of the psalmist into the image of ritual banquets at the sanctuary.

"I pour out my soul within me," reminds us of water *poured out* in the temple ritual (1 Sm. 7:6; Is. 57:6).

"Procession," *"loud cries of joy and thanksgiving,"* and *"the multitude keeping festival"*—all reminders of the happy celebrations in the temple of which the psalmist is now deprived.

"Why are you so downcast" occurs with a Hebrew word which is almost the exact expression for prostration in worship and adoration before God. "Downcast" reads in the Hebrew *shaḥaḥ* (in which the dot below the letter "h" indicates the letter *ḥeth*, a heavily accented "h." The word for worship or prostrate, *shaḥah*, lacks the dot over the final "h" and stands for a different letter of the Hebrew alphabet, *hē*. In other words the psalmist *almost* says, and certainly implies, that the sorrow which bends the soul in anguish is another form of offering

liturgical adoration. Yet, it is the absence of the psalmist from the liturgy which is responsible for the overwhelming sadness.

"The spirituality of Psalms 42–43," as I have written in a commentary on the Psalms (Michael Glazier: 1983), "centers around thirst and longing, a reaction all the more painful and poignant the closer anyone may be to the source of living water," the living God whom we encounter very intimately in the liturgy. Psalms 42–43 have occupied a prominent place in various liturgical approaches towards God—and almost always the accent is upon *approach*. Not united with God, yet drawing very close, separated from someone who is very near, Psalms 42–43 combine liturgical symbol with mystical prayer.

Before the reform of the Mass at Vatican II, this Psalm was recited at the foot of the altar before the priest ascended the steps to the altar. These Psalms occur frequently in the Divine Office or liturgical prayers for the deceased. These suffering souls of purgatory are consumed with longing for God who is so close that they are assured of full union and yet are far enough away that their burning desire becomes painful and purifying. On Holy Saturday after the blessing of the baptismal water and during the procession to the baptistry, Psalms 42–43 were sung by the catechumens who are at the border of full union with the church in the sacrament of Holy Communion and yet are separated by mighty waters.

Water can be life-giving and it can be destructive. For this reason Psalms 42–43 reflect very well the theology of baptism, which plunges a person into the death of Jesus "so that the life of Jesus may be manifested in our mortal flesh" (2 Cor. 4:11). Finally, mystics have interpreted Psalm 42:8, "Deep calls unto deep in the roar of your cataracts," to mean that the "depth [of human weakness and sinfulness] is calling out to the depth [of divine strength and goodness]."

Still other examples of "the deaf and silent God of mysticism and liturgy" (subtitle of an article prepared for *Biblical Theology Bulletin*, July, 1982), can be found in other Psalms of lament, like Psalm 22, and in the prophetical writing of Jeremiah. We think particularly of the confessions of Jeremiah in which the prophet's question to God, "Why does the way of the wicked flourish?" (Jer. 12:2) is recorded in the Bible and therefore qualifies as the word or answer of God. This situation becomes all the more enigmatic when the answer of God to Jeremiah's question never addresses the question of Jeremiah but rather demands further faith in the midst of no answer:

> If running against human beings has wearied you,
>> how will you race against horses?
> If in the land of peace you seek confidence,
>> what will you do in the jungle of the Jordan (Jer. 12:5)

In this enigmatic reply God cruelly taunts Jeremiah with exalted poetic imagery, to say that things are going to get worse before they get any better. Jeremiah has not yet hit bottom, in order to come up. Up until now he has been running against other human beings and he is complaining; God is now pitting him against horses, as though the trials will become still more superhuman in their magnitude. We can hear the divine answer only if we wait long enough in prayer to hear the silent God within the gnawing question of the prophet.

In Psalm 22 we see again how God's word consists in the psalmist's anguished question: "My God! My God! Why have you forsaken me?" God remains silent and dead; the psalmist exclaims, "You do not hear me." After a long lament in vv. 4–19 with its questions and desperation, its momentary hope and then deeper sorrow, we meet the pivotal verses that turn the poem into an expression of thanksgiving. Verses 20–22 repeat three key words of the opening call of pain:

vv. 2–3	vv. 20–22
distant	do not be distant
from my salvation (Hebrew)	save me (same Hebrew word)
you do not hear	you hear me (Hebrew text)

Unfortunately, many modern English-language translations change the final words of v. 22 from "you hear me" (*anitani* in the Hebrew) to "my poor self" (*aniyati* as the Hebrew reading is corrected in the Greek Septuagint). Because of the impressive "inclusion" or repetition of key words, we maintain the Hebrew or masoretic reading. Once the psalmist realizes the *God hears* what the psalmist is suffering and shouting to the heavens, the psalmist at once sings a song of thanksgiving in which all the poor and lowly of the world, even those Gentiles at the end of the earth (v. 28), and most surprisingly of all the sick and possibly the dead who were prohibited from entering the sanctuary (v. 30) are asked to participate. We note in passing that the psalmist relied heavily upon the prophet Jeremiah and upon ancient liturgical texts in the composition of Ps. 22.

If I may quote from my article in *Biblical Theology Bulletin*:

For the psalmist, an answer came from the very source that seemed to betray him and plunge him into agony. Mysteriously enough, from the very liturgical and prophetical traditions which the psalmist found cruelly deficient, he finds the Lord once more listening to him.

I admit at once that the psalmist could just as easily have been a woman and the pronouns could be reread in the feminine gender.

At times then the Bible asks us to wait in suspense upon a silent God. This waiting, like that of Jesus on the cross, becomes our most active moment of faith; silence speaks the loudest answer from God. The absent God is directing our most profound union with the God-head and inspiring our most genuine prayer. The religious educator must be willing to wait for an answer; he or she needs to have the right instinct when to be silent so that the student, adolescent or adult, in the classroom or in parish instruction, learns the art of prayer and waits upon the Lord. The Bible may not always supply the immediate answer in statements or in replies to our questions; it hopes to lead beyond statements and replies to the person of God, whose love, goodness and wisdom reach far beyond our rational discourse.

Conclusions

This chapter, outlining biblical approaches toward prayer for the religious educator, has relied upon a hermeneutic which refuses to interpret the Bible as normally providing at once and without reflection the absolute will of God. Traditional Roman Catholicism has always maintained that the Bible is to be explained within the context of church teaching. We have expanded upon that "context" with special insistence upon prayer.

Prayer is basically God-mindedness. Prayer is the spirit by which we breathe God's spirit ever more consciously within the daily events of life. To perceive God's presence in between the sequence of words and actions that comprise our life, we generally need longer periods of time in which we are absorbed alone with God. In this chapter we have used the word "prayer" for these more extended spaces in our lives.

While faith opens the door of Scripture as the Word of God, prayer indicates our willingness to remain beyond that door in the sacred space, the Holy of Holies, where we come ever more intensely before the "face of God."

Four ways have been drawn from the Bible to prepare ourselves to contemplate God within this Holy of Holies. First, we hear the word of Scripture, not simply as a statement or doctrine, but primarily *as spoken by God* in whose living presence we find ourselves. Even the Decalogue or Ten Commandments are much more than a moral code. They express the hopes of a personal God for God's family and elect people. Each syllable contains a mystery of compassionate love, as God calls out his secret name, the Lord! the Lord! Moses arrived at this contemplative posture on Mount Sinai only after forty days and forty nights of prayer and fasting.

Moses also returned to the base of the mountain and made the divine word live intensely, even fiercely, within the reality of the people Israel. This *adaptation of the divine word to the human situation* can be seen whenever the Bible interprets the Bible or translates the Bible! Each new contemporary scene adds a necessary ingredient either to the context of what was being quoted from tradition or even to the actual quotation. The normative meaning of the Bible is reached, not simply by repeating the sacred word, truly God's word, but also by hearing that word as God's people struggle with it, the religious leaders explain it and the word at large, God's magnificent creation, challenges and enriches it. Again a religious educator needs time and a large dose of humility to integrate all of these factors and to decipher the divine melody within such a symphony of voices. Prolonged prayer, we suggest, is required so that God's voice emerges as the integrating force and that God's person be the center of activity.

Prayer too is all important as a religious educator ponders the canonical and liturgical arrangement of biblical passages. The *relationship* of parts makes its own contribution to what God is saying to us. Once more we need time to wait upon the Lord, as we reread a passage from the viewpoint of key words or from the juxtaposition of other biblical selections.

Finally, *God speaks loudest in our moments of silence.* At first, we are confused by pain and discouragement. If we persevere, prayerfully sustained by our desire for God as our personal savior and our sweetest reward, then we will hear a message in the word of God beyond our human ability to understand. Yet, it is true that our finest moments as teacher come when students or listeners admit that they have discovered God, not just a message about God, even when they have been drawn into silence beyond our rational explanations, when the mystery of God enables them to return to the base of the mountain as stronger God-minded people.

CHAPTER 7

Justice

Horacio Simian-Yofre

Asking the Bible Questions

Before beginning a study of any biblical theme, we must be clear about our expectations. What can we hope to gain from such a study?

This clarification is all the more urgent when we are investigating a notion like justice. There are two reasons for this. First, in dealing with justice in the Bible we immediately run into a semantic difficulty. The Hebrew terms in the Old Testament and the Greek terms in the New Testament, which in some passages may quite legitimately be translated as "justice"—like the Hebrew ṣedeq/ṣᵉdāqâ or the Greek *dikaiosúnē*—have to be translated very differently in other passages. For example, the Revised Standard Version very frequently translates *sedeq/sᵉdāqâ* as "righteousness," where it indeed means what the English words "righteousness," or "justice,"mean. But in other passages the same word is translated as "vindication," "deliverance," "saving deeds," "saving help," "righteous help," "equity," "right," "uprightness," "truth," "triumph," "victory," or "prosperity." Similarly, *mišpāṭ* in the Old Testament is often translated as "justice," especially when it appears with *ṣedeq/sᵉdāqâ* in the Hebrew literary structure known as parallelism. But *mišpāṭ* can also call for translations like "judgment," "court," "process," "sentence," "execution of judgment," "right," or "rectitude." And finally, in the New Testament *dikaiosúnē*, frequently translated in the RSV as "righteousness," can require translations like "justice," "piety," "justification," or "right," while the adjective derived from it can be translated as "righteous," "just," "innocent," "sincere," or "upright."

Thus there is no precise semantic correspondence between the origi-

Translated by Robert R. Barr

nal languages of the Old or New Testaments and English. The same holds true for the other modern languages. Neither of the great biblical languages has any single way of saying "justice," so that we could conduct an investigation of "justice in the Bible" merely by looking up the biblical passages that used the word "justice." Further: even in English, "righteousness" and "justice" have more than one meaning. Thus, even if *ṣedeq* or *dikaiosúnē* had always been translated in the same way—by the word "justice," for instance—the problem of determining the precise reality underlying that word would still remain.

The second difficulty with a study of the meaning of justice in the Bible arises not from terminology, but from the concept itself. Unlike other ethical or religious notions, the concept of justice has undergone a development that has been independent of its biblical meaning. The elements of justice set forth in the Old and New Testaments have not been adequate to resolve all the problems arising in connection with the antithetical concepts of "just" and "unjust." When the teaching authority of the Roman Catholic Church undertakes to make a pronouncement on labor, for example, it can have only the briefest recourse to Scripture. The cultural universe of the Old and New Testaments simply did not pose these kinds of problems.[1]

The New Testament, especially, seems to have very little to say in matters of public morality—such as justice in economics or politics. To take a well-known example, the New Testament does not explicitly condemn slavery, although the words of Jesus concerning the equality of human beings before their Father ought to lead to this conclusion.

Jesus himself could appear to be a conformist in the matter of national sovereignty ("Give back to Caesar what belongs to Caesar"), or an outrageous pacifist ("All who draw the sword will die by the sword"). This is not the case, of course, because what Jesus is interested in in such expressions is what immediately follows in each of them: Give to God what belongs to God, and the Father's will is to be accomplished. It is true that Jesus does not consider it part of his mission to resolve the problems of foreign invasion or legitimate self-defense. Does it follow from this that such problems are not important from a Christian viewpoint, so that a Christian is free to think just as he or she pleases in these areas?

The Old Testament is religious literature. At the same time, however, it is also a literature that legislates for a particular people. Hence it is concerned with problems of public order, but it does not establish principles that can be applied to other cases. For that matter, even the individual concrete laws laid down in the Old Testament manifest a broad ethical diversity.

We are touched by the austere delicacy of Deuteronomy's (20:5–7) legislation concerning the conscription of newlyweds. But a few verses further on we find the horrible legislation on the treatment of captured cities (20:10–18). If the inhabitants have given up without a fight, they are merely to be subjected to forced labor in the service of Israel. If they have resisted, the men are to be executed, and the women and children taken prisoners of war. But in the case of Israel's neighbors, who could be more dangerous, men, women, and children are all to be slaughtered.

Thus we are faced with a double difficulty, and an apparently insoluble one. If we wish to accept all of Scripture's norms of conduct as the expression of the will of Yahweh, the will of God, our reason and our hearts rebel. It is impossible to reconcile such legislation with the notion of God propounded to us by any sane metaphysics. It is understandable, then, that exegetes of the Old Testament, in particular, maintain a practical divorce between their philosophical exigencies—if they have them—and their fundamentalist and conformist propositions about Yahweh. Actually, however, though they do not coincide completely, the philosophical and the biblical picture of God cannot contradict each other if the former is healthy and the latter mature.

Well, then, suppose we attempt to extricate ourselves from our difficulty by gathering together all the concrete norms we can find, and distilling from these a series of general principles that will be valid for other cultural contexts. But here we run the risk of finding ourselves with a bundle of propositions as general as, "One must love and defend one's country," or, "One must be generous toward one's fellow citizens." Why then, use the Bible at all, if our only ethical propositions will be common sense truths to which all peoples have come, with the Bible or without it?

And even so we have not handled the unacceptable propositions. To pretend to conclude from passages like the one just cited from Deuteronomy a principle like, "Justice is to be observed in war," is simply a travesty of intellectual honesty.

This whole series of difficulties seems to spring from a single root: from our attempt to obtain precise answers—all genuine answers must be precise—to questions we ask Holy Scripture which Holy Scripture is in no position to answer because it has never posed them. In particular, in dealing with matters of social justice, the usual danger is that we come before the high court of Scripture with a series of propositions, legitimate or not, that we have obtained from economics, sociology, or political science, or from political and social confrontations, seeking the *nihil obstat* of the Word of God.[2]

Since Scripture is not prepared to "take an examination" on certain contemporary questions, it answers imprudent questions with generalities, with mutually contradictory statements, or simply with silence.[3] We can readily imagine the frustration of a Christian political scientist who would like to base a justification of the parliamentary or democratic system on Scripture.

In undertaking an investigation of a scriptural theme, then, there would appear to be but one legitimate point of departure: Not to arrive on the scene armed with explicit, detailed questions, but simply to open our hearts and our understanding to what Scripture has to say to us. Any intellectual activity must of course be undertaken with some question in mind. But our question here can be a very broad one, broad enough to permit Scripture to develop its response in the direction it deems most appropriate. For centuries, Christian exegesis frequently made the mistake of reading the Bible for answers to questions from the natural sciences: How did the earth come to be: Does the earth revolve around the sun, or the sun around the earth? It would be no less fatal an error today, for biblical studies as well as for the fruit which Scripture ought to produce in the reader of goodwill, were we to commence to interrogate Scripture on matters of political science.

A broad question will avoid technicalities tending to prejudice the response. Hence it will surely not be appropriate, for instance, to ask what the attitude of the prophets was regarding imperialism, or real estate investments. Imperialism involves politico-economic elements of which the biblical authors doubtless had no idea. The Bible concretely condemns cruel domination by a foreign power, but the Bible's concept of cruel foreign domination does not necessarily coincide with the notion of imperialism.

Let us not ask, then: Is such or such a comportment, or social structure, or political relationship today just or unjust? Let us ask instead: What relationships of particular persons or groups does Scripture characterize as just or unjust? Or: What relationships does Scripture approve or disapprove of, so that we may take them as falling under our modern categories of just and unjust? For what reason are these relationships endorsed or condemned?

In this way our field of investigation will be limited. We shall be concentrating on justice as an interpersonal relationship, among particular persons or groups, and we shall be able to prescind from other problems, which touch more exclusively on the relationship between the human being and God, like: Can Ancient Israel, or the Christian today, be said to be just before God? Why are the needy and indigent considered just in the Old Testament? What is the function of covenant in the Old Testament with respect to God's justice? What does it mean to be justified by and in Christ?

Still, the interpersonal relationship of justice does have its repercussions on the relationship between the human being and God. These repercussions, then, will also be the object of our study.

The Biblical Understanding of Justice

Justice is a concept that has been subjected to a variety of of cultural and religious conditioning. But it is a basic ethical category, one by which we judge all interpersonal relationships: of individuals with one another, between individuals and groups, and among groups. Wherever there are two persons, there can be the question of a just or an unjust relationship.[4]

Scripture speaks to us about justice in a number of passages. The "legislative" passages in the Bible establish what is just or unjust in determinate situations, and prescribe the manner of punishing injustice. But we would illegitimately narrow the field of our investigation if we restrict ourselves to one single type of passage.

1. The biblical concept of justice in *interpersonal relationships* is actually presented most expressively in the patriarchal and historical narratives. Indeed it is likely that the purpose of some of these narratives is precisely to set human conflicts in relief, along with how they are solved.

The long history of Esau and Jacob (Gn. 25:19–33:20)[5] is that of an ambitious person completely taken up with his own interests and ready to fight for them even by illegitimate means. But he is ambitious in a "toned-down" sort of way—he is not violent, or a murderer, but a person of craft and cunning.

Jacob's dishonest purchase of the birthright of an eldest son in chapter 25 is a typical example of his behavior. He lays no trap, but neither does he let slip by an opportunity presented to him on a silver platter . . . or rather, in a dish of lentils.

Jacob's inability to deal openly and aboveboard even in defense of his genuine rights appears in the episodes involving his uncle, Laban. Once more, Jacob's revenge will be one of craft and deceit: The complex story of the increase of his own flock at the expense of his uncle's, the secret flight, and the theft and concealment of the idols is graphic evidence of Jacob's character. Injustice toward his brother, his father, and his uncle, will ever be part of Jacob's behavior.

If this were all the account had to say to us we would not see what its meaning is in the Bible as a whole, or why we do well to take it as an example of a biblical consideration of justice in interpersonal relationships. But Yahweh, too, plays an important role in the story of the deceits of Jacob. Jacob is an atheistic personage—in the purest sense of the word—as the story opens: he has no god but his ambitions.[6] Yahweh is mentioned only rarely in chapters 25 and 27, and not mainly by Jacob. Jacob's first reference to Yahweh is almost disparaging: "'It was Yahweh your God,' he answered, 'who put it in my path'" (Gn. 27:20), when his father Isaac wondered how Jacob—disguised as Esau—had so quickly found some game to offer him.

The account in Genesis 28 of the dream about the ladder makes it clear that this is really the first time Yahweh and Jacob have ever met. Genesis 28:16 should be translated, "Truly, *there was* Yahweh in this place, and I never knew it." This is the only occurrence in the Bible of the Hebrew impersonal form *yēš*—"there is," "hay," "il y a," "es gibt"—having the name of Yahweh as its object. The expression—difficult to explain as a literary lapse, as if an author or copyist had merely become distracted—indicates the ambiguity that the name "Yahweh" had in Jacob's mind: first it is a common noun, and then a proper name, for him. Along this same line of interpretation, verse 17, in order to convey Jacob's feelings of confusion, should be translated: "This is nothing less than a house of a god," or "a dwelling of gods." Jacob had not yet realized that Yahweh was God, or at least not *his* god. Witness his vow—his conditional vow—by which he manages once more to turn the situation to his advantage: "If God"—really, "this god"—"goes with me . . . if . . . and if . . . then Yahweh shall be my God" (Gn. 28:20–21).

Jacob's silence regarding God will continue in chapters 29 through 31, to be interrupted only by his declaration: "If the God of my father, the God of Abraham . . . had not been with me, you would have sent me away emptyhanded" (Gn. 31:42). Yahweh is not yet Jacob's god, but he is the God of his "father," Abraham. Only when God's help has become absolutely necessary, as the brother-enemy approaches, does Jacob have recourse to humble, grateful, anxious prayer (32:10–13), and in this prayer recognize Yahweh as his God. But the moment his prayer is ended, he prepares to buy Esau's forgiveness with lavish gifts (32:15–22). Finally, unsure of the success of his enterprise, he decides on flight (32:23–25).

Then occurs the mysterious encounter with "one" who, as it were, baptizes Jacob with his new name, Israel—because he has "been strong against God." Jacob has been vanquished now, but the memory of his mighty struggle with God ought to be reason for gratitude from now on (32:23–32). This encounter in Peniel ("because I have seen God face to face") will lay the groundwork for Jacob's reconciliation with his brother. When Jacob goes forth to meet Esau he expresses his new attitude with the words, "I came into your presence as into the presence of God" (33:10)—a clear allusion, as we see by the words, "into the presence of" (literally, "before the face of"), to the account of Genesis 32:23–32. The encounter with the mysterious figure, which in some ways has been an encounter with God, and the reconciliation with that figure in which he has submitted to Yahweh, have been Jacob's preparation for his reconciliation with his brother. For once Jacob has acted with true generosity. For once he has given of what is his for the sole purpose that the other receive it, lavishing his gifts upon Esau even though Esau had already demonstrated his willingness to be reconciled with him. The brothers' relationship of justice—corrupted since their birth, we are given to understand, or at least since Jacob's "purchase" of Esau's birthright—are reestablished now.

Sober allusions in key moments in the biblical account seek to inculcate in us the concept that there is no justice or reconciliation apart from encounter with God. Human relations that are pure, harmonious, perfect, but atheistic, would be a self-contradiction.

2. Other biblical accounts portray relationships of justice or injustice at the level of the individual.

The story of David, Bathsheba, and Uriah (2 Sm. 11–12), or of Ahab, Jezebel, and Naboth (1 Kgs. 21), are similar in a number of respects. The personages in each instance are a king, a woman, an enemy, and a prophet. The drama opens with the lascivious or greedy caprice of the king, who is not content with what he already possesses. Now the king commits a double crime—he takes for himself the woman, or the enemy's land, and then has the person from whom he has taken them killed, by sending him into a trap. The prophet denounces the king's crime to his face, declaring that the punishment will be such and so. The king repents, and the punishment is mitigated.

The difference between these stories and that of Jacob is that now we are no longer watching a process of interior growth on the part of the central personage—a growth which will permit him, at a given moment, to act more in conformity with the will of Yahweh and justice toward his neighbor. David and Ahab manifest a profound spiritual and ethical meanness. Only a formal denunciation and the announcement of a punishment lead them to consider that they may have committed a crime.

David is hardly an undemonstrative person. He can weep and fast for the child of his adultery who is about to die. He will rend his garments at the death of Amnon, and groan inconsolably at that of Absalom. However, in reply to Nathan he utters a confession of sin that is just a little more than perfunctory: "I have sinned against Yahweh" (2 Sm. 12:13). Ahab performs even more acts of penance than David, and Yahweh looks on him with satisfaction (1 Kgs. 21:27–29). But in both cases the relationship between the king and Yahweh is formal, external. It is as if it sufficed for the kings to perform an external act of acknowledgment of guilt, an outward penitential act, and to offer a present or future sacrifice to Yahweh in order for justice to be reestablished.

The spiritual richness here, the scandal, perhaps unique among the cultures of the time, is that there is a personage who, in the name of Yahweh, gathers the courage to condemn the king openly. Ahab's greeting to Elijah leaves no doubt as to their relationship: "So you have found me out, O my enemy!" (1 Kgs. 21:20). The solitary moral grandeur in these accounts is that of the prophets, who take the risk of denouncing the powerful. The sole justice manifested is that of Yahweh, who, through his prophets, strides forth in defense of the stranger, and the one who is less strong.

3. Ancient Israel had a very clear awareness that the poor, strangers, orphans and widows—those who could not count on the support of a

group—were the most exposed to injustice. The "dispensation of justice" could be transformed into a source of oppression, and Israel knew it. Hence the same legislation provided for instruments for ensuring that the courts functioned rightly and honestly.

Exodus 23:1–3,6–8 provides elementary, but important and basic, norms whose observance could surely guarantee that courts would function fittingly even today: not to make false depositions or declarations, not to attempt to defend the guilty by such false witness, not to be towed along by the majority in a trial so as to side with an unjust decision. This last prescription calls on all who are involved in a trial, judges and witnesses alike, to have the courage to stand up to the multitude if need be. Then follows another prescription, along the same lines of respect for impartiality: not to take the part of the poor when they are in the wrong. The danger of someone's taking sides unjustly with the one who has the least—and hence can show the least gratitude materially—is no doubt more remote. But it is not out of the question. This norm seeks to prevent injustice arising out of sentimentality. In 23:6, on the other hand, it is injustice *against* the poor that is proscribed. Verses 7 and 8 forbid false accusation and bribery.

These general norms are complemented elsewhere by more precise, more developed prescriptions. Deuteronomy 19:15–19 lays down the requirement that there be more than one witness in a case, that witnesses whose testimony is suspect be themselves investigated, and that perjured witnesses be severely punished.

A general exhortation to justice, and an admonition against partiality and bribery, accompanies the directive that judges sit in all cities (Dt. 16:18–20)—ending with the words, "Strict justice must be your ideal, so that you may live."

Transgression of the law, and injustice, can be the deed not only of those who have a part to play in court procedures, but of anyone in authority. Accordingly, the norms for the appointment of the king (Dt. 17:14–20) provide that the latter have a true copy of the law (Deuteronomy itself) and all its dispositions, and that he "read it every day of his life," lest his heart "look down on his brothers." The implicit principle of government as a service activity, and the rigorous observance of the law, so that persons in power "swerve neither right nor left" in the administration of justice, are the basic elements in the establishment of a just system of government. In this way a king "will have long days on his throne."

4. But the Old Testament is not naive when it comes to what human beings are capable of. There are laws, then, indicating to judges and governors the exact manner of acquitting themselves of their duty. But there are prophets, too, who consider it a prime component of their own task to exhort those in power to the observance of these norms and to denounce their infidelities.

When the prophet Jeremiah announces the scourge to come (Jer. 5:20–29), he cites the presence of wicked persons among the people.[7] Who are these persons and in what does their wickedness consist? The prophet sets up an antithesis: Yahweh is the powerful God who has set limits to the sea, he is the provident God who grants rain when rain is needed and who determines the time of harvest. Nature is subject to Yahweh's norms. The term "law," or "norm," occurs twice and "limit" once, as the prophet develops his theme. But what nature does not permit, certain persons among this people of Yahweh, persons labeled "stupid and thoughtless," blind and deaf, set about doing with a will. Their inability to recognize God's activity is identified with not fearing Yahweh—that is, with not acknowledging his dominion over the universe. And so, when human beings have disqualified God as Lord of creation, they establish their own laws, laws of the exploitation of human beings. "Your crimes have made all this go wrong," verse 25 tells us—all these dispositions of God's wisdom. The indictment lodged immediately after the reference to rain which falls in due season, declares that the law of human beings, when placed above the law of Yahweh, prevents the people as a whole, the whole human race, from enjoying the nature that has been placed in their service. The same thought is concretized in the next verses.

Verse 26 is not easy to translate, but its sense seems clear enough: The wicked are those who set traps for their brothers and sisters, their fellow-citizens. The possible allusion to lying in wait for persons falling into their nets, like those who snare fowl—the occurrence of *mirmâ*, "fraud," or "cheating," with its broad spectrum of meanings, in verse 28; the accusation that these wicked persons grow rich and prosper through this behavior of theirs—all seems to indicate the evil of economic techniques developed in order to enrich some persons at the expense of others: usury, sales fraud, inadequate or withheld wages. That this statement is not the product of gratuitous exegetical imagination is clear from the various legal norms providing that abuses not be committed in this area.[8]

But "people hunting" goes further still. It is also a means of making economic progress, through abuses in the dispensation of justice, taking advantage of the weak, and ignoring the rights of orphans and the poor in judicial processes. The passage concludes with this tremendous threat, placed in the mouth of Yahweh: "Must I not punish them for such things . . . or from such a nation exact my vengeance?"

Jeremiah 5:20–29 is a good example of the way the prophets taught. It not only provides a list of typical victims in social life, with a summary but graphic description of the common forms of exploitation, it exposes the deep root of this universe of injustice: the abandonment of Yahweh and the assuming of his functions as the one who guides the universe.

The exploiters themselves are not very precisely described. But the context suggests who they are: the powerful, the rich who have gained their riches precisely by means of exploitation. See also Amos 5:7,10–13.

Jeremiah 5:30–31 may not have originally belonged here with 5:20–29. But it is in the spirit of the prophets to allude to two influential groups in the society of these times, the prophets and the priests, and to ascribe to them a share in the guilt of the powerful. The prophets are accused of prophesying lies—that is, of cooperating with the cheating denounced in verse 27. In all likelihood the prophets' lie consists in an ideological justification of the status quo and a call for peace and tranquillity. (We shall have something to say about this later.) Doubtless they have been invoking the "will of Yahweh," and the importance (for the poor only) of accepting one's suffering.

Micah 3:5–8,11 is more explicit in its association of priests and prophets with the rulers of the people. The latter judge for a bribe, while prophets utter their oracles for money and priests teach for a fee (v. 11). Micah is reproaching those who use the influence they have with the people to set forth a doctrine calculated to persuade the exploited to acquiesce in their fate and thereby to permit the exploiters to continue their exploiting with impunity. The prophets are accused of crying, "Peace!" (Mi. 3:5; cf. Jer. 6:13–15, 8:10–12). This may have meant that this is what the prophets say they see—"We live in peace, there are no problems in our land"—or it may mean they are exhorting the people to conform—"One must live in peace." Micah inveighs against both interpretations and announces the punishment that will come upon such prophets: a real silence on the part of God

(vv. 6,7), which will throw them into total confusion. They have been unwilling to denounce injustice when they have seen it—very well, then, they will be incapable of distinguishing between justice and injustice in the future. Micah takes his stand against such prophets as someone who can denounce sins and transgressions because he is led by the strength of the spirit of Yahweh (v. 8).

But the prophets know very well that the true danger for society—and, from a religious point of view, for the believing community—does not lurk in individual injustices, but in the fact that corruption has reached the very institution charged to guard justice.

As Elijah and Nathan have done in concrete cases, Micah 3:1–4,9–10 explicitly confronts the rulers of the house of Jacob and the judges of the house of Israel, who, after all, have the obligation to know what right and justice are. The accusations include "loathing justice" and "perverting all that is right" by pronouncing sentence in consideration of bribes received. The most concrete allegation, however, is that of "building Zion with blood, Jerusalem with crime." Just as Amos 3:10, 5:11, and Jeremiah 22:13–14 have done (Amos is probably referring to the rich of the land rather than to the rulers), Micah connects Jerusalem's luxury building-projects with injustice. Only by exploiting people, he says, could someone grow rich enough to build things like that.

Jeremiah is not content, however, with railing against exploiters in general. He directly attacks the rulers and the king himself—something prophets before him have not dared to do.

Jeremiah 22:13–19 is a harsh criticism of Jehoiakim, the son of Josiah. Josiah had been the king who had initiated a religious reform by applying Deuteronomy's legislation, and the passage is built on the contrast between the two figures. Verse 13 brings in a threat that might seem at first to be addressed to no one in particular: "Doom for the man who founds his palace on anything but integrity," "without ṣedeq," and "his upstairs rooms on anything but honesty," "without mišpāṭ." But then this warning is concretized in the second part of the verse: "who makes his fellow man work for nothing, without paying him his wages." Verse 14 gives us to understand that it is not a matter of just any house, nor even of just any rich person's house. It is a matter of a real palace, with panels of cedar! Then suddenly in verse 15 the audience realizes that the prophet is addressing the king: "Are you more of a king for outrivaling others with cedar?" Some king, and his father, are being spoken of. Josiah, the father of Jehoiakim, had been able to lead a pleasant, comfortable life (v. 15b), a life of banquets and the like. And yet he had been a king who was pleasing in Yahweh's eyes, for he had dealt in *mišpaṭ* and *ṣᵉdāqâ*, "honesty and integrity" (ibid.), and "examined the cases of poor and needy" (v. 16a). In this line—set in stark contrast with verse 13, and physically central to the passage from the point of view of composition—lies the sense of the oracle. The prophet's characterization of the just king par excellence is accentuated by the twice-repeated refrain, "All went well."

Now verse 17 explicitates the accusation being lodged against Jehoiakim: attention to his own interests alone, without any regard for oppression or crime. Verse 18 echoes the initial woe with four more— the lamentations which will *not* be pronounced at Jehoiakim's death, for he will have been buried as one buries a donkey.

Acting in *mišpaṭ* and *ṣᵉdākâ* or not so acting—this is the criterion by which this pair of kings, father and son, are distinguished. The Revised Standard Version translates, "do justice and righteousness." H. Cazelles prefers, "justice et prospérité."⁹ We are dealing with two terms of very broad meaning. It is impossible and unnecessary to try to determine their basic meaning. But it is important to keep in mind that the two terms are not strictly synonymous and that they imply a certain area of activity. Texts like 2 Samuel 8:15, a transitional verse describing David as reigning over all Israel and doing *mišpaṭ* and *ṣᵉdāqâ* to all his people; or 1 Kings 10:9, where the Queen of Sheba concludes her eulogy of Solomon with a blessing on Yahweh, who has made him King of Israel "to deal out *mišpaṭ* and *ṣᵉdāqâ*"; or the passage from Jeremiah we are examining; or the exhortation in Ezekiel 45:9—each of these passages makes it clear that we are hearing of the acts of a king who obeys Yahweh and acts in conformity with his norms. More in detail we might say that, in a context of the theology of the monarchy, *mišpaṭ* is "a legal sentence which manages to ensure social peace in the midst of opposing interests" (Cazelles). It is Moses, under the inspiration of Yahweh, who is the first author of such sentences, and it is along their lines that the decisions of the kings are to be taken. *Ṣedāqâ*, on the other hand, is "the properly royal virtue permitting the anointed of Yahweh to offer a sufficiently prosperous life to the members of his nation."

"Dealing in *mišpaṭ* and *ṣᵉdāqâ*," then turns out to be intimately connected with "defending the cause of the poor and needy." A king who would not only repudiate this, but attend exclusively to his own interests, ignore the common welfare, and trample on the rights of his weakest subjects, would be attacking the very basis of his royal function. Such a king could not be buried within the walls of Jerusalem.

The nucleus of our text, taken in a context of the praise of Josiah, contains another key proposition for us: "Is not that what it means to know me?—it is Yahweh who speaks" (Jer. 22:16b).

The unity between knowledge of Yahweh and behavior toward one's neighbor is explicitated in at least one other passage in Jeremiah. This time the prophet is referring to the common person—to the people as a whole, considered as a band of traitors and adulterers. We refer to Jeremiah 9:1–8 which identifies the essential element in the distortion of human relations as the lie, the falsehood, *šequer*. *Šequer* appears twice in the passage; *'ĕmet/'ĕmûnâ*, "truth, loyalty, fidelity," likewise occurs twice, in negative statements; *mirma* "deceit, fraud, false oaths, false testimony," occurs three times; *tōk*, violent oppression (cf. Psalms 10:7, 55:12, 72:14), occurs twice (in a reading accepted by a number of authors) the root *'QB*, referring to the name of Jacob, who defrauded his brother (Gn. 27:36), twice; *TLL*, to deceive, to delude with false promises, to go back on one's given word, the verb used to characterize the comportment of Pharaoh toward Moses, or of Laban toward Jacob, once; and *'ārab*, to lie in ambush, once.

In the emphasis by concentration so characteristic of biblical language, almost every line of the text contains an expression indicating a lack of truth in relations with one's neighbor as the reason for the punishment announced in verse 8. The immediate consequences of this situation are portrayed in verse 3. The prophet himself exhorts his audience to be on guard against their neighbors, not to trust them—for the lie, in all its forms, reigns supreme.

Balanced against all this, we read: "But Yahweh, they do not acknowledge him," and, "They refuse to acknowledge Yahweh." Jeremiah's thought is clear. No band of traitors and adulterers (these two nouns, again, denote falsehood, disingenuousness, whether in one's public relationships or in private life) can know Yahweh. Or conversely, a society that has excluded the knowledge of Yahweh, that has refused to discover God, is condemned to the lie, on all levels of its relationships. The central thought that we have discovered in the story of Jacob and Esau is now transformed into an organizational principle of society. Jeremiah does not begin with a general ethical or dogmatic

doctrine. The experience of the twin truths, deceit and forgetfulness or
negligence of Yahweh, is what leads him to formulate his conclusions.

5. Isaiah 3:1–15 is a forceful passage, laying out the effects of injustice on the structure of society.[10] It justifies the punishment to
come with a most jejune expression, and one which occurs only well
into the text: "Their words and deeds affront the Lord" (v. 8). What
arrests our attention is the detailed description of the punishment.

The punishment can be summed up in two categories: hunger and
thirst (v. 1) and social chaos (vv. 2–7). The disintegration of society
involves primarily the disappearance of the people who usually see to
law and order in the country: Verses 2–3 list warriors, "captains" or
squad leaders, judges and prophets, counselors and elders. We must
suppose that these have either died or fled in despair. But other personages are longed for as well, whose functions are suspect and whom
society generally rejects: "diviner . . . sorcerer, soothsayer." These,
the passage suggests, could have replaced other, better authority. But
even these are missing.

With no one able to wield power legitimately, it will be adolescents,
victims of their own passions and caprices, who will seize it. The
immediate result is the disorder of which verse 5 speaks. And then in
the last act of the tragedy anyone of good will and initiative will seek
out someone who still has something, some goods, or even who still
lives in his house, and propose to him that he take up the reins of
power. But the latter, conscious of the gravity of the situation, will not
be willing to accept. Someone would be needed who would be capable
of healing deep wounds in the whole social order, for this is what this
people has suffered (v. 7).

Verse 12 provides a forceful summary. You are being governed by
the impotent and weak. Those who should be healing you are actually
misguiding you. Only the intervention of Yahweh as judge of his
people can resolve this situation of corruption and destruction. Verses
13–15, then, charged with a massive vocabulary of Yahweh's judicial
and salvific intervention, help us deepen our understanding of what is
involved in the problem of justice. In verse 13, "Yahweh is taking his
place to make an accusation (rîb)" (Limburg); "he stands up to arraign
(dîn) his people." Verse 14 indicates that Yahweh "calls to judgment
(BW' bemišpāṭ) the elders and the princes of his people."

Each of these three Hebrew expressions, which are sometimes translated synonymously, has its peculiarity of meaning, and we should

respect it. "Call to judgment," or "enter into judgment with," is the most generic of the expressions and can refer to human beings as well as to God. It denotes participation in a judicial process, a trial. *Dîn*, on the other hand, is the expression used of a judicial decision, a sentence pronounced by duly constituted authority, and binding on all parties concerned. Finally, *rîb* is a term whose rich meaning has been subjected to a great deal of discussion[11] and in the Old Testament constitutes the primordial element of the so-called "*rîb*-pattern"—the prophetic lawsuit speech, or "réquisitoire judicielle prophétique." For our purposes we may prescind from the controversies. At all events it is clear that, in a large number of passages, *rîb* implies the accusation made by the offended party against the offender. This is the meaning of *rîb* in numerous nontheological passages in the narrative books.[12] It consistently appears in the prophetic texts as well.[13] There is no reason then to conclude that Isaiah 3:13 describes a different situation; i.e., Yahweh is making an accusation as the attorney for his people. On the contrary, the insistence on "my people" suggests that Yahweh fully identifies himself with the oppressed and the troubled. As in the other prophetic indictments, Yahweh considers himself the offended party. In verse 14 it is clear that the offenders are the elders and princes—a generic manner of designating the public authorities or influential persons listed in verses 2–3. The offended party is designated twice in verses 14–15: the poor, denoted by the term '*anî*. This is another concept that has been the subject of a great deal of exegesis. But A. George's description of its meaning can be considered commonly acceptable: '*anî* means someone in a situation of current or ongoing misery—economic poverty, for example—but also illness, prison, or oppression.[14] In Isaiah 3:13–15, "my people" appears in parallel with "the vineyard," who are the people of Israel as a whole, as is clearly seen in Isaiah 5:1–7. But "vineyard," as well as "my people," appear in parallel, respectively, with "poor" in the singular and "poor" in the plural. Thus the whole people of Yahweh are identified with the poor and are contradistinguished from the ancients and the princes. To put it another way, it is the poor who truly constitute God's people. See also Isaiah 10:2, 14:32.

The notion that the "poor" are favorites of Yahweh, his protegés, occurs abundantly in the Psalms. Yahweh hears them, he forgets them not, he hides not his face from them, he saves them (Pss. 22:25, 34:7, 35:10, 74:19). It is not just Isaiah 3:15, then, that so decidedly asserts that the poor belong to Yahweh. See also Exodus 22:24, Isaiah 49:13, Psalm 72:2,4.

The expressions, *rîb* (accusation lodged by the injured party), *dîn* (sentence pronounced by the one in authority), and "call to judgment," or "enter into judgment with," which we have seen all coming together in Isaiah 3:13–15, set in relief *God's intervention in favor of his people* when the "judges"—the authorities—of this earth are incapable of performing this function. The conjunction of this vocabulary is not likely coincidental. In 1 Samuel 24:13,16—a passage probably antedating our passage from Isaiah—we find the same eloquent concentration of vocabulary, at a crucial moment in the history of the mortal enmity between David and Saul. David, resisting the temptation to take advantage of the opportunity to put his enemy to death, invokes the intervention of Yahweh three times: "May Yahweh be the judge and [may Yahweh] decide between me and you; may [Yahweh] take up my cause and defend it and give judgment for me, freeing me from your power." And David refuses to take any action against Saul himself, abandoning his cause to God that justice may be done.

This profound confidence in the justice of Yahweh-God, who will annihilate the injustice of human beings, is a prime element in biblical thought. See also Zephaniah 3:1–5,12–13, which is similar to Isaiah 3:1–15.

6. The profound relationship among God, society, and justice, is set in succinct but sharp relief in Isaiah 1:21–28. Society, represented by Jerusalem, is accused in verse 21 of having become a prostitute. The image of prostitution, used in Hosea 2:9, for example, to characterize idolatry—loving and running after the baals—is employed here with another connotation: selling oneself for money.

The fidelity of bygone days, says the prophet, was manifested by the continuing and abundant presence of justice and right in the bosom of the city (v. 21b). Now, however, silver has become slag, and the city's marvelous wine has lost is authentic savor. Thereupon the silver and the wine are at once identified with the princes of the city. Next comes the reason for the use of the image of prostitution: By running after gifts and bribes the princes of the city have sold themselves. The rulers have left off doing justice to the orphan and defending the cause of the widow. The punishment foretold, beginning in verse 24, involves the purification of the dross, of the slag. (The image of the wine is not repeated. Only the purification of the dross is spoken of.) Verse 26 leaves it unclear whether the judges and counselors who will be "as in bygone days" are the same as have been designated previously, but who have been converted, or whether they have been replaced. But at all events the city will regain its character and title of city of justice, the faithful city. Verses 27–28, probably a commentary on the passage, emphasize the "redemption," the liberation, of Jerusalem by justice and integrity.

It is interesting to note that the city, society as such, is called a prostitute because of the venality of its judges and counselors, and then, when the judges and counselors are purified, the city has its epithet changed. In other words, Jerusalem's evaluation depends on the ability of its courts to hand down just judgments.

It is possible that verse 21b does not mean merely that once upon a time justice was the normal thing in Jerusalem. It may mean that Yahweh dwelt in the temple there, in the midst of his own. Yahweh the Just dwelt there. Hence the judges are all the more guilty for not having been capable of adapting their conduct to the presence of God in the midst of the city. Our suggestion finds support in Isaiah 5:16: "Yahweh Sabaoth will increase his glory by his *mišpaṭ*, the holy God will display his holiness by his *ṣᵉdāqâ*." The two attributes constituting the permanent specificity of Jerusalem, then, the two attributes by which Jerusalem will be redeemed and liberated, are the attributes of Yahweh himself, by which he manifests himself as the holy God.

How is the identity between the prophet's characterization of the city and the judges to be explained? Without a doubt, the "corporate personality," so familiar to ancient cultures and so strongly present in ancient Israel, plays a role here. Even today judgment is passed on the legitimacy of a nation's attitude according to the legitimacy or illegitimacy of those in authority there. But there is a social factor to be taken into consideration too, which is likewise observable in both the ancient and modern worlds. The morality or immorality of those in authority determines, in large part, the ethical tone of the nation. Why should an ordinary individual submit to the difficulty of acting in conformity with the law when he or she sees that "the great ones" of the land profit from its transgression?

Isaiah 3:1–15 insisted that peoples receive the government their behavior deserves. Isaiah 1:21–28, conversely, stresses the influence of government on the ethics of a society.

7. The relationship of justice between a human being and his or her

neighbor, on the one hand, and between the human being and God, on the other, come into sharp focus in worship. Worship offered to God can conceal the deficiencies of one's relationship with one's fellow human being. This is what the prophets so bitterly criticized on a number of occasions.

Hosea 8:11–13 is regarded as a classic case of this. Ephraim—Israel—multiples its altars, but these only serve as an occasion of sin, and victims immolated there are not pleasing to Yahweh. This reproach is an integral part of a series of condemnations which include Israel's self-sufficiency in designating its authorities (Hos. 8:4), idolatry (vv. 4b–6), seeking the support of Assyria with the resulting loss of identity as a chosen people unique among nations (vv. 7–10), and reliance on economic development for the security which Yahweh alone can bestow (v. 14a).

In the context, the condemnation of worship does not represent an attack on worship as such, but worship organized and performed (like the other political and economic activities labeled criminal by the prophets) behind Yahweh's back—worship that ignores or flouts his laws. The whole series of indictments is sandwiched in between two references to ignorance of Yahweh's will as expressed in his dispositions: "They have violated my covenant and rebelled against my Law" (v. 1); and "My precepts would be paid no more attention than those of a stranger" (v. 12). Both references to Yahweh's law imply a breach of his covenant, as verse 1 explicitly states, as well as ignorance of Yahweh himself. The people may cry, "God of Israel, we acknowledge you" (v. 2), but in reality Yahweh has become a stranger to his people.

The only worship that could be pleasing to Yahweh would be one that would be integrated into a cohesive whole consisting of just relationships with God. But these relationships would have to affect social life globally. Our passage does not speak explicitly of injustices committed against one's neighbor, but the prophet obviously has no hope that any advantage may accrue to individuals as the result of a series of initiatives born out of legitimate wedlock between Yahweh and his people—be these initiatives a matter of government, political alliances, or economic or military development (v. 14a). Collective abandonment, or at least official abandonment, of Yahweh will bring with it the atrophy and the dissolution of all just social relationships.

The antithesis erected between, on the one hand, right and justice (*mišpāṭ* and *ṣᵉdāqâ*), and, on the other hand, the sacrificial victims, music, solemnity, and songs of official worship, is explicit in passages like Amos 5:21–24 or Micah 6:6–9. Amos 4:4–5, 5:4–6a bitterly criticizes pilgrimages to traditional sanctuaries which do not signify a return to Yahweh.

In Isaiah 58:1–7 the prophet addresses the people on the subject of fasting. The fast that is pleasing to God, he says, is not the one that leads to external postures of submission to God, but the one that leads people to toil for the freedom of the oppressed (v. 6), and to assist those in need by sharing their own bread and shelter.

The tension between worship and justice reaches a climax in Isaiah 1:11–17 with the detailed description given there of various kinds of cultic celebrations, sacrifices, and liturgical acts and the final exhortation: "Learn to . . . search for justice, help the oppressed, be just to the orphan, plead for the widow." Justice is manifested in the defense of the poor and the weak, and worship should not have priority over it.

Before proceeding to a global evaluation of the data we have gathered in our consideration of justice in the Bible, we must of course sound out the New Testament on the matter, even if only very briefly.

We shall not have the space to discuss all the many aspects of our subject in the New Testament, where there is surely abundant material. We shall concentrate our attention on two pivotal passages which demonstrate the continuity of Jesus' teaching with that of the prophets and at the same time show his radical modification of the notion of norm and law.

8. The Beatitudes have come down to us in two different versions: that of Matthew 5:3–12, as an introduction to the Sermon on the Mount, and that of Luke 6:20–26, as the first part of the discourse on the plain. It will not be possible for us to take up the question of the relationship between the two texts here—whether one depends on the other, or both have a common source, or, finally, whether each represents an independent tradition going back ultimately to Jesus himself. What is certain is that Matthew and Luke reflect two different, but complementary, elements that are basic to Jesus' thinking.[15]

Luke has only four Beatitudes, as compared with Matthew's nine; and he adds four woes, in a one-for-one correspondence with the Beatitudes, which Matthew does not have.

The four Lukan Beatitudes correspond in subject matter to four of Matthew's, but appear in a different order. It is the difference in formulation, however, that indicates the theological peculiarity of each of the evangelists.

In order to visualize the differences better, let us schematize them:

THE FOUR BEATITUDES COMMON TO LUKE AND MATTHEW

LUKE	MATTHEW
1. You poor	1. The poor in spirit
2. You who are hungry now	4. Those who hunger and thirst for what is right
3. You who weep now: you shall laugh.	2. Those who mourn: they shall be comforted.
4. People hate/drive out/abuse/denounce on account of the Son of Man—rejoice and dance for joy when that day comes.	9. Abuse/persecute/speak calumny on my account—rejoice and be glad.

Matthew has hung up a veil of universalization here, of distance, in the expressions he uses—and of moderation, both in the situation that is considered "blessed" and in his description of the attitude of the persecutors.

Luke's "poor" become "poor in spirit" in Matthew. "You who are hungry now" become "those who hunger and thirst." The double expression "hunger and thirst," like other reduplications in the Old and New Testaments, indicates intensification. In view of the object of the hunger and thirst—"what is right"—the meaning is something like "those who ardently desire what is right" (*dikaiosúnēn*, "justice"). Luke's "you who weep now" is more direct and immediate than Matthew's "those who mourn," those who are sorrowful. "Mourning" precedes "weeping" in certain other passages (Mk. 16:10, Lk. 6:25), as if to indicate a crescendo." "Laughing" is more incarnate than "being comforted." "Drive out" may refer to the religious ostracism of one who is excluded from a group—as could happen to Jews who followed Jesus—or, more probably, to the social ostracism of a person who is ignored because he or she does not share the viewpoints of the group. In conjunction with "hate," Luke's "drive out" is more intense and dramatic than Matthews "persecute."

Luke uses the word "now" in two of his Beatitudes. And he uses the form of direct address, the second person, instead of the third.

We may conjecture that the Matthean text sounds the way a Sunday homily would have sounded in a traditional Christian community. Luke has preserved the energy of prophetic denunciation.

Our impression is strengthened by the tone of the Beatitudes proper to Matthew, the ones Luke does not have: "Happy the gentle . . . the merciful . . . the pure in heart . . . the peacemakers." These refer exclusively to the spiritual condition of both the person and the reward. Luke, by contrast, has woes of an entirely different tenor: "Alas for you who are rich . . . who have your fill now . . . who laugh now . . . when the world speaks well of you."

The introduction to the sermon on the plain (Lk. 6:17–19) describes, among those present, not only Jesus' disciples, but the people in general. It suggests that there were rich and poor in the audience: persons important in the eyes of the people, and nameless wretches or outcasts; well-dressed and well-fed people, and the dregs of humanity. This is the heterogeneous audience to whom Jesus says, "You rich," and "You poor."[16]

It seems correct to say that, in Matthew's version, the kingdom of heaven, the "kingdom of the skies," is presented as the reward of those who would make themselves worthy of it by their internal dispositions and their manner of living the Gospel message.

But just because Matthew insists more than Luke on interior dispositions, we may not simply rest satisfied with asserting that Luke presents the kingdom of God as the just compensation of those who have no share in the felicity of the present world—hence, as a consolation.[17] What is peculiar in the Lukan version is its emphasis on the fact that there are certain situations in human existence which do not easily find a horizontal, intrahistorical solution. Luke refers not only to the poor, the hungry, and the suffering, but also to the rich and satisfied.

The Lukan promises, "You shall be satisfied . . . you shall laugh," are framed by the first and last promises, "Yours is the kingdom of God," and "Your reward will be great in heaven." That is, the context is that of God's presence in the life of a human being.

The Lukan Beatitudes promise no change in the earthly situation of those it addresses. There is no question of an economic and social revolution which will simply make today's exploited into tomorrow's exploiters. But neither do these Beatitudes postpone the hopes of suffering people to some future solution, promising a magical cure-all tomorrow for the sake of solace today.

No, instead, "Yours *is* the kingdom of God" indicates that these particular poor and needy, in their present situation itself, enjoy a de facto nearness to God with which the rich and satisfied are not favored.

The first Lukan woe contains no explicit condemnation of the rich, but only makes a tragic observation, likewise referring to the present time: "You are having your consolation now." Your universe is shut in upon yourselves. And there is no place for God there. We may conclude, therefore, that the categories of rich and poor in the first Lukan Beatitude have neither a simple socio-economic sense—as if these categories could be determined by real income above or below a "poverty line"—*nor an ethical sense*—as if this Beatitude referred to the poor who had accepted their poverty for the sake of the kingdom of the skies, or for the sake of the "Son of Man," while the rich "do not look beyond the satisfaction of their own desires."[18] Rather, the first Lukan Beatitude has an *ontological sense.* Jesus directs his woe not against the rich in general, nor against the unjust rich, but against the very situation of being rich. Being wealthy excludes God from the human being's horizon, since it de facto excludes the neighbor from that horizon.

The parable of the rich person taking his satisfaction in his banquet and the poor person at the gate, which we find only in Luke (16:19–31), gives no hint as to whether the rich person was just or whether the poor person had accepted his poverty for the sake of the kingdom of heaven. One could almost suppose the contrary—that the poor person envied the rich person's wealth, for he surely "longed to fill himself with the scraps that fell from the rich man's table" (Lk. 16:21). The reason for the rich person's punishment is probably to be found in verse 20: Lazarus was at the gate, outside the house. In other words, the rich person's house, and heart, without being particularly evil or unjust, are simply closed to anyone who does not happen to have been invited to the banquet.

As Raymond Brown has incisively observed, in the Lukan conception "the only proper use of wealth is to get rid of it."[19] To the extent that the rich person really delivers himself or herself from his or her wealth, with all that this implies—to the extent that a rich person becomes poor—he or she can have access to the kingdom of heaven. By contrast, the situation of the poor person is one of openness toward God: only in the measure that he or she becomes rich, by covetousness and envy, is he or she estranged from the kingdom.

The condemnation of wealth in itself does not authorize the Christian preacher to send all rich persons off to hell. But neither is it permitted to banalize this condemnation by restricting it to a condemnation of the *unjust* rich person.

The relationship prevailing between the kingdom of God and poverty and between the kingdom of God and justice (cf. Mt. 5:6) shows how Jesus' teaching resumes that of the prophets. Injustice is tightly, if not indissolubly, linked to the possession of the goods of the earth. Other passages in Luke, especially by comparison with their Matthean parallels—for example, Luke 12:16–21 and 12:33 (Mt. 6:19–20); Luke 14:13 and 18:22 (Mt. 19:21)—clearly establish that the following of the Gospel of Jesus, the Magna Carta of Christian justice, necessarily involves renunciation of the goods of this earth.

This may seem a hard saying. But we have only to think how, at the root of nearly any dispute among persons or nations, there is a problem involving material goods, and how the best intentions toward one's neighbor, or neighboring country, vanish like smoke when it is realized that these intentions involve even partial renunciation of one's own goods.

Jesus' thinking concerning wealth and its inherent injustice also connotes a realistic pessimism. Neither the rich heir of Luke 12:16–21 nor the rich gourmand of Luke 16:19–31 are invited to alter their lifestyle. The rich youth of Luke 18:22 receives an admonition and rejects it. And of course "Alas for you who are rich" sets forth an established fact. The power of the goods of the earth, the true god of this world, is such that it is very difficult for anyone who has fallen into its toils to break free again. "How hard it is for those who have riches to make their way into the kingdom of God!" (Lk. 18:24).

9. The Old Testament establishes legislation for a community, as in the books of Exodus, Leviticus, Numbers, and Deuteronomy. Jesus does no such thing.

Instead, he has left a series of principles, gathered together in Matthew 5–7, intended to govern the behavior of his disciples. They regard fasting, prayer, almsgiving, and the use of material goods (ch. 6). The emphasis is on prayer, avoiding judging one's neighbor, and adapting one's conduct to the principles thus established (ch. 7).

But it is Matthew 5:17–20, especially, that attracts our attention as we consider justice in the Bible.

The moment a human group is able to use writing it tends to consolidate its organizational principles into written norms. The oldest evidence of a literate culture always seems to include a legal code. A code makes legislation clearer and more precise. It makes for easy application in ordinary cases, and interpretation in difficult ones. But it is probable that as legislation is codified the perception of relationships of justice and injustice are altered. Written law ceases to be the expression, albeit necessarily imperfect, of deep, basic needs rooted in human nature itself, whose interpretative criterion should therefore be the human beings themselves. Instead it tends to acquire an autonomy of its own, it breaks free of the tutelage of the human beings who have created it, and, like some science-fiction computer, ends by enslaving them. The process is all the more cruel and irreversible in proportion as society, along with its juridical apparatus, becomes more complex.[20] At the same time the individual loses a sense of what is just or unjust—which ought to coincide with the aspirations and needs of the human being, as an individual and in society—and introduces a new pair of basic categories into human intercourse: the permitted and the prohibited. And these are related directly to written law.

This same process has its effect on the human being as a religious being, as well. The permitted/prohibited dichotomy replaces that of just/unjust in relationships with one's neighbor considered as a creation of God, as well as in our manner of conceiving our relationship with God.

In Matthew 5:17–20 Jesus denounces this process of the subjection of the human being to the dictatorship of law, and restores both terms of the juridico-religious reality to their legitimate places.[21] Jesus knows that society, whether civil or religious, cannot function adequately without laws. To abolish them would mean to usher in the reign of arbitrary whim. "Do not imagine that I have come to abolish the law or the prophets," Jesus says (Mt. 5:17). "Abolish," in the original Greek, is *katalûsai*, a very strong expression designating an activity whose purpose it is to withdraw and liberate human beings from the authority of law. It is not simply a theoretical refutation of law.[22]

In conjunction with his generic defense of the law, Jesus introduces a second element: "or the prophets." Some manuscripts, instead of the disjunctive "or," use the copulative conjunction, "and," here, as in Matthew 7:12, 11:13, and 22:40—while in other passages it is indeed "or" that is used in the same expression. The variant may be of no particular significance; but in Matthew 5:17 it may indicate an intimate oneness between the law and the prophets. In any case, as we shall see, Jesus is seeking to complement, to complete, the law, in a very particular way, by understanding it in the light of the prophetic teachings.

It should also be noted here that, in Matthew 7:12 as in 22:40, "the law and the prophets" are defined by means of the golden rule of Christian ethics (7:12), and by the commandment of the love of God and neighbor (22:36–39).

"Do not think that I *have come. . . .*" Jesus begins—using another of the Gospels' technical terms, one which designates his mission as such, which he accomplishes in his teachings and in his deeds. Jesus "has come," then, to "complete"—to accomplish, to fulfill by means of words and works—the will of the Father as manifested in the-law-and-the-prophets. Jesus is thus constituted the interpretative criterion of the teachings of the Old Testament, now through his reading of the law in the light of the principle of love, and now through his nuanced accomplishment, his personalized interpretation and observance, of the law in conformity with each set of circumstances.

This interpretation of verse 17 opens the way for an understanding of verse 20. (Verses 18–19 must be read in the context of verses 17–20: otherwise verses 17–20 become contradictory and unintelligible.) Verse 20 reads: "If your virtue goes no deeper than that of the scribes and Pharisees. . . ." The original Greek has *dikaiosúne* here for "virtue"—our "righteousness," or "justice"—and so is to be understood as meaning the demand God makes on the human being, and consequently the proper comportment of the human being before God. The virtuous, the righteous, are those who obey the law. Both "law" and *dikaiosúne* provide a provisional point of contact between the Judaic religious conception and the specific, exclusive teaching of Jesus.[23]

Inasmuch as it is not an abstract concept of justice that is in question here—which would not admit of gradations of "more" and "less"—Jesus can require of those who wish to follow him that their obedience to the law be "deeper," better, than that of the scribes and Pharisees. "Deeper" here means that his disciples are to have come to an intimate grasp of the sense of the law, of its validity, its value—and at the same time of its limitations when it comes to regulating relationships among human beings and their relationship with God.

Now Jesus goes on to show what this "deeper virtue," this better observance of the law, this better obedience to the demands of God, means. He sets up six antitheses, six contrasts, each couched in the

formula, "You have learned . . ." (or the like), "But I say to you . . ."
(Mt. 5:21–28, 31–46). In the first term of each contrast he cites a law
we read in the legislative books: successively Exodus 20:13,14, Deuteronomy 24:1, Exodus 20:7, Leviticus 19:12, Exodus 21:24, Leviticus
19:18. In the second term of each contrast he proposes his own authoritative interpretation.

Jesus' own interpretation of the law in each case consists of his
intensification of a particular law (murder, adultery, love of enemy), or
its de facto suspension (oaths, the law of retaliation), or indeed his
overt contradiction of the law, with his reason for contradicting it
(divorce).

We cannot undertake an adequate investigation of the tension between Jesus' declaration, "I have come not to abolish but to complete"
the law and the prophets, and his rejection of certain laws, such as the
repudiation of one's wife. But we shall briefly examine Jesus' understanding of "completing the law" in the case of the law against murder,
and rest satisfied with that as an example of his whole approach to the
old law by way of complementing it.

Jesus begins by quoting Exodus 20:13, "You must not kill" (Mt.
5:21), and goes on to cite other Old Testament laws concerning
murder, all in the same verse of Matthew—Exodus 21:12 (which is
almost identical with Leviticus 24:17) and Numbers 35:16–25. The
three texts he cites represent three successive stages in the evolution of
a consciousness of ethics and justice: The first establishes the basic
principle of respect for human life apodictically, without exceptions or
casuistry. The second and third provide for a first exception to the
general law: capital punishment for murder. And the last lays down in
some detail the conditions under which not only a court, but even the
so-called "avenger of blood" (Nm. 35:19) may exact appropriate retribution for homicide.

Jesus' words in verse 22 are sometimes interpreted as expressing a
gradation of offenses (anger, calling someone a fool, calling someone a
"renegade") and their punishments (court, Sanhedrin, hell fire). Thus
Jesus would be setting up a casuistry—one different in content from
Numbers 35:16–25—and more severe penalties, but similar in form.
But this opinion does not seem to be correct. Notice that Jesus is using
heterogeneous terms. There is no gradation between calling a person a
fool, which was the worst of insults, and a "renegade," which denoted
apostasy, the worst of sins. Meanwhile, anger is an interior process of

the emotions, which can be violent without showing on the surface. Similarly, in spite of our translation ("court"), *krísis*, "judgment," refers not to any particular court, but to the judicial sentence itself, without specifying the tribunal from which it issues. And "hell fire" is not a court but a penalty, that of eschatological condemnation.

Jesus is not establishing a new casuistry, then, nor a new gradation in crimes and punishments. On the contrary, he is returning to the simplicity of the Ten Commandments: Thou shalt not kill—ever. But he is enriching and deepening this precept. He is demonstrating its breadth by paraphrasing it. Aggression against one's "brother"—and this is the main point, that he or she is your brother or sister—is basically the same whether it occurs in internal anger that does not show, or harsh words, or its paroxysm in murder. Therefore every form of this aggression ought to result in the culprit's being hailed before the tribunal of human beings ("judgment," *krísis*) and condemned by God's judgment. Jesus succeeds in showing how broad the commandment, "You must not kill," is and how much it covers. It is not observed simply by omitting homicide in deed. On the other hand, Jesus is not suggesting that it would be possible to eliminate all aggressive reactions completely in all circumstances, or that it would make sense to bring everyone who becomes angry to trial. Nor is he suggesting that God's judgment would regard an outburst of uncontrolled anger and a premeditated and meticulously executed act of revenge as equally wrong.

By eliminating degrees of culpability and presenting courts and sentences all on one level, Jesus is seeking to eliminate the juridical mentality which says, "I have not killed anyone, so I am just." Jesus wishes to replace this attitude with one that says, "I have entertained a sentiment of anger toward my brother, so I am not just." In other words, Jesus is striving to destroy all limits to observance of the law. Underlying the precise formulation of the law, "You must not kill," is a demand without limits, in whose accomplishment a human being can employ all his or her energy. Only law understood this radically is an expression of the will of the Father, who is perfect and who wishes human beings to be perfect. The urgency of reconciliation, to the point where one must interrupt the very act of worship, is an explicitation of the unlimited nature of the demand not to "kill."

All the other antitheses here, all the other pairs of contrasting attitudes toward the law, are to be read in the same way. Jesus proposes one example after another of people's behavior toward their brother and sister and toward the Father. "You must not commit adultery" means control of one's hidden desires, too. "You must not break your oath . . ." is based on a broader norm: not to depart from truth and simplicity in your assertions—even emphasis can be a way of deceiving! In place of revenge, Jesus establishes the principle of being willing to give up your own rights as a way to win over your brother or sister. Love of neighbor ought not to lead to sectarianism. Rather it ought to dispose us positively toward our very enemy.

Justice and Religious Education

Let us attempt to summarize the main traits of the conception of justice offered to us by the Old and New Testaments in the few passages we have briefly considered here.

Ancient Israel manifests a concern to set up a body of laws and norms which will make it possible to safeguard institutions, especially the administration of justice. This is done in the consciousness that the correct functioning of the courts of the city means the defense of the weakest. At the same time it sets limits to the potential arbitrariness of the king.

The importance of these laws and norms for Israel is clearly shown in the way this juridical corpus is conceived in the Old Testament. Its laws have been transmitted by Yahweh to Moses. On various occasions, in various Old Testament texts, the whole corpus of the laws of Israel is considered as a mere development of the legislation entrusted to Israel by the divinity directly. Accordingly, there is no question here of any profane, secular, lay reality. This is a set of norms, including the most minute dispositions concerning worship, food, and ritual purity, considered to be the direct expression of the will of God.

This reliance on the juridical organization of the nation and its religion, an organization which ought to have been conducive to a life of harmonious relationships, showed itself on more than one occasion to be illusory. The accounts of Israel's wanderings in the wilderness, which can be read in the Book of Numbers, are in large part the history of this people's infidelity to the decrees which, according to biblical tradition, they had only just received from God. Nor will the history of Israel from the time of Solomon on show a different picture. Israel's laws demonstrate their incapacity to deliver what they promise. Laws have no value unless they are observed. Despite the goodness of the legislation itself, ultimate responsibility for the functioning of society rests with the individuals and groups who accept or reject it. It is probably fair to assert that Israel's prideful, tragic flaw was to believe that this wonderful legislation ("What great nation is there that has laws and customs to match this whole law that I put before you today?" Moses asks in Deuteronomy 4:8) was sufficient of itself to assure that nation's salvation.

The mission of the prophets, on numerous occasions, is to point out the grave and continuous insult to the basic points of this law: the oppression of the weak by the iron heel of the mighty, the wealthy, the unjust authorities. The prophets denounce instances of omission, too, such as court prophets or venal priests who, in spite of their influence, dare not raise their voices to demand a remedy for oppression.

For the prophets, then, just relationships depend in large part on the influential, the powerful, those in authority. The prophets know that a certain balance of power among the parties is an advantage when it comes to fostering just relationships—which will then be forthcoming from necessity and convenience, if not just from virtue. Correlatively, injustice is directly proportional to the inequality of the parties concerned. This is why, while the prophets so frequently inveigh against injustices already committed, they also strongly condemn, if less frequently, concentrations of wealth and power, whether of individuals or of nations, that open the way to new injustices.

Condemnations of the concentration of power or wealth in the hands of nations are to be found in some of the so-called "oracles against the Gentiles." Isaiah 14:4b–21, for instance, does not seem to be directed against any person or power in particular, but against the arrogance of anyone, person to nation, seeking by means of a concentration of power to take the place of Yahweh. By way of example, Israel's ancient enemy, Assyria, is cited in verses 5–8, where Assyria is associated with a mythical figure, Helal, son of the Dawn ("Daystar, son of Dawn"), who sought to erect his throne in opposition to the throne of God (vv. 12–14).

Isaiah 14 summarizes, explicitates, and universalizes the teaching of Isaiah on the fatal flaw of the pride of might—a might that is intimately bound up with military and political power ("you who enslaved the nations," v. 14; "who . . . leveled cities, who never to his captives opened the prison gates," v. 17).

Ezekiel 32:17–32 likewise condemns, by name and with specifics, some of the nations who have embarked upon the venture of universal, arrogant power. The passage is a long, monotonous list of tirelessly repeated but never quite indentical, expressions. The purpose and meaning of this tiresome philosophico-religious meditation on the fleeting power of nations is given in the obsessive refrain, the dramatic words associated with the names of the nations: Such and such a nation "is there . . . all killed . . . with all her troops around her tomb . . . yet she once spread terror."

Ezekiel 28:2–10 (to cite one last example along these lines) is the condemnation of a state (Tyre), together with its prince, that has used its commercial skill to master other nations by the power of its wealth, and to assume—like a god—the control of nations.

The prophets are aware that the corruption of the influential and powerful leads to the corruption of the lowly, and eventually to the destruction of the whole of society. Hence the prophetical condemnations are not leveled against evil individuals alone. Nor do the prophets criticize primarily and per se the two great institutions of their time, the temple and the monarchy. But they do see and denounce the structures of corruption in society. These may well originate with individuals. But at a given moment they become independent of them and begin to constitute an objective evil rooted in society itself. From that moment on it is all but impossible to resist their corruption. The prophets are not anarchists or revolutionaries in the extreme sense, but they certainly are not conformists when it comes to a conception of justice and injustice. They are far from the misconception that justice and injustice reside in the wills of individuals alone. Rather, the good or evil that each one does has its repercussions and influence on the whole body of society.

When the prophets threaten a national castigation in the area of politico-military relationships for crimes that are largely "private"— oppression of the poor, luxury beyond all bounds, and the like—they are demonstrating that no hard and fast line between the private and the public, between the individual and the social, exists for prophetical thought. Justice's space is unitarian, homogeneous. The interaction between the seemingly private and the public is total.

Therefore the prophets do not dawdle over a casuistry or codification of multiple and varied individual relationships—of master and slave, employer and wage-earner, family members, officers and soldiers. It suffices to lay down a single paradigmatic comportment: that of powerful king or judge vis-à-vis powerless subject or plaintiff. All rules for just comportment are laid down in this one relationship. The justice that Yahweh demands of the king toward his subject is the same as he demands of the master toward his slave.

This is why the prophets are not explicitly interested in a "structural reform" of society. They are convinced (Yahweh's conviction) that the human intelligence and heart will find current societal structures adequate if only they will accept the basic principle of societal coresponsibility—of the responsibility of the stronger for the weaker.

There is an element of profound realism here, and an acute perception of social psychology. Human reality is such that there will always be some who are more powerful than others. There will always be some who are more intelligent, or more persuasive, or more imaginative, or more enterprising than their fellows. And so the problem of justice cannot find its ultimate solution in a utopian equalization of human qualities. The ultimate solution of the problem of justice will be found in the persuasion on the part of individuals and groups that it is their inalienable responsibility to take the weakest into their care.

Since injustice is so closely bound up with the various forms of power, the prophets insist on Yahweh's preference for the little ones, the defenseless. He identifies with them, they warn, and they trust in his intervention to heal the corruption afflicting them.

How do the prophets concretely imagine that Yahweh's intervention in favor of the needy will take place? Some passages seem to expect some manner of apocalyptic intervention on Yahweh's part. But prophetical realism relies mainly on the very history of peoples for the castigation of groups and nations that allow themselves to be swept away by unjust leaders, by governors who are disloyal to God's word.

The prophet Hosea, for example, sums up his condemnation of his nation's politics of alliance with foreign powers (5:12–14, 7:11, 8:9, 12:2) in one lapidary expression: "Assyria cannot save us" (14:4). It is not that the prophet considers the foreign alliance, immediately and in itself, a punishment by means of a political power. It is from a religious point of view that the prophet opposes such an alliance, because it signifies idolatry—theologically, because his nation is placing its trust in a power of this world and not in God; and from the point of view of worship, because of the risk of contamination by foreign religious practices. But besides all this it is likely that he opposes this alliance because he foresees that an alliance between unequal powers is simply not viable and is soon dissolved in the subjugation of the weaker party—Israel, in this case—to the stronger. The alliance with Assyria, then, will not only be infidelity to Yahweh, but punishment by Yahweh.

Other prophets explicitly view the danger of a foreign enemy as a punishment for Israel's unfaithfulness—punishment of a nation that has placed all its confidence in political means. First, Isaiah attempts to convince the king by means of reasonable arguments (Is. 7). But then he explicitly threatens him with the danger represented by Assyria (7:17). In Isaiah 10:5, Assyria is spoken of as the very lash with which Yahweh chastises Israel. (Assyria itself, for its part, will then be castigated for its own excesses.) In Jeremiah 6:22–26, the historical punishment which threatens is tinged with apocalyptical traits. But the danger is a concrete one, and is to be punishment for concrete injustices. The reader will recall the Jeremiahan passages examined above.

Doubtless the prophets did not imagine that a foreign invasion would suffice for the reestablishment of an order of justice. On the contrary, it was possible that internal injustices would actually increase under the protection of favoritism and the pressure of agreements struck between the forces of occupation and their subjects. But in the face of a situation of such broad corruption, the prophets foresaw no solution—and perhaps indeed there was none—except total destruction so that everything might begin all over again.

Indeed, could there have been any other solution to the extreme decadence and corruption of some of the great Western monarchies but the revolutions that put an end to them?

The biblical understanding of justice is so solid, so basic, so simple:

• An intimate connection between power and riches, and injustice.

• Yahweh's resultant predilection for the weak.

• The responsibility of the mighty toward the weak.

• The influence of individual injustice on the body of society.

• The consequent coresponsibility for injustice.

• Knowledge of Yahweh as dependent on the practice of justice.

- Consequently, the obligation of justice toward one's neighbor as first among human responsibilities, hence as antecedent even to the duty of worship.

- Yahweh's reestablishment of the order of justice, at determined moments, and severely, by means of historical processes.

As we have shown, the prophets do not consider it their obligation to establish precise norms for particular cases. They know that those who allow the truths they preach to permeate their bones and blood will find the just path in the concrete event—the proper, adequate reaction for each particular case.

Jesus' teaching is the prolongation of that of the prophets. He refers to the received religious tradition in Israel as "the law and the prophets" advisedly. But he goes a step further. The prophets have established their demands with the law in brackets, as it were. They prescind from laws, they make no mention of them, they do not discuss them. Jesus, on the contrary, proposes himself as the interpretative principle of the law. But his interpretation is only exemplary. It is not exhaustive. Jesus does not limit his demand—that he himself be acknowledged as the ultimate norm of the law, that he be regarded as the principle governing the law itself—to the few laws explicitly interpreted in the New Testament. If "man is the measure of all things," then a Christian will insist, even more, that there is no basic law, in the church or in society, other than the word and action of Jesus himself, the perfect image of the Father.

Like the prophets before him, Jesus refuses to establish a new code of norms. It is difficult indeed to decide, with the Gospel in hand, whether democracy or monarchy is the political theory more in accordance with Jesus' teaching, whether liberal or state-controlled economics is the more adequate theory for a people to develop its whole potential, and so on. But we can certainly decide, with the Gospel in hand, whether such and such a particular regime or concrete economics is achieving its purpose of being at the service of the community.

It goes without saying that the mechanisms and relationships of modern society are enormously more complex than those of the first-century society in which Jesus preached the Good News. A modern state that would seek to replace all its legal codes with the Gospels, or the Old Testament (or, while we are speaking along these lines, the

Qur'an) would be found to be without adequate instruments for the fruitful organization of the life of the nation.

Nevertheless, the totalizing demands of the Christian faith give us the assurance that all aspects of national life, the multiple confrontations and collisions of international relations, and the disagreements of individuals and small groups, ought to be able to be judged by the yardstick of the Gospel. If this were not the case, Christianity would have to renounce its just claim to offer not only a "path to heaven," but—inextricably intertwined with that path—a path upon earth.

One element in the complexity of the modern world is the interpersonal relationship. No individual can organize the world about himself or herself independently of multiple influences. This means that no one can build a space of justice, his or her own "faithful city," in isolation from others.

Most probably, then, in a world where not all profess, let alone live, the Christian faith, it will be impossible to establish a regime of relationships that are strictly faithful to the Gospel. Instead, the Christian's task will be to grow in his or her ability to "discern the various situations," to judge them according to the Gospel, and to obtain a final result as close to the Gospel as possible. Over and above all this, he or she must accept the limitations imposed on the realization of this result—all in the hope in a Kingdom of unlimited justice, however.

Education in the Christian meaning of justice, then, cannot consist in acquainting students with the various passages in the Old Testament and the few in the New Testament which bear upon a concrete ethical problem, pointing out the biblical solution, evaluation, or norm proposed in each passage, and teaching them how to apply it logically to a contemporary situation. This would be to forget that laws, while they are more concrete than principles of attitude, are also more tightly bound up with an unrepeatable historical situation so that they are inapplicable in another situation. This intimate connection with historical circumstances is the only thing that keeps us from taking scandal at laws prescribing the extermination of one's enemies in Deuteronomy 20:10–18, or the racist precepts of Esdras 9:12. But it also prevents us from accepting them.

Education in the Christian meaning of justice will be authentic in proportion as students are taught to discover in Scripture the deeper elements that determine the structure of a just or unjust relationship— some of which we have noted in this chapter—and then to recognize the presence (or absence) of these elements in the contemporary situation or institution under examination.

Scripture thwarts our efforts to use it as a catalogue of behavioral norms handed down identically from generation to generation and timelessly normative in its immediate content. Scripture is given to us as the living Word of the living God, when its text, inspired by God but anchored in a bygone historical moment, is received by the community of faith under the inspiration of the same Spirit who presided at its composition and who enables us to read both the present situation and the ancient word and set them in mutual confrontation. The text of Scripture should sharpen the reflection, and the response for today, that God seeks to stir up in the reader by means of these passages.

Our immersion in the word which we accept as the Word of God means ultimately that we are trying to enter into a different universe from our categories today—a universe where power, wealth, might, and beauty are not definitive values—in fact are not values at all. This is perhaps the final, the most decisive, word that Scripture has to say to us on the subject of justice: that our efforts to build a new world will never be anything but—at best—naive babbling until we really make up our minds to enter into this other universe, this true universe of justice. This is probably how we should read the parable of the eleventh-hour laborers in Matthew 20:1–16: not as a defense of the most liberal concept of the right to property, but as a statement that there is an order of justice in which the "latecomer," the "new arrival," the handicapped person, the person who needs a "head start," the foreigner, the member of another race or religion or sex, has the same rights as the person whose rights are already established. But this order is intelligible only in the universe of Jesus crucified.

Notes

1. For example, *Laborem Exercens*, the encyclical of John Paul II on labor, September 14, 1981, has only one biblical reference out of about a hundred in chapters 3 and 4, which deal with the conflict between labor and capital and the rights of the worker, and are the most technical of the chapters. By contrast, there are seventy-eight biblical references in chapter 5, on the elements of a spirituality of labor—mostly appearing in No. 26, where the subject is Christ as a laborer. These latter citations are not doctrinal in the proper sense, but simply point out that Old Testament societies and Jesus' world alike were societies of working people.

2. Much just criticism of the "theology of liberation" is directed against its rather capricious use of Scripture to justify positions indeed valid in themselves, and demonstrable from *other* premises.

3. A reader who is willing to be objective and not force the data will acknowledge the difficulty of finding in Scripture a consistent and explicit response to a "modern" problem like imperialism. See for example J. L. Sicre, "La actitud profética ante el imperialismo," *Proyección* (Granada) 26 (nos. 114–15): 171–80, 313–23. Rather than speaking of *the* biblical answer we ought to speak of the answers of Jeremiah or Ezekiel, Nahum or Zechariah. See also Sicre's p. 323.

4. This statement has no pretenses of being a definition of justice, either at the ethical or the anthropological levels, both of which fall outside the scope of this work. We are simply advancing a partial anthropological characterization for the utility it will have in delimiting the area of our study.

5. For a useful study of this text see J. P. Fokkelman, *Narrative Art in Genesis: Specimens of Stylistic and Structural Analysis*, Studia Semitica Neerlandica 17 (Assen/Amsterdam, 1975).

6. For an adequate understanding of the patriarchal narratives it is important to avoid transferring concepts from one textual level to another. Jacob's atheism in a more folkloristic narrative cannot be set at naught by a redactional theological formula like "the God of Abraham, Isaac, and Jacob," frequently though the latter may occur throughout Scripture.

7. On the prophet Jeremiah see the recent work by L. Wisser, *Jérémie, Critique de la vie sociale*, Le monde de la Bible (Geneva, 1982), especially pp. 53–64 on Jeremiah 5:29–29, pp. 23–31 on 9:1–8, and pp. 96–107 on 22:13–19. For a treatment in English see J. Bright, *Jeremiah*, The Anchor Bible 21 (Garden City, N.Y., 1965).

8. See for example Exodus 22:24–26, Deuteronomy 23:20–21, 24:10–15, 17–18.

9. "Bible et politique, *Revue des Sciences Religieuses* 59(1971), pp. 497–530; cf. p. 507.

10. It is difficult to determine whether we are dealing with a textual unity here, or with two texts (verses 1–9 and 13–15, with verse 12 as a transition). At all events the thematic unity is very strong. Verses 10–11, on the other hand, seem to be a marginal commentary.

11. For a good synthesis of the problem see J. Limburg, "The Root *rib* and the Prophetic Lawsuit Speech," *Journal of Biblical Literature* 88(1969), pp. 291–304.

12. For example, Judges 6:25–31, 8:1, and in the accounts of Isaac and Jacob in Genesis 26:17–20, 31:33–36.

13. See, besides the passage we are examining, Isaiah 1:15–17, Jeremiah 2:5–9, 25:31, Hosea 2:4–17, 4:1–3, 4–6.

14. See the article, "Pauvre," in *Dictionnaire de la Bible*, Supplement, vol. 7 (1961), col. 387.

15. A detailed discussion of these problems will be found in I. Howard Marshall, *The Gospel of Luke: A Commentary on the Greek Text*, The New

International Greek Testament Commentary (Exeter, 1978), pp. 243–57. The whole book is an excellent general aid to reading the Gospel of Luke.

16. For a state of the question on who the rich and poor are in the Gospel of Luke, see Robert J. Karris, "Poor and Rich: The Lukan *Sitz im Leben*," in Charles H. Talbert, ed., *Perspectives on Luke-Acts* (Danville, Va./Edinburgh, 1978), pp. 112–25. Karris thinks the hypothesis that the rich of the Lukan woes are members of the Lukan community rests on shaky grounds (p. 118). For a defense of this hypothesis see Marshall, *Gospel of Luke*, p. 242.

17. Marshall, *Gospel of Luke*, p. 246, embracing the opinion of Jacques Dupont, *Les Béatitudes* (Paris, 1954), pp. 298 ff.

18. Marshall, *Gospel of Luke*, p. 246.

19. Raymond Brown, in his brief but positive article, "The Beatitudes According to St. Luke," in *The Bible Today Reader* (Collegeville, Minn., 1973), p. 305. The general discussion is on pp. 302–306.

20. This is the situation described so magnificently by Franz Kafka in his novel, *The Trial*.

21. One final, good commentary on this passage we may cite is D. Marguerat, *Le jugement dans l'Evangile de Matthieu*, Le monde de la Bible (Geneva, 1981), pp. 110–41.

22. Pierre Bonnard, "L'Evangile selon Saint Matthieu," in *Commentaire du Nouveau Testament*, 2nd ed. (Neuchâtel, 1970), 1:71.

23. See B. Pryzybylski, *Righteousness in Matthew and His World of Thought*, STNS Monograph Series 41 (Cambridge, 1980), pp. 99, 103, 123.

CHAPTER 8

Sin

Alice Laffey

I. An Introduction

To write a short essay elucidating the nature of sin from a biblical perspective is no easy task. A course on the Bible might systematically treat the vocabulary of sin—*ḥattâ'*, *pesha'*, *'awōn*, *'amartano*, *'anomos*, *'adikia*, etc.—and analyze the nuances of each term.[1] Fleshing out such vocabulary might include a systematic analysis, even a cataloging, of relationships—Yahweh and Israel, Jesus and his church, humans dealing with one another. And one would need to begin with some commonly accepted definition of sin, such as, "an action or omission in opposition to rules, accepted values, common good; a rejection of relational bonds, a rejection of another, others, the Other."[2]

These things the Bible teaches. But the Bible's way of revealing and teaching is not primarily systematic and analytical. Rather, it is symbolic and experiential.[3] Biblical insights into the nature of sin emerge out of vivid descriptions of concrete persons and the dynamics of relationships which are classic types.[4] They emerge out of impassioned outbursts of prophetic anger and human pleading for forgiveness and reconciliation.

A biblical perspective of sin is one which begins with love and caring and sharing, the contemporary language of bonding. Love spurned, caring refused, sharing repelled—this is the Bible's story of sin. Nor is such rejection always simple and absolute. It is often the product of weakness and temptation, of decision making amidst ambiguity. Having once chosen God (what contemporary moral theologians today refer to as the "fundamental option"), one may deviate from the fullness of fidelity. But to one who has so compromised, the door remains open to repentance and forgiveness. The Gospels assure us that Jesus

234

came to forgive sins (e.g., Mt. 1:21; 9:2.5.6; 26:28; Lk. 7:47–49; 24:47; Jn. 1:29).

A. God's Initiative

Of one thing the Bible is quite certain: God calls. God calls into creation, God calls Abraham forming him into a people, God calls out of slavery, God calls into relationship and therefore to fidelity, God calls to repentance. . . . The initiative is God's. A brief glance at the history of the Old Testament clearly shows the Israelites' experience of God as Giver (Gen. 15:18–19; Jos. 1:2),[5] as source of life and death (Deut. 30:15) as well as of blessing and curse (Gen. 12:3; Deut. 28:1–19; 30:1), as Lord who is One (Deut. 6:4) and jealous (Jos. 24:19). Only those caught up in this call, the people whom God has created, only they can be guilty of sin.[6] And the community or individual which has heard and believed, who has said "yes" to this God who calls, these especially[7] may choose to reject the One who gives, and thereby, to sin.

B. The Community of Israel and the Individuals Who Form It

There is an intricate relationship between the community and the individual, even for the earliest Israelites. Adam's sin somehow affects more than Adam (Gen. 3:17–19); Abraham's call is somehow for an entire people (Gen. 12:2); Joseph's leadership is for the others (Gen. 45:4–8) as is the great prophet Moses' (Ex. 3:4–10). Prophets speak in the name of God but to the people (e.g., Jer. 1:9–10; Is. 6:8–9; Ez. 2:3–4); priests sacrifice with and in behalf of the people (e.g. Lev. 3); kings rule over and govern the people (e.g., 2 Sm. 8:15; 1 Kgs. 3:9). It is traditionally noted by biblical scholars that Israel's earliest sense of itself was as a people, as a community, rather than as individuals. As such, fidelity was expressed by the community (e.g., Jos. 24:16–18), as was sin or the rejection of God's call (e.g., Jgs. 2:11).

Gradually Israel began to understand itself also as individuals within a community. As part of the community, one is responsible to that community as well as to God (e.g., Jos. 7); one is responsible as a decision-making entity (e.g., Ez. 18:20–24; 33:18–19). The individual comes to understand that he or she bears responsibility for his or her choices, whether for good or ill, faith or disbelief, God or idols.

The New Testament, though it recognizes Israel's more ancient belief that one could suffer for a parent's sin (e.g., Jn. 9:2–3), transcends the idea; the materials presume individual responsibility. The writers do, however, continue the Old Testament emphasis on the additional responsibility which Jewish leadership bears. It is for this reason that the Pharisees (e.g., Mt. 23:1–36; Lk. 11:37–44; 15:7–9.14), the scribes (e.g., Lk. 20:46–47), and the lawyers (e.g., Lk. 11:45–52) become the special objects of Jesus' condemnation.

C. Responsibility

To what extent are people really free? That question has been hotly debated by psychologists and psychiatrists for the past hundred years.[8] Though the query had been raised by theologians long before that (e.g., the medieval debates regarding God's foreknowledge and human free will), human potential for free choice has been consistently affirmed.[9]

The biblical authors of the Old Testament affirmed human freedom. Individuals and communities might bear the effects of the sinful decisions made by their predecessors (e.g., Ex. 34:7; cf. Rom. 5:19), but they also had within their power the opportunity to choose a destiny. Both Deuteronomy 30 and Joshua 24 exhort Israel: "Choose life!"[10]

The New Testament's approach is only slightly more sophisticated. Paul wrestles within himself because he knows that he does not always do the things that he knows are best (e.g., Rom. 7:15–23). Choosing for him is not always simple; one senses his struggle. Yet the better choice is possible in Paul's theology (e.g., 1 Cor. 10:31–11:1; Phil. 2:2–3). The letter to the Ephesians exhorts, "Choose a life worthy of the calling to which you have been called." (4:1; cf. 5:1–3).

D. Conclusion to the Introduction

No biblical study of sin can begin without presuppositions and these need explicit expression. They include, first of all, that it is a loving God who first calls his people and offers to them a relationship. Without an understanding—more than that, an appreciation—of the notion of genuine relationship, freely offered and freely accepted, one's understanding of sin will be a misunderstanding, limited to legalism, very specific do's and don'ts, and fear of punishment. Second, no biblical study of sin can ignore that relationships do not exist in a vacuum. Just as individuals are always, in some way, part of one community or another—families, neighborhoods, nations, and for us, religious affiliations—so also we participate in relationships both as a community and as individuals. Third, a biblical perspective includes a humankind which is capable of free choice, sometimes conditioned or limited or difficult, but free. Healthy people are therefore responsible for the decisions they make—as a community and as individuals. Finally, the Bible is not, nor was it meant to be, a set of doctrines. There is no biblical doctrine of sin.

This introduction merely sets the stage for the drama which is the love story between God and his people, between lover and beloved, a love story which, sad to say, includes infidelity, betrayal, and compromise. Yet the love story will not end there. Sin is not the final word. Rather, punishment, forgiveness, reconciliation—these too form an essential part of the picture[11] and sin cannot be properly understood or appreciated for what it truly is apart from these continual expressions of the God who initiates, the God who is Love.

II. The Old Testament: a Sampling

The Old Testament's reflections on sin can only be understood within a context of covenant. A motley group of nomads fled Egyptian bondage and experienced their deliverance as the work of a liberating God. This God they claimed as their own and to him they pledged loyalty and obedience.

The Old Testament rarely speaks of sin except within the context of this relationship. "I am your God, you are my people, says the Lord" (Jer. 31:1, 33; cf. Ex. 19:4–6a). The Israelites eventually[12] came to understand that their God whose name was Yahweh was a jealous God who demanded that they acknowledge only him as their God and him as the only God. Israel must put aside all idols. Obedience to Yahweh meant also an obedience of justice. The God in whom they believed, who had shown his power and who continued to act on their behalf called them to treat one another with respect. They were not to steal or lie or hurt or envy or abuse one another in any way (Ex. 20; Deut. 5).

The self-revelation of this caring God called for the free response of a just and faithful people. The brevity of an article such as this prohibits an examination of all the Old Testament encounters in which Israel "missed the mark" (the original meaning of the Hebrew word "sin"). Yet at the risk of excluding key insights into the nature of sin, I have tried to select incidents and elements which are *most representative* of Israel's love story.

A. David and Bathsheba (2 Sm. 11–12)[13]

Too much passion? Too much power? Is that what got David into trouble? Was his sin that he began to trust less in God and more in himself?

The biblical narrative portrays David as the ideal king, faithful to Yahweh and ruling justly. He is credited with a military victory over the Philistines, and with uniting Israel and Judah. The Lord had even promised him a dynasty. Yet he who seemingly has everything—wives, children, riches, power, prestige—wants more. The man whom Yahweh had chosen to shepherd his people takes another man's wife and covers up his adultery with murder. These are pretty serious crimes, even today. And one might note, too, that he had become lazy (2 Sm. 11:1) and deceitful (2 Sm. 11:8–10, 15). We might conclude that the most serious aspect of David's sin was the fact that he was so preoccupied with not getting caught by people that he was oblivious to the gravity of his actions before God.

The laws which David violated were concrete expressions of Israel's freely chosen covenant with Yahweh. David did not just "do bad things against people"; rather, David acted out a "forgetting" of the Lord, a "rejecting" of the covenant bond, an indifference to a respectful way of relating to people, in this case, to Uriah and Bathsheba and Joab.

Two things must be said in David's defense, however. The first is that the sin seems to be an isolated episode. The preceding narrative has consistently described him as "a man after the Lord's own heart" (e.g., 1 Sm. 13:14). And David has elsewhere prayerfully acknowledged his dependence on the Lord (2 Sm. 7:18–19). The second is that David's sin did not end there. He was caught in it by his God who knew what might otherwise have gone undetected and undenounced. The prophet Nathan elicited from David a condemnation of a rich man who cruelly took from a poor man and then declared to David that he was that man (2 Sm. 12:7). Having thus named his own sin and condemned himself, David moved to ask God's forgiveness.

But recognition and sorrow do not cancel punishment; it loudly proclaims that decisions have consequences. David's son dies and he is warned that the sword will never depart from his house (2 Sm. 12:10). Punishment, however, is not incompatible with forgiveness. David is restored to God's favor. He who was loved much yet betrayed that love is reconciled to his Lord and shown God's steadfast kindness. (e.g., 2 Sm. 23; 1 Kgs. 1:48; 3:6).

B. Adam and Eve: The Fall

The story of Adam and Eve is David's story (and probably both accounts can be traced back to the tenth century B.C.). It tells of having a lot—all one could want, really—yet wanting more. Not satisfied with the gifts given—creation, the animals, a garden of de-lights, human companionship—not appreciative and making the most of them, these characters, like all of us at times, demand more. Eve was persuaded to taste the fruit of the tree of the knowledge of good and evil which the serpent promised would make her like God, a forbidden fruit, a fruit which she shared with Adam.

Obedience to the Lord's command, "Of this tree you may not eat." (Gen. 2:17), they no longer perceived as unqualified good, but rather as limitation, restriction, binding obligation. Having "almost" every-thing, at the suggestion of a lesser being, they turned their backs on the known Giver of Good. It sounds absurd, but it's so real and so com-mon. That's what David had done. (That's what turning from God to worship idols is all about, as the continual repetition of this theme in Israel's history demonstrates.)

Perhaps it was reflection on common human experience and, in particular, on David's experience, that occasioned incorporation of "the fall" into the story of creation. And the consequences or punish-ment for such sin—regardless of sorrow and forgiveness—take on in the story the forms of human labor and childbirth pain, apparently understood in the tenth century B.C. as unfortunate aspects of the human condition. The biblical account demonstrates, therefore, that right from the start, those who had received all that they possessed reached for and demanded more, paying the price of infidelity to their Lord.

Theology has developed a doctrine of original sin based on Genesis 3 to explain how sin first entered our world and how it is that we also participate in sin.

C. The Deuteronomistic Pattern of Sin

The final editing of seven books of the Old Testament—Deuteronomy through 2 Kings—has been attributed to one writer[14] or school of thought,[15] who compiled and organized more ancient materials into a consistent whole. This segment of the Bible is unified by a recurring theme, the "deuteronomistic theology of history." Briefly stated it is this:

> Israel, blessed by God, sinned.
> As a consequence, the Lord became angry and punished her.
> Then Israel called out to the Lord for deliverance.
> The Lord heard Israel's prayer and sent a savior.
> Then, once again, Israel, blessed by God, sinned.
> The Lord again became angry. Punishment followed.
> The Israelites, in sore distress,
> cried out to the Lord for deliverance.
> The Lord again heard their plea
> and sent a savior. . . .

We note here, too, that sin is not the final word!

Moses perceived Israel's reluctance to take possession of the hill country of the Amorites as its *not trusting the Lord* who went ahead on the journey to find a place for the camp (Deut. 1:33). For this they were punished, but not irrevocably: the Lord's promise of the land to Israel would be fulfilled, but it would be delayed until "that evil generation had all died" (vv. 35–36).

When Joshua died the Israelites did wrong and worshiped the Baalim; their bowing down to other gods provoked the Lord's anger (Jdg. 2:14) so that he punished them. They then became the prey of bands of raiders and plunderers and each of their battles resulted in defeat. But the Lord sent judges to rescue them, relenting when he heard their groaning under oppression and ill-treatment (v. 18). During the judges' lifetimes the Lord kept Israel safe from her enemies, but as each judge died Israel relapsed into corruption and gave allegiance to other gods. This, inevitably, aroused the Lord's anger and punishment ensued: the nations left in Canaan at the time of Joshua's death remained, a thorn in the Israelites' side (cf. Jgs. 10:6–16).

Beginning with Solomon, the monarchy's primary sin, from the viewpoint of the Deuteronomistic historian, is idolatry. And we can trace its continuation in Abijam (1 Kgs. 15:3), Jehoram (2 Kgs. 9:27), Jotham (16:2–3), Manasseh (21:2) and others, as well as in the northern kings who follow in the way of Jeroboam's sin. Israel thus turned from the Lord to include and even prefer other gods.

For the Deuteronomistic historian Israel's sins—principally idolatry but also those against one another (e.g., Deut. 15:7–11; 24:10–13; 1 Kgs. 12:13–15) and even the stranger (Deut. 10:19)—eventually arouse the Lord's anger to the extent that punishment takes the form of exile (2 Kgs. 25:11). The fact, however, that this cycle of sin and pardon reappears in the postexilic writings (e.g., Ez. 9:6–15; Neh. 9:6–37) and finds itself readily on the lips of Job's so-called friends (e.g., Jb. 4:7–11; 8) testifies to Israel's belief that even the exile was not irrevocable punishment. On the contrary, exile is conducive to Israel's acknowledgment of sin and then to its repentance and deliverance. The exile, understood as the consequences of Israel's sin and the expression of her punishment, is precisely what gives birth to the hope which Isaiah expresses and ultimately to Israel's redemption (Is. 40–55).

The practice of idolatry, though it is vehemently and consistently condemned throughout the Deuteronomistic history (and, for that matter, throughout the entire Old Testament) is rampant in our own time. The only difference is how we name our gods. No longer are they Asherah and Baal, but rather, power, prestige, success, money. . . .[16]

D. The Prophetic Consciousness

The prophetic literature names sin in three major ways: idolatry, not trusting the Lord, and injustice to other people. Again one hears echoes of covenant violation. Each of the prophets speaking at a specific time, in a particular place, addressing precise historical situations, calls the Israelite community to fidelity to its chosen covenant partner and Lord. Exhortations take the form of pleas and threats. The particulars of Israel's sin vary from situation to situation and individual prophets emphasize different aspects of Israel's infidelity, but that these actions are expressions of attitudes of indifference or lack of confidence in Yahweh is quite clear.

Idolatry, as the Deuteronomistic editors also point out, is folly. It is folly not only because of its consequences, but it is an absurdity to worship the work of one's own hands:

> The carpenter . . . cuts down cedars;
> or he chooses a holm tree or an oak
> and lets it grow strong among the trees of the forest;
> he plants a cedar and the rain nourishes it.
> Then it becomes fuel for a man;
> he takes a part of it and warms himself,
> he kindles a fire and bakes bread;
>
> also he makes a god and worships it,
> he makes it a graven image and falls down before it.
> Half of it he burns in the fire;
> over the half he eats flesh,
> he roasts meat and is satisfied;
> also he warms himself and says,
> "Aha, I am warm, I have seen the fire!"
> And the rest of it he makes into a god, his idol;
> and falls down to it and worships it;
> he prays to it and says,
> "Deliver me, for thou art my god" (Isaiah 44:14–17).[17]

Rejecting the Lord and choosing other gods can only lead to Israel's demise, to the exile. It is their choice. Yahweh and other gods are mutually exclusive. He is a jealous God.

In the eighth century B.C. Northern Kingdom of Israel and the sixth century B.C. Southern Kingdom of Judah and consistently throughout Israel's history, idolatry functions as both symbol and reality. Idolatry in the twentieth century A.D. may not take the form of Baal worship or sacrifices to Molech, but the notion functions as symbol in a very real way. What we prize above all, what values determine our judgments and become the bases of our decision making—if these are not godly, they are idolatrous.[18]

The prophetic naming of sin finds expression also in Israel's choice of foreign alliances. These alliances occur, according to the prophets' understanding, because Israel does not believe firmly enough that their

Lord—although he had shown his power countless times in the past on their behalf—can and will protect them now. Not sufficiently trusting God, Israel seeks to bolster its political and military strength with foreign help—human power—even at the risk of consequent idolatry.

Isaiah warns Judah not to ally itself with Assyria as defense against Syrian and Israelite aggression, but rather, to trust in the Lord. The foreign powers it fears will themselves be brought to nothing (Is. 7:7–9; cf. 37:6). Both Isaiah (31:1–3) and Jeremiah (2:17–19, 36–37) warn also against trusting in Egypt:

> Have you not brought this upon yourself
> by forsaking the Lord your God,
> when he led you in the way?
> And now what do you gain by going to Egypt,
> to drink the waters of the Nile? (Jer. 2:17).

> You shall be put to shame in Egypt
> as you were put to shame by Assyria.
> From it too you shall come away
> with your hands upon your head,
> for the Lord has rejected those in whom you trust,
> and you will not prosper by them (Jer. 2:36–37).

Hosea longs for the day when Israel will say,

> "Assyria shall not save us,
> we will not ride upon horses;
> and we will say no more, 'Our God,'
> to the work of our hands" (Hos. 24:3).[19]

Israel's sin finds expression in alliances; the sin itself, however, is lack of trust.

For us to identify with Israel's experience, we must try to understand its political predicament. A small fragile people vulnerable to the constant power shifts of its neighbors, it was frequently endangered. At one point Judah feared that refusal to ally itself with Assyria would mean its defeat at the hands of Syria and the end of the Davidic kingdom. Later, Judah allied itself with Egypt. This it saw as the lesser of evils. The alternative it feared was destruction by Babylon. Though the historical particulars are peripheral to the purpose of this paper, the background is necessary if we are to appreciate the pain of Israel's plight, the intensity of its fear, the anguish preceding its choices. Yet the prophets portray trusting in the Lord not as virtue but as necessity. The covenant relationship demands total confidence in God. There is no room for the idolatry of national security.[20]

Finally, but hardly less important, are the countless instances where the prophets name social injustice as sin. Because of one's chosen relationship with the Lord, one has consequent responsibilities to other people. Failure to treat other Hebrews, and also the stranger, in a manner worthy of their human dignity—is consistently condemned. Though the expressions of this failure vary—shedding innocent blood, sexual abuse, bribery, theft, deceit, etc.—the basic attitude which the prophets condemn is one of indifference to others, treating them as a means to one's own ends, as things.

One need only cite a few examples, but the prophetic literature is replete with them:[21]

> Thus says the Lord:
> For three transgressions of Israel, and for four,
>   I will not revoke the punishment;
>   because they sell the righteous for silver,
>   and the needy for a pair of shoes—
> they that trample the head of the poor
>   into the dust of the earth,
>   and turn aside the way of the afflicted;
>   a man and his father go in to the same maiden,
>   so that my holy name is profaned;
> they lay themselves down beside every altar
>   upon garments taken in pledge;
>   and in the house of their God they drink
>   the wine of those who have been fined (Am. 2:6–8).

> Woe to those who decree iniquitous decrees,
>   and the writers who keep writing oppression,
> to turn aside the needy from justice
>   and to rob the poor of my people of their right,
>   that widows may be their spoil,
>   and that they may make the fatherless their prey (Is. 10:1–2).

> Woe to him who builds his house by unrighteousness,
>   and his upper rooms by injustice;
> who makes his neighbor serve him for nothing,
>   and does not give him his wage;
> who says, "I will build myself a great house
>   with spacious upper rooms,"

and cuts out windows for it,
    paneling it with cedar,
    and painting it with vermillion.
Do you think you are a king
    because you compete in cedar?
Did not your father eat and drink
    and do justice and righteousness?
    Then it was well with him.
He judged the cause of the poor and needy;
    then it was well.
Is not this to know me?
    says the Lord.
But you have eyes and heart
    only for your dishonest gain,
for shedding innocent blood,
    and for practicing oppression and violence (Jer. 22:13–17).

Because Israel understood its identity as communal, Israel's leadership bore great responsibility for not guiding the people in the Lord's way and for leading them astray. The kings,[22] the priests,[23] the prophets[24]—each find themselves the object of prophetic censure.

In addition to Israel's communal identity, at least one prophet, Ezekiel, emphasized individual responsibility; no one is punished for another's sins:

The word of the Lord came to me . . .
Behold, all persons are mine;
the father as well as the son is mine;
the person who sins shall die. . . .

The person who sins shall die.
The son shall not suffer for the iniquity of the father,
nor the father suffer for the iniquity of the son;
the righteousness of the righteous shall be upon himself,
and the wickedness of the wickedness shall be upon himself (Ez. 18:3, 20).

In stark contrast to the prophetic naming of sin, Micah succinctly describes faithful covenant behavior. What the Lord requires of his people is this:

To act justly,
to love tenderly, and
to walk humbly with God (Mi. 6:6–8).

III. The New Testament: Forgiveness of Sin

The New Testament takes its name from the New Covenant which, according to the text of Matthew, Jesus makes with humankind when he sheds his blood for the forgiveness of sins (Mt. 26:28). For Christians this relationship intensifies, extends, and completes the covenant bond God established with His people Israel.[25] The initiative taken, this time by Jesus, takes the form of incarnation and redemption.

The Holy Spirit declares to Joseph that Mary's son Jesus will save his people from their sins (Mt. 1:21). And John records the Baptizer's sentiment on seeing Jesus, "Behold the Lamb of God, who takes away the sins of the world" (Jn. 1:29). Each of the Synoptic writers presumes Jesus' authority to forgive sins (Mt. 9:6; Mk. 2:10; Lk. 5:24), a power understood to be God's alone (Mt. 2:7; Lk. 5:21; cf. Lk. 7:49). Luke's Gospel concludes with Jesus' exhortation to his followers to preach the forgiveness of sins in his name to all nations (24:47).

Yet Jesus' disciples are also to participate in the forgiveness of sins. Both Matthew and Luke express the early Christian community's conviction that forgiveness of one another is to know no limits: "not seven times, but seventy times seven times" (Mt. 18:22), "seven times a day, if need be" (Lk. 17:3–4). Jesus' disciples are to pray to his Father, "Forgive us our sins in proportion as we forgive those who sin against us" (Mt. 6:12; Lk. 11:4). And Stephen, in the record of Acts, prays that the Lord will forgive the sin of those who are stoning him (7:60).

At least two organizational principles will be applied to the New Testament literature in our efforts to arrive at a better comprehension of the nature of sin from a biblical perspective. The materials will be dealt with chronologically, from the oldest to the most recent writings, i.e., the Pauline letters, the Gospel accounts and Acts, and finally, the pastoral Epistles. The picture which this approach gives is helpful, because it enables us to become aware of consistency as well as theological development. Yet such an approach is inadequate unless it is augmented by a literary one. The literary suggestions made here entail an analysis of narrative structure, a delineation of narrator, of saying, and of story. The narrator may "objectively" set forth observations regarding sin and sinners while sayings about sin are found on the lips of key personages. Finally, the Gospel writers couch Jesus' teachings in story form, in parables. These literary techniques are also examined here in the hope that they, too, will increase our appreciation of New Testament insights regarding the reality of sin.

A. A Chronological Approach

1. The Pauline Letters

Paul declares that Christ died for our sins (1 Cor. 15:3; Rom. 5:8), that he "gave himself" for our sins (Gal. 1:4), and that it is in him that we have redemption, the forgiveness of our sins (Col. 1:14). Faith in Jesus is a logical consequence of these assertions.

Yet Paul was very much a Jew. As such, he struggled with the relationship between Torah and Jesus and later, between Jew and Gentile. How were Jews affected by Jesus' death and resurrection? How were Gentiles affected?

It is clear from his letters that Paul believed that everyone was guilty of sin (e.g., Gal. 3:27; Rom. 2:12; 3:9, 23; 5:12). He describes this debased state of humankind most emphatically in Romans 1:24–31 as including "wickedness and covetousness, malice, envy, murder, strife, deceit, malignity, gossip, slander, insolence, pride, disobedience, folly, heartlessness, ruthlessness, impurity, idolatry, immorality. . . ." Yet Paul is quick to warn that his hearers must not judge one another about these things, because the self-appointed judge is also guilty of doing the same things (Rom. 2:1)!

Paul's reflections lead him to conclude that the Gentiles could have perceived God and righteousness from their experience of creation, yet they had chosen "ungodliness and wickedness" (Rom. 2:18–20). The Jews had received God's further revelation in the Torah, yet the Law had not served to lead them in the ways of righteousness, but rather, had only named more explicitly the evils of which they were guilty (Rom. 7:7). For Paul, then, both Jew and Gentile had been given opportunities to affirm God, and both had failed. Though the Jew had been privileged to receive additional revelation in Torah, the Law had proved inadequate. Against the background of these poignant affirmations of humankind's sinfulness, Paul makes his assertions regarding Jesus. His preaching centers on faith in Jesus. It is through Jesus' obedience that many are made righteous (Rom. 5:19); the death Jesus died he died to sin, once for all (Rom. 6:10). It is the law of the "spirit of life in Christ Jesus" which has set Paul free from sin and death (Rom. 8:2).

What Paul has to say about sin is basically summarized above. Everybody sins and our only hope of deliverance from sin is faith in Jesus Christ; faith in him leads to obedience and righteous living.

Frequently enough, Paul speaks of particulars, various attitudes and actions which express one's faith in Jesus, or which indicate that one's faith is weak or lacking. Most of the content of Paul's letters takes the form of exhortation and encouragement: "This is how to live one's life in a manner pleasing to God." But occasionally also Paul names attitudes and actions which express idolatry—in his language, the desires of the flesh as opposed to the desires of the Spirit—and injustice to oneself and others: "fornication, impurity, licentiousness, idolatry, sorcery, enmity, strife, jealousy, anger, selfishness, dissension, party spirit, envy, drunkenness, carousing, and the like (Gal. 5:19–21).[26] These, of course, can lead to ruin. The idolatry we are familiar with from the Old Testament, as well as the acts against human dignity. Paul explains why these attitudes and actions are not acceptable: The fruits of the Spirit are love, joy, peace, patience, kindness, goodness, faithfulness, gentleness and self-control (vv. 22–23).

2. The Gospels and Acts

At least three themes emerge from the gospel teachings regarding sin:

a. Faith in Jesus is almost always associated with forgiveness of sin;
b. Jesus associated with sinner.
c. A potential for humility is also a potential for conversion.

a) Faith in Jesus

Jesus was moved by the faith of the paralytic whose friends lowered him from the roof into the crowd. Seeing their faith Jesus forgave the man's sins (Mt. 9:2 and par.). Luke names the sinner's "love" as the reason Jesus forgave the sins of the woman who washed his feet (Lk. 7:47–49), and the further comment, "But he who is forgiven little, loves little" seems to imply that one is forgiven in proportion to one's love. Jesus dismisses her with the words, "Your faith has saved you; go in peace" (v. 50). The blind man who "obeyed" Jesus' command to wash in the pool of Siloam received his sight (Jn. 9:7).

Jesus' formal teaching, according to John's Gospel, includes the statement: "I told you that you would die in your sins, for you will die in your sins unless you believe that I am he" (8:24). Because Jesus came and spoke to the world[27] and even did among them the works that no one else did, yet they would not believe, they have no excuse for their sin (Jn. 15:22, 24). When the Counselor comes to convict the world of sin it will be because they did not believe in Jesus (Jn. 16:9).

It is here that we must insert "the sin against the Holy Spirit" (Mt. 12:31). This dread evil is, for Matthew, rejection of Jesus. Since forgiveness comes through Jesus' death and resurrection and through our faith in him, one's refusal to believe amounts to a choice not to be forgiven.[28] What is here condemned as unforgiveable is refusal to believe, not ignorance.

Luke records a proclamation of Peter, after Jesus' resurrection, to the early Christian community:

> To him all the prophets bear witness that everyone who believes in him receives forgiveness of sins through his name (Acts 10:43).

And Paul is recorded as making a similar proclamation:

> Let it be known to you, brethren, that through this man forgiveness of sins is proclaimed to you, and by him everyone who believes is freed from everything from which you could not be freed by the law of Moses (Acts 13:38–39).[29]

b) Jesus Associates with Sinners

That Jesus associated with sinners is clear. A traditional interpretation of this idea cites those whom society named outcasts: Matthew, the tax collector who became one of the Twelve (Mt. 9:9); the woman who washed Jesus' feet (Lk. 7:37–50); Zaccheus, the chief tax collector (Lk. 19:1–18); the woman caught in adultery (Jn. 8:1–11). And it is true that Jesus affirmed these people.

The Gospel records also make a point to generalize: "Now the tax collectors and sinners were all drawing near to hear him" (Lk. 15:1; cf. Mt. 11:19; Mk. 2:15–17; Lk. 5:30–32; 7:34). In addition to these references regarding Jesus' association with sinners is the implied more general recognition of sin. Those who come to him for physical healing are often told that their sins are forgiven, that they are to go and sin no more (e.g., Mt. 9:5; par.; Jn. 5:14; 9:24). (Yet it is not the sin which has caused their physical ill, cf. Jn. 9:2–3.) And Peter, after the unexpected catch of fish, exclaims, "Depart from me for I am a sinful man, O Lord" (Lk. 5:8). One concludes from this that Jesus knows just how pervasive sin is.[30]

c) Humility and Conversion

Finally, it is those who recognize need and unworthiness, those who seek, who become candidates for conversion and forgiveness of sins.

This is best exemplified in the prayer of the tax collector: "God, be merciful to me, a sinner" (Lk. 18:3), and Jesus' comment that everyone who exalts himself will be humbled whereas he who humbles himself will be exalted (v. 14). This attitude is explicitly contrasted—whoever exalts himself will be humbled and whoever humbles himself will be exalted (Mt. 23:12)—with the hypocrisy of the Pharisees whose false sense of self-righteousness leads them to neglect the weightier matters of the law, justice, and mercy and faith (Mt. 23:1–36).

3. The Later Epistles

The first letter of John contains an affirmation similar to Paul's: We all have sinned (1:10). And the first letter to Timothy notes that Christ came into the world to save sinners (1:15). These statements are complemented by a passage from Ephesians: You he made alive when you were dead through trespasses and sins (2:1).

Since these later letters are of diverse authorship, addressing different communities and situations, each piece of literature deserves its own hearing. However, sin is not a major theme and is, in fact, mentioned only rarely in much of the later material. We will examine, therefore, only those two letters in which the theme of sin has a somewhat prominent position: the letter to the Hebrews and the first letter of John.

The letter to the Hebrews makes Jesus the High Priest who entered once for all into the Holy of Holies. He is both priest and spotless victim. As victim, he made purification for sins (1:3; 2:17). He did what bulls and goats could not do (10:4; 13:11). These sin offerings God takes no pleasure in (10:6); they can never take away sin (10:11). In contrast, Christ offered himself as victim, for all time a single sacrifice for sin (10:12); he effected forgiveness (v. 18).

As High Priest, Christ was to offer sacrifices for sin (5:1). Because he himself did not succumb to sin (4:15; 7:26), there was no need for him to offer sacrifice for his own sins, but rather, for the people's sins (5:3). As High Priest, he interceded for the people, asking God not to remember their sin (8:12). The sacrifice he offered he offered once for all (7:27; 9:26, 28). Whereas annual sacrifices are a reminder of sin (10:3) there is now no need for these since those whom the High Priest has cleansed no longer have any consciousness of sin (10:2).

The final chapters of this letter detail examples of Israel's leaders who proved themselves outstanding for their faith in God. The letter exhorts: Surrounded by these examples, lay aside sin (12:1); do not give up the struggle against it, even to the point of death (12:4). And finally, gain courage from the consideration of him who endured hostility against himself for sinners; do not grow weary or fainthearted (12:3).

This letter is important to our understanding of sin because it affirms both Jesus' once for all victory over sin and our continual struggle against sin. The letter's central thrust, however, is Jesus' victory, the power of his death to effect forgiveness of sins. From this victory flows the author's exhortation to his hearers: reject sin.

The first letter of John also polarizes faith in Christ and sin. Yes, we all have sinned (1:8), but if we "walk in the light," that is, if we believe, then the blood of Jesus cleanses us from all sin (v. 7); if we confess our sins, God will forgive our sins (v. 9).

Christ, in whom there was no sin (cf. Heb. 4:15), came to take away sins (3:5). John sharply contrasts sinning, which he identifies with the devil (3:8) and not sinning, which he identifies with God (3:6, 9; 5:18). He urges his hearers not to sin, but if they do, he assures them that they have an advocate with the Father, Jesus Christ (2:1), who is the expiation for both his hearers' sins and for the sins of the whole world (v. 2; cf. 4:10).[31] For God's sake, their sins are forgiven (2:12).

At the risk of great simplification, I am tempted to suggest, from this perusal of New Testament literature, that what had been Old Testament "idolatry" becomes New Testament "sin." Refusal to acknowledge only Yahweh becomes refusal to believe in Jesus. And the expressions of this idolatry or sin are, as Paul so clearly points out, violations of other people. Lack of confidence in Yahweh becomes lack of faith.

B. A Literary Approach

The writers of the New Testament express their perceptions of sin in three literary genre: comments of a narrator, statements on the lips of characters within the narratives, and parables. A brief look at each of these literary forms can further clarify biblical insights into the nature of sin.

1. The Narrator

Frequently in the letters, the author and the narrator are one. Such is the case with those who declare that Jesus came to forgive sins (e.g.,

1 Cor. 15:3; Rom. 5:8; Gal. 1:4; Col. 1:14); such also is the case with Paul's teaching on sin in his letter to the Romans. He adds a further insight in 1 Corinthians 8:12 when he equates sinning against one's brethren with sinning against Christ.

The narrator of the Gospel accounts, setting the scene for Jesus' appearance, describes the work of John. He preached a baptism of repentance for the forgiveness of sins (Mk. 1:4–5; Lk. 3:3). Many who came to him "were baptized in the Jordan confessing their sins" (Mt. 3:6). The only other narrative statement in the Gospels related to sin is the assertion—also in each of the Synoptics—that "many tax collectors and sinners came and sat down with Jesus and his disciples" (Mt. 9:10; Mk. 2:15; cf. Lk. 15:1).

2. The Sayings

Almost all of the statements on the lips of personages in the New Testament texts are found on the lips of Jesus.[32] He forgives sin and exhorts people to refrain from sinning;[33] he ridicules the Pharisees' condemnation of his attitude toward sinners;[34] he calls his disciples to forgive sin;[35] he associates sin with lack of faith in him.[36]

Since Jesus' sayings, especially those recorded in more than one tradition, are thought to be the oldest and most authentic Gospel passages, there can be no doubt since there is no inconsistency: Jesus recognized the reality of sin and perceived his mission as forgiveness.

The personages who, after Jesus, speak most frequently of sin are the Pharisees. In contrast to Jesus, they take it upon themselves to declare other sinners and to criticize those whom they consider unfit.

3. The Parables

Jesus frequently teaches in parables. Though these passages are also found on the lips of Jesus, their form is quite precise. Each is a simple story containing a moral. Among Jesus' parables regarding forgiveness of sin are those found in Matthew 18:12–14 (cf. Lk. 15:3–7) and Luke 15:8–10; 11–32, and 18:9–14.

After warning his listeners of how serious sin is—it is better to lose a foot or an eye than that either of these lead you into sin!—and how serious it is to influence another toward sin, Jesus tells the story of a man who has lost one of his hundred sheep. Leaving the ninety-nine, he goes out in search of the lost one and rejoices greatly when he finds it. *In the same way*, says Jesus, heaven will rejoice over one sinner who repents.

Then Jesus tells of a woman who lost one of her ten silver coins. She lights a lamp and sweeps and searches diligently, and she rejoices immensely when she finds it. *In the same way*, Jesus says, the angels of God are joyful when one sinner repents.

Jesus then goes on to tell another story, this time about a young man who deserts his father and wastes his share of the family fortune. When he recognizes his wrongdoing and returns, his father is filled with great joy and calls for an elaborate celebration. By this time the message is clear to his hearers so it need only be implied: There is rejoicing in heaven over one sinner who repents.

The final parable for our consideration is the one Jesus tells about those persons who trust in themselves, who think they are without sin and then despise others. It is the parable about the two men who go into the Temple to pray. The Pharisee thinks himself righteous and prays accordingly: God, I thank you that I am not like others, extortioners, unjust, adulterers, tax collectors. I fast, I give tithes. . . . In contrast, the tax collector acknowledges his unworthiness before God, and this posture resounds in his prayer: God, be merciful to me, a sinner. Jesus then concludes with the moral he intends: The tax collector, not the Pharisee, was justified; the one who exalts himself will be humbled, but the one who humbles himself will be exalted.

The morals of Jesus' stories are consistent. Jesus, who came to forgive sin, longs for the repentance of sinners. The one who audaciously feels no need of repentance is not the one whom the Lord will exalt.

IV. Conclusion

The biblical perspectives on sin which I have tried to present here do not give explicit answers to some of the most difficult ethical questions of our own time. There is no narrative about nuclear war, no saying regarding abortion, no parable dealing with the ordination of women. Yet there is given a clear and consistent framework out of which to make moral choices. Faith in God must hold priority; trust in God must be part of all responsible decision making. There can be no room for idolatrous values, no place for attitudes and actions which diminish human dignity. Then and now, all forms of idolatry and injustice are sin.

Notes

1. Eugene Maly has made such a contribution in his study, *Sin: Biblical Perspectives* (Dayton, Ohio, 1973), a book especially written for religious educators. Cf. the small book by Albert Gelin and Albert Descamps, *Sin in the Bible* (New York, 1965), and "Sin," in Paul Ricoeur, *The Symbolism of Evil* (Boston, 1967), pp. 50–98.
2. Karl Menninger, M.D., *Whatever Became of Sin?* (New York, 1973), p. 18, quotes a definition from Webster: "Sin is a transgression of the law of God; disobedience to the divine will; moral failure; failure to realize in conduct and character the moral ideal, at least as fully as possible under existing circumstances; failure to do as one ought toward one's fellow man."
3. One notes especially Brian McDermott's article, "From Symbol to Doctrine: Creation and Original Sin," *Chicago Studies* 19 (September, 1980), pp. 35–50, and Paul Ricoeur, "Sin."
4. My use of the term "classic" here is that used to describe classical literature in general, and derives from David Tracy's use of the term in *The Analogical Imagination* (New York, 1981), in particular.
5. For a comprehensive examination of this idea, see J. F. Kane, *God Who Gives: A Verbal Study of the Actions Attributed to God in the "Deuteronomic" School, with Speical Attention to God's Giving* (Pamplona, 1973).
6. Though not covenant partners with Yahweh, others who reject him, his power, his people, etc., may be guilty. For example, the peoples of Tyre, Edom, Ammon, and Moab in Amos 1–2; the pagans in Romans 1:18–23.
7. The closer the bond, the graver the offense. E.g., Judah more than Israel in Ez. 16:51; the Pharisees and Jerusalem in Mt. 23:29–39.
8. Never resolved, some believe we are almost totally conditioned and unfree (e.g., B. F. Skinner in *About Behaviorism* (New York, 1976); and *Beyond Freedom and Dignity* (New York, 1972), while others (e.g., Karl Menninger, *What Became of Sin?* claim *a certain degree* of personal responsibility in all human acts, good and bad.
9. Contemporary theologians continue to debate the issue. For example, Jacques Pohier, in his article, "What Purpose Does Sin Serve?" *Theology Digest* 26 (September, 1978), pp. 24–28, declares: "The reason why man is a sinner is not sin but the fact that man is man" (p. 27), while John H. Wright, "Problem of Evil, Mystery of Sin and Suffering," *Communio* 6 (Summer, 1979), pp. 140–156, presumes human freedom.
10. Exodus 7:3; 9:12, seem problematic: the Lord hardens Pharaoh's heart. The object of these statements, however, is not to deny free will, but to assert God's power and his willingness to control history on Israel's behalf.

11. In fact, an adequate study of the semantic field which includes "sin" requires also an examination of the term's linguistic polarities.

12. Passages such as Genesis 31:34–35 indicate that the people who became Israel at first tolerated other gods.

13. Literature on David abounds. See especially Walter Vogels, "David's Greatness in His Sin and Repentance," *The Way* 15 (October, 1975), pp. 343–354; D. M. Gunn, *The Story of King David*, JSOT Supp. Ser. 6, (Sheffield, 1978); Keith W. Whitelam, *The Just King*, JSOT Supp. Ser. 12, (Sheffield, 1979).

14. Martin Noth, *The Deuteronomistic History*, JSOT Supp. Ser. 15, (Sheffield, 1981).

15. Moshe Weinfeld, *Deuteronomy and the Deuteronomic School*, (Oxford, 1972).

16. Matthew's Gospel declares this explicitly: "No one can serve two masters; for either he will hate the one and love the other, or he will be devoted to the one and despise the other. You cannot serve God and money" (6:24). Cf. Rom. 6:16–18.

17. See also Am. 2:4; 5:4–6, 26; Hos. 3:1; 4:12–13, 17–18; Is. 2:8, 18; 10:11; 31:6–9, 42:7; Mic. 1:7; 5:12–14; Hab. 2:18–20; Zep. 1:4–6; Zech. 13:2; Jer. 2:10–13; Ez. 22:3; 23:30, 49.

18. The prophets often equate idolatry with adultery; Israel's true spouse, Yahweh, is rejected for false lovers, e.g., Hos. 1–3; Ez. 16; 22.

19. Cf. Is. 37:6; 39:1–8.

20. Complementing Israel's lack of trust in God is her pride and arrogance. Isaiah repeatedly condemns these attitudes, e.g., Is. 2:12; 13:11; 28:1.

21. Cf. Am. 5:7–12; 6:12; Hos. 5:11; 6:7–9; Is. 1:15b–17; 3:12, 15; 5:22–23; 26:10; 32:6–7; Jer. 7:5–6; Ez. 9:9; 12:19.

22. E.g., Jer. 23:1–5; Ez. 34:1–6.

23. E.g., Hos. 5:1.

24. E.g., Jer. 23:15–24.

25. Cf. Acts 2:38; 5:31.

26. Cf. 1 Cor. 5:1–2a; 6:17–18; 10:6, 14.

27. John's Gospel frequently uses the term "the world" to designate those who reject Jesus.

28. Cf. Heb. 10:26–27; 1 Jn. 5:16.

29. Cf. Acts 22:16; 26:18.

30. John will later write that the one who says that he or she is without sin is not telling the truth (1 Jn. 1:8).

31. Both the author of the letter to the Hebrews and John realized that, despite expectations, the Parousia had not yet arrived. They must therefore incorporate into early Christian teaching the reality of sin both after the resurrection and after the individual's conversion.

32. In all four Gospels and Acts, the speakers are overwhelmingly Jesus and the Pharisees when the topic is sin. John the Baptist, Judas, and Paul each speak only once. John declares, "Behold the Lamb of God, who takes away the sin of the world"; Judas acknowledges that he has sinned in betraying

innocent blood; Paul, when defending himself to Festus, affirms that he has sinned neither against the law nor against Caesar. Peter speaks twice of sin, when he declares himself a sinner and when he asks Jesus what the limits of forgiveness are.

33. E.g., Mt. 9:2, 6 and par.; Mt. 9:13 and par.; Mt. 12:31; 26:28; Lk. 7:47–48; 24:47; Jn. 8:11; cf. Jn. 5:14.

34. Mt. 11:19; Lk. 7:34; cf. Jn. 19:11.

35. Mt. 18:15, 22; Lk. 17:3–4; Jn. 20:23.

36. Jn. 8:21, 24; 15:22, 24; 16:8–9.

CHAPTER 9

Reconciliation

Robert Barone

It would certainly not be overstating the case to say that the central theme of the entire Bible is reconciliation. A loving and faithful God pursues a resistant people and an alienated world to snatch them from the course of disaster on which they are plunging headlong. The Scriptures witness to the passionate pursuit by which the Mysterious Creator and Redeemer seeks to bring home a recalcitrant child who never understands the destruction towards which he is heading.

Salvation History

Themes of covenants made and broken with prophetic voices promising hope to repentant sinners who return to covenant commitments characterize the traditions shaped and transmitted down through the ages of salvation history. The Bible is replete with a history of a people who have been experiencing the unmerited and gracious presence of a God who desires communion more than his fickle worshipers. He miraculously creates his people Israel in the liberating event of their Exodus from Egyptian bondage and sustains them down through centuries by visionary spokesmen who taught them to hope for salvation. These prophetic figures perceive the Almighty's saving hand in the course of Israel's history and reinterpret the events of their experience to testify to his continuing concern for their welfare and his own loyalty to his covenant promises. He is faithful and, despite the apparent catastrophes of their lives, he has not abandoned his beloved but rather graciously provided beyond their wildest dreams.

The literature of promise (the Old Testament) transmits the hope of Israel in the books of the Law, the prophets and the Writings. These sacred Scriptures all in some way relate to the Exodus that Israel saw as its creation experience. (Israel is first mentioned in the inscription of

the Stele of Merneptah about 1220 B.C.) The scrolls of Judaism contained the constitution (the Law), the insightful interpretation (the
prophets) and the practical wisdom (the Writings) of the assembly of
God's holy people. The promise of God's love and providential care
was enshrined in the books of the Old Testament. The people had
experienced his powerful hand in their history and the prophets had
bequeathed to their contemporaries and future generations their own
illumined vision of his saving purposes.

In continuity with the more than one thousand years of history
reflected through the Old Testament literature, the writers of the primitive Christian communities gave witness to the person and events they
understood to fulfill the hope of the prophets. Their apostolic letters
(the Epistles), their proclamation portraits (the Gospels) and their theological histories (the Acts of Apostles and the Book of Revelation)
focused in upon the Palestinian peasant from Nazareth. They saw him
as the centerpiece of human history and his life, death, and resurrection as the apex of God's saving activity. Their writings spanned only
the decades of the first century of our era, but their testimony re-
sounded down through the centuries as the basis for all church life and
doctrine. Their eye-witnesses (the Apostles) of the Risen One were the
prophets of the new covenant and the books of their New Testament
proclaimed the final age had been definitively inaugurated.

The Eye-Witness

Our vision of the theme of reconciliation in the New Testament
must be guided by the writings of the only man who has both contributed directly to the New Testament and witnessed the Risen Lord
Jesus: Paul of Tarsus. Only this writer was himself an Apostle! If any
man can be said to have understood the mind of the Master from
Nazareth, it was the rabbi from Tarsus. Paul looms like a giant in the
pages of the New Testament. Every reader and student of the New
Testament knows that the mystical genius who encountered the Risen
Lord on the road to Damascus became his most visible and vocal
disciple.

From a human point of view the two men had very little in common. Jesus was about fifteen years Paul's senior but Jesus was a Palestinian Jew from the rural, northern region of Galilee. Paul was a product of diaspora Judaism and had resided in the city of Tarsus in Asia

Minor (modern Turkey). We have no sources from which to conclude that Jesus had any formal education, but he probably spoke Aramaic as did his Palestinian contemporaries. Paul was clearly an educated individual who studied in Jerusalem under the famous rabbi Gamaliel and moved easily among both Jewish and Gentile people.

Jesus taught in the simple language of parable to rural people who worked as fishermen and farmers. Paul taught in synagogues and public halls to freemen and slaves. The former addressed himself to "the lost sheep of the House of Israel" while the latter addressed himself to people of every nation. Jesus was characterized by his regional, Galilean dialect. Paul was a bilingual citizen of Rome itself.

We have no reason to conclude that the two men ever met. It is not impossible that one of the annual Jewish pilgrimage feasts brought them both to Jerusalem at the same time, but our sources recount no such meeting. But it would be difficult to overestimate the impact that Jesus of Nazareth had upon Paul of Tarsus. In his letter to the churches of Galatia Paul refers to a "revelation" experience that he had on the road to the city of Damascus in Syria. He does not normally make this experience part of the content of his "gospel." In fact we must really scan his Epistles quite closely to find explicit references to what has been called 'the conversion of Paul.' The impact it had upon the man is everywhere present in his preaching and catechesis, but he is so focused in on the death and resurrection of the Master that his own "turning point" has faded into the background. He recounts (Gal. 1:15–16) what can only be called the "effects" that the encounter had upon him. It made clear to him that he had not earned the revelation; that it set him apart from others; that it was a calling and it was for him to preach among the Gentiles. In 1 Corinthians 15:8 he refers to it as an "abortion." We cannot be sure what he is intending to say, but perhaps he is referring to the sudden and violent character of the religious experience.

The Apostle's journeys and Epistles all grew out of this mysterious encounter with the Risen Lord, and he was deeply convinced that through the death and resurrection of the Lord a great reconciliation had taken place. In various places we read his eloquent testimony:

> For if, when we were God's enemies, we were reconciled to him by the death of his Son, it is all the more certain that we who have been reconciled will be saved by his life (Rom. 5:10).

Not only that; we go so far as to make God our boast through our Lord Jesus Christ, through whom we have now received reconciliation (Rom. 5:11).

He died for all so that those who live might live no longer for themselves, but for him who for their sakes died and was raised up.

Because of this we no longer look on anyone in terms of mere human judgment. If at one time we so regarded Christ, we no longer know him by this standard. This means that if anyone is in Christ, he is a new creation. The old order has passed away; now all is new! All this has been done by God, who has reconciled us to himself through Christ and has given us the ministry of reconciliation. I mean that God, in Christ, was reconciling the world to himself, not counting men's transgressions against them, and that he has entrusted the message of reconciliation to us. This makes us ambassadors for Christ, God as it were appealing through us. We implore you, in Christ's name: be reconciled to God! For our sakes God made him who did not know sin to be sin, so that in him we might become the very holiness of God (2 Cor. 5:15–21).

In 2 Corinthians St. Paul says that he is an ambassador for Christ. He has a message for the people, and this message is the good news that in Christ the old order has been overcome and a new creation brought into existence. He speaks of our being reconciled to God in Christ. He understands the world as previously alienated from God and filled with people who live for themselves.

To really appreciate the Apostle's words (2 Cor. 5:15–21) we must understand his deep convictions about "the old order." By the old order Paul means the world as it existed before Christ. This old order is the deadly state of a world at enmity with its God. We need only recall that an "alien" is a foreigner and an alienated world is a foreign world. He envisions that being at peace with God is a matter of being "at home" while being filled with transgressions is a matter of "being away." We then would be "away."

The apostolic teaching of St. Paul actually reflects Jesus' parable of the Prodigal Son. Paul himself gives no indication that he knows this parable, but its message is quite synonymous with his "message of reconciliation." The loving father of the parable is so anxious to have the erring son return to him. He can think of nothing but preparations for that son "when as yet he was a long way off." The graciousness of the father is also reflected in his attempt to get the older son to overcome his envy and enter into the joy of the return. The parable does say that the erring son "came to himself" and realized that things would be better in the father's house, but the attractive figure is really the father himself. He loves the son and wants him to "come home." The teaching of the ambassador is rooted in the preaching of the Master. But this message of reconciliation is not only the content of the Master's thoughts, it is actually an interpretation of the significance of the Master's life and death. Paul says: "We were reconciled to him (God) by the death of his Son" (Rom. 5:10). Paul understands Jesus' death not to have been in vain, but rather to have been effective to bring the world home to God! He goes on: "We go so far as to make God our boast through our Lord Jesus Christ, through whom we have now received reconciliation" (Rom. 5:11).

So the Christian believer is to understand the "newness" of his existence and see himself and the world as having passed out of an "old order" and in Christ become a new reality.

This obviously points the Christian in the direction of a whole self-understanding. It does not merely indicate that Christ has achieved a great liberation over death for himself but that he has constituted an entirely new order of grace into which we have all been invited. We can never understand ourselves in quite the same way as non-Christians understand themselves. He died and rose so that our life might be for him rather than ourselves. He has become the centerpiece of our consciousness and the foundation of our daily existence. Under the "old order" self-service was the norm and sinfulness was the pattern of behavior. In this "new order" service of God and neighbor is the norm and peaceful self possession is the pattern of behavior.

"We implore you, in Christ's name: be reconciled to God!" (2 Cor. 5:20). With these words Paul exhorts the people of Corinth to cooperate with the work accomplished by the Lord's death and resurrection. He does not think that the work of Christ can substitute for the faith of the people. He knows that only if they understand what has happened in Christ and choose to enter into this mystery will they be saved. Paul writes: "For our sakes God made him who did not know sin to be sin, so that in him we might become the very holiness of God" (2 Cor. 5:21). He says, "We might become the very holiness of God" because he knows that this was the intention of Christ but it still will require the response of the believer's life.

But the heart of Pauline theology on reconciliation lies in the effect of "freedom" that has been produced for those who now live "in Christ." The great witness to the Apostle's thought on this matter is the vitrolic letter he wrote to his converts in the area of Galatia. He had founded Christian communities in the northern region of central Turkey (around modern Ankara). After Paul had moved on in his missionary travels, a message reached him that clearly infuriated the Apostle. He heard that individuals had followed up upon his apostolic work and instructed his converts that it would be necessary for them to adopt Jewish ways in addition to their faith in Jesus as Lord and Christ. He set out to correct this matter in a fury that makes the Epistle to the Galatians the most passionate book in the New Testament. He literally screams at them, telling them that they are fools! He says: "You foolish Galatians! Who has cast a spell over you? . . . How could you be so stupid?" (Gal. 3:1, 3). He says that they have put him back in labor and that they have him at a complete loss. He is absolutely amazed at how soon they have deserted Christ who called them to faith. He tells them that they were progressing so well and asks who has diverted them! We cannot imagine a bishop or pastor being more irate than Paul is in this Epistle. He knows full well that they are novice Christians (the Epistle is usually dated about 54 A.D. and the founding visit about 50 A.D.) but that they got off the track so soon shocks him all the more.

He has preached Christ crucified to them and they have received the gift of the Spirit. Under the influence of troublemakers they have hankered after the security of the Jewish Torah (Law) with its prescriptions of circumcision and kosher life. They have abandoned faith in Christ alone, and like little children they want a "monitor" to hold them by the hand! They have fled the responsibility of mature faith and preferred the slavery imposed by a Law that commanded righteousness but did not empower them to attain it.

Having been reconciled to God by the work of Christ, the Galatians have been set free. No "Judaizers" are now to take away the freedom that comes with reconciliation. He sees the return to the Law as a pollution of the mind and a return to the flesh. Christ's reconciling death and resurrection has liberated people from all bondage (sin, death, law). Christ has made it possible for people to receive their inheritance as true sons of Abraham according to the freeborn woman. Slavery to sin has been left behind, and slavery to a Law that could not grant salvation is left behind as well.

He confronts the Galatian churches when he says: "Have I become your enemy just because I tell you the truth?" (Gal. 4:16). He found it necessary to remind his converts of their former devotion to him. He felt that once they had possessed an openhearted spirit, but now they are a disappointment to him. He anticipates the pain and difficulty with which this corrective will fall upon their ears. He knows that they might possibly turn against him for the truth he speaks. Nothing stings so much as the truth! Nevertheless, he has the courage to confront them on their quest for "another gospel." He has to administer the harsh words: "I fear for you; all my efforts with you may have been wasted" (Gal. 4:11). This must have been a frightening sound as it came to them from the one who had traveled so far and worked so hard that Christ might be born in their midst. Abuse from an outsider is one thing but stern correction from a loving father is another!

The fury of the Saint seems to have come from a man who felt that the danger to their faith was so great that there was really nothing to lose. If this stern admonition and instruction did not sway them from their present course, he must have envisioned nothing less than the demise of Christian faith in Galatia. They were on a path that would mean that for them "Christ died to no purpose" (Gal. 2:21). They were treating God's gracious gift as pointless, and he had to put a stop to it. He tells them that "it was for liberty that Christ freed us" (Gal. 5:1). They must recognize the gracious gift of the One who has given them the power of the Spirit and enabled them to call upon God as "Abba." Their intimate relationships with God in Christ has removed the yoke of sin; the yoke of death; the yoke of law. They are no longer slaves but sons of the freeborn woman. They are heirs of freedom. The lesson so powerfully defended by the Apostle is that you can be free and not know it. You can have within the expansive power of the Risen One and still cling to those realities that provide security. We have been gifted with freedom, but we may not know it. We are liberated, but we need to hear it and be exhorted to risk our lives in faith in Christ.

In the incident at Antioch the Apostle found it necessary to point out Kephas' inconsistency. He must not seek to be accepted by those who do not grasp the total sufficiency of Christ. Those from James are evidently Christian believers from the Judeo-Christian community at Jerusalem. Their presence in Antioch could cause trouble for Kephas if he behaves in a way they do not approve. If he eats with Gentiles, he is not observing Jewish kosher laws. They feel these laws are still binding on believers. Peter knows better but understanding is one thing, while being a witness to the truth of the Gospel is quite another. If you witness to the truth of the Gospel, those who do not grasp that truth will not treat you well. They will cause trouble for you. They will not see you are living in the freedom of the sons of God but simply feel you are not clinging to those precepts in which they have found so much security. To the group of visitors from Jerusalem, Kephas may well have looked like a "libertine." But if the Gospel's truth is that Christ is sufficient and he is free from kosher prescriptions, then his association with Gentiles would be a witness against their grasp of the essentials of Christian faith. He would be throwing off the security blanket of the Jewish Law. He would be venturing into human experience without the "monitor." His behavior would be a direct challenge to their piety. He would have been completely counting on Christ for justification and to "those from James" this was a bit too risky.

The faith they had received in Christ had not only set them free but literally "condemned them to freedom." This freedom could be scary business and living it out in service could be far more challenging than the "security" of the justification based on legal observance.

The testimony of the Apostle is that responsible freedom is precisely the outgrowth of the dynamic power that dwells within the heart of the believer. That Spirit within will transform until the believer can say with the Apostle "I have been crucified with Christ and the life I live now is not my own: Christ is living in me" (Gal. 2:19–20).

Christological Diversity

The authentic Epistles of the Pauline corpus have provided us with direct apostolic testimony on the theme of reconciliation and its consequent effect of freedom "in Christ." This witness was born and recorded before the great Gospel portraits of Jesus were produced. Contemporary exegetes are in agreement that the rest of the New Testament is the product of postapostolic Christianity. The Gospel accounts according to Mark, Luke, Matthew, and John were written in the last third of the first century A.D. and strongly reflect the situations of the churches of that era. In other words, the Gospel portraits are like verbal mosaics put together after the death of the Apostles but out of preexisting units that were transmitted through the churches. These traditional materials bore the stamp of the Apostles' point of view that Jesus was indeed the Lord and Christ and in him the hope of the prophets had come to pass. The accounts were therefore clearly not biographical in perspective but proclamatory. They sought through each story to portray him in the light of their faith contentions about him and bring others to salvation by their preaching. The oral proclamation of the apostolic authorities colored the way in which the churches envisioned Jesus and the Gospel accounts they produced reflected this "post-resurrectional insight."

For this reason we can begin to speak of the phenomenon of "Christological diversity" as we investigate the Gospels for the theme of reconciliation. We are simply recognizing the fact that each church had its own particular perspective on how Jesus was the Christ and what this would mean for discipleship. The Gospels of the New Testament are artistic creations. They are sacred literature which the church holds to be inspired by the Holy Spirit and normative (canonical) for faith. But because the Spirit inspired human agents we can fruitfully examine the Gospels as literature. We can see them as great artistic compositions of Christian faith.

The four Gospel accounts reflect a compositional technique that we can refer to as a "time-collapse." When they present the figure of Jesus from the beginning of the first century, they blend together his historical ministry with concerns from the churches of their own times. Artists frequently employ this technique and Renaissance fresco painters combined biblical subjects with persons and scenes from sixteenth-century Italy. Raphael did exactly this when he was painting the walls of chambers in the Vatican palaces. He was painting the "School of Athens" on the wall while his rival, Michelangelo, was putting the great fresco of the creation on the ceiling of the Sistine Chapel. In spite of the rivalry between the two painters, Raphael so respected Michelangelo's genius that he represented him right in the midst of the ancient Greek philosophers and intellectual giants. All the figures in Raphael's painting are from the ancient world, but still Michelangelo, his own contemporary, is placed in the "School of Athens." More than eighteen centuries have collapsed in the painting so that the viewer can see Michelangelo from Raphael's point of view.

Sometimes artists intermingle details from one event with details from another and by this mixture bring together separate historical events. Cosimo Rosselli painted a scene on the side wall of the Sistine Chapel. It is part of a sequence on the prophet Moses. It was done in the late fifteenth century. An army is depicted drowning in a body of water. The water is red and the soldiers wear fifteenth-century Italian uniforms. Is this Pharaoh's army being drowned in the Red Sea at the exodus from Egypt? Is this in any way related to the recent papal victory at Campomorto (1482)? The answer to both questions is "yes." It is the 1482 papal victory and it is the drowning of Pharaoh's army in the Red Sea. Over twenty-six centuries have collapsed in the painting so that the viewer can see the association that Rosselli wants to make. He has not distorted the truth but rather artistically represented his point of view.

Any theme being pursued in Gospel study must take seriously the nature of the composition process by which the documents were formed. To ask the Gospel writers about the theme of reconciliation demands that we respect the nature of the writings that we are investigating. The Gospel accounts of Mark, Luke, Matthew, and John manifest this same technique of time-collapse that the painters utilized. The authors are Christian believers of the postapostolic era. When they record incidents from the life of their Lord, they do it with the conviction that the mystery of salvation is relevant to their own times and people. They express his word and deeds but always in a way that shows that he is as significant in the late first century as he was in his own time.

The Lion

When we now turn to the earliest of the Gospel accounts, the Gospel according to Mark, we encounter a literary work quite interested in the Christ as a liberator from demonic powers and a Suffering Servant who must be followed by those who would be his disciples. We see the Markan Jesus whose ministry of proclaiming and establishing God's reign was threatened and opposed by Satan and demonic powers at every turn. To Mark Jesus was the great exorcist and his work was to roll back the Satanic forces that held all as their prey. The alienation of the would-be-disciple is caused by evil beyond his power to control. The great liberator Son of God is able to effect communion between God and men through faith in Jesus the Christ. Without the requisite faith, even the Christ can do no great work. He could not heal at Nazareth without faith, and he cannot heal Mark's Christians without their faith. But this healing of those sorely afflicted is the form the theme of reconciliation takes in Mark's Gospel. To be healed by Christ is to be reconciled to God.

The role suffering plays in the Markan Christology also is quite significant for reconciliation. The Christ is a humble servant who numbers himself among sinners at his baptism, throughout his ministry, and at the scene of his death. He three times prophesies his passion; he rebukes Simon for not judging by God's standards and he teaches his disciples that they must take up their own crosses. To accept the Christ is not to look for God to manifest himself through miraculous liberations from suffering but rather to follow the path of suffering. Mark's Christians are suffering, and the power to endure this human rejection is available through faith. Suffering is the road to reconciliation. It is the path of discipleship in the Markan church and those who would follow Jesus are being instructed that all alienation will be overcome.

The Ox

The Gentile Gospel of Saint Luke is accompanied by a companion volume presenting a theological history of the early church: the Acts of the Apostles. The two works come from the same pen and are suffused with themes of the universal character of salvation and the providential growth of the faith in the Gentile world. The first volume (the Gospel) recounts all that Jesus said and did prior to his ascension, while the second volume (the Acts) recounts all that Jesus said and did through the Spirit after his ascension.

Most scholars place Luke-Acts in the 80s of the first century and consequently locate it in the second generation of Christianity when the apostolic generation has died out. The obvious preoccupation of the work is its desire to be loyal to the original witness of the Apostles and recount how the Spirit of the Risen and Ascended Jesus was directing the growth of the church. The Christ is presented as the savior of the world and his linage was to be traced back to Adam as the father of all men. Luke is greatly interested in a history of salvation which he sees to have had three distinctive phases. The first phase was the period of the Old Covenant, while the second was the period of the life of Jesus. The period of the church encompassed the third phase. The Old Testament Scriptures bore witness to the hope of the first period and Luke's Gospel and his Acts of Apostles were the narratives treating the second and third phases respectively.

The theme of reconciliation is treated in Luke as a salvation that God has extended to all people. The Gospel of the churches is not merely good news for the people Israel but rather good news for all people. It is the good news for the nations.

But apart from the vertical dimension of reconciliation (between God and all humankind) Luke is interested in a horizontal dimension. He is interested in a reconciliation between Jewish Christians and Gentile Christians. His Acts of the Apostles present preaching to both Jews and Gentiles and indicates that some converts were made from both groups. His idyllic picture of the early church (Acts 2:42) is so harmonious that we can hardly imagine he is talking about the same people as the Pauline Epistles. Galatians indicates that there were very deep feelings of hostility (Gal. 5:12) between Christians over the importance of observing the Jewish Law after baptism. This problem does not appear so severe in Luke's Acts. It is entirely possible that the problem was more acute in one area of the early church and less in another; still, a very different picture emerges. Luke is either saying that the Spirit of the Risen Christ has already reconciled Jew to Gentile or that the Spirit can reconcile Jew to Gentile within the church if both will just open their hearts!

But perhaps the most vivid picture of reconciliation that appears in the New Testament is Luke's parable of the Prodigal Son. No other evangelist records this magnificent piece of pedagogy. Jesus' association with prostitutes and sinners is the context for this extraordinary story. He is either among the sinners because he is one of them or he is among them because in his ministry the rift between sinful humankind and God is being dissolved right before their eyes.

The well-known parable depicts a loving father, a loyal son, and a prodigal son. This latter son takes his share of the father's goods, leaves home and wastes everything until he repents of his behavior and returns to the father. The loyal son stays behind and works for the father but feels jealousy when the loving father eagerly accepts the erring son home with open arms. The parable is clearly dealing with unmerited gracious treatment. The prodigal son had the right disposition to avail himself of his father's loving kindness, but no one would say he earned the kindness. It was certainly grace.

Many exegetes feel the association of Jesus with an "unclean" element was the reason he defended himself by means of the parable. God was extending through Jesus an unmerited acceptance. The only requirement was repentance. The prodigal son "came to himself" says the parabler. This is all that is required for reconciliation. The mercy of the father had made the alienation of sin a negligible factor. Reconciliation is possible if only humankind will repent. If the Jewish community can be seen in the figure of the older son, then the message is that reconciliation is a gift and even centuries of observance of the Jewish Law do not merit salvation. To be reconciled is a gratuitous matter.

The Angel

Dating from 80–90 A.D. comes the Gospel according to Matthew. This proclamation of the good news of salvation presents Jesus as a second Moses who definitively reinterprets the Law of Judaism. Christ is the great teacher and speaks in Matthew through five discourses that may be meant to resemble the five books of the Law of Moses. Matthew is very interested in the church and its accountability to Christ as the judge who will evaluate its loyalty at the end of time. His Jesus sets forth a revelation in many words. The Lord talks far more in this account than in the Markan account which Matthew utilized as a literary source. The great popularity of this orderly Gospel may well be accounted for precisely because the Rabbi of the New Covenant can be heard so vividly.

The Gospel was written after the fall of Jerusalem in 70 A.D. and the relocated rabbinic school of the Pharisees at Jamnia may be the rival center of religious authority to Matthew. The Jamnia rabbis had neither Holy City nor cult, and so their authoritative interpretations of the Law were to become the foundations of all subsequent Judaism. Matthew's church feels a great tension with these teachers, and the loyalty he upholds is to the apostolic interpreters. His easy reference to Jewish things has led many scholars to contend that Matthew's church was at least in part a Jewish-Christian community. Their interests would be in demonstrating the continuity between prophetic hopes and church proclamations about Jesus. The portrait of the Master is very Jewish and the conflict with the Pharisees is very pronounced (Mt. 23).

If Moses stood on the mount of Sinai receiving the stipulations of the Old Covenant, then Jesus sits for his great sermon on a mount and gives the stipulations of the New Covenant. This compendium of Jesus' teachings has been organized by Matthew to instruct the church that it is the New Israel and its New Moses charts the course for the disciples who would live by that covenant. The covenant background and imagery is the linguistic of reconciliation in Matthew's Gospel. The covenant was an accord for harmony between Israel and God and the church as the New Israel is being summoned to live that harmonious (reconciled) life.

Matthew's church seems to have its own admixture of Jewish and Gentile elements and his reworked parable of the Great Feast (Mt. 22) indicates that "appropriate" wedding garments (faith) will be required of all. The Lord before whom the church will one day stand to be judged demands that no one rest simply upon his election. Jews were rejected after the sendings of the prophets, but now Gentiles must not imagine nothing will be required of them. Faith will be required of all who stand before the Son of Man.

The Eagle

The latest of the four canonical Gospels is that attributed to Saint John. Many contemporary exegetes now speak of a Johannine school stemming from the apostolic work of the Apostle. His tradition would have been preserved in a Johannine church and placed in final form by some disciple late in the first century. It has been called a "spiritual" Gospel because of its lofty conception of the Christ as God's Word made flesh. Its author was clearly a reinterpreter of Christian tradition. Scholars debate whether the Gospel's author had access to the accounts according to Matthew, Mark, and Luke. The Risen Lord speaks throughout this Gospel and he becomes the protagonist of the Johannine church's views about him.

Scholarship (J. L. Martyn, R. E. Brown, C. K. Barrett) has been engaged in the fascinating process of trying to discern the prehistory of the Johannine church in the pages of the Gospel. The exegetes have been quite attentive to the interests of the sacred author in his contemporary church problems and how these concerns shine through the text. They have spoken of a bilevel reading of John. On one level the author is talking about Jesus' ministry but on another he is talking about the struggles of his own church in the late first century.

What emerges from their scholarship is a picture of a church that thought of itself as a community of disciples. Their church offices and structures would not have been as important to these Johannine Christians as their common goal of discipleship. A certain "Beloved Disciple" figure mysteriously appears in this Gospel and is clearly the model of a "Spirit-directed" Christian life. He is their superior disciple.

These Christians held that Jesus was the preexistent Word of God and was, in fact, God himself! They often present the Lord as using the divine "I am" language familiar to the Bible reader from the Sinai theophany recorded in Exodus. Reconciliation between God and the world had been effected, according to this Johannine church, by the Word becoming flesh. They are hereby referring to the whole immersion of the Word in human history. It was not just his conception or birth or death that redeemed the world, but the whole process. He was "enfleshing" himself in the world, and when finally he was lifted up upon the cross he could draw all to himself because the hour had come and the process was completed. Now he could pour out the gift of the Spirit (from the cross) on Good Friday because the sacrificial lamb had been slain and the world's Passover was at hand. The resurrection does not have the role in the Johannine Gospel that it has in the other accounts. Not that they denied that he had risen, but rather that they focused in upon the cross. Believers were to look upon him and be saved.

The Johannine church struggled to maintain that Jesus had indeed come down from heaven, but he was truly human flesh. From within their ranks came some who denied that he was actually fully human but the Epistles of this church sought to correct any false impression on the matter.

This Gospel believes that "God so loved the world that he gave his only begotten Son." This Son was the bearer of the gift of eternal life. They proclaimed their faith in him and were prepared to oppose all who opposed them. They did encounter opposition on all sides, not the least of which came from the late first century synagogue. They had many Jewish converts in the Johannine church and found themselves being ejected from orthodox Jewish belief for their contentions about the Christ. This caused a great deal of bitterness toward the synagogue in the Johannine church and the Gospel account reflects the anti-Jewish sentiment.

The Johannine Christians felt that a true disciple had to be ready to publicly profess his faith in Jesus and also pay the cost of discipleship. No reconciliation would be possible between these Christians and those citizens of the world or synagogue who expected compromise. They were unbending in their loyalty to the insight of their tradition.

They are prepared for another kind of reconciliation in that they pray to be one with some "other sheep" of the divine shepherd. These are probably the Christian churches founded by Paul and the other Apostles. We cannot be sure, but it seems they are praying for an eventual communion of fellowship with churches that they respect and love.

The survey of the preceding pages has contended that the witness of the Apostle Paul and the four Evangelists on reconciliation is woven into the fabric of the individual author's theological thought. One must have some feel for the dominant themes of a given literary work in order to see how the sacred writer expresses himself on reconciliation. The more precisely one understands the individuality of the sacred author, the more one is able to recognize what he is saying and what he is not saying. Nothing can substitute for detailed study of the sacred passages.

The Teacher-Communicator

Teaching is an art and communication is a skill. We can be trained and coached by others, but in the final analysis the dynamic of any teaching situation is heavily dependent upon the gifts, efforts, preparations, and enthusiasm of the teacher. The teacher can greatly facilitate that emergence process by which the student is led into the questions involved and taught by some kind of mysterious sympathetic vibration to become interested in the subject. This is as true in religious education as it is in any other area of education. The student must be "led out" of his simplistic conceptions, and even with a necessary amount of confusion be brought to realize that there is a great deal more to it all than he previously suspected. He is, in a certain way, brought gently and carefully to realize his own ignorance and the possibilities for growth that lie before him. He has not been "snowed," but he must be challenged and intrigued. Because I firmly believe that this is how learning happens, I really cannot delineate some specific methodology by which the biblical theme of reconciliation can be extricated from the Sacred Scriptures and inculcated into the prospective student. Each teacher will have to develop his or her own peculiar style (and the best teachers are frequently the "peculiar" ones!) and utilize the reading, background, and experience at his or her disposal.

But all teachers owe preparation to their students. Remote preparations are necessary and proximate preparations are essential. The student must sense order and progression or the cause is hopeless. The teacher must know clearly what he is trying to say and how he is trying to say it. I offer here only my suggestions on what I would stress if teaching on the biblical theme of reconciliation. I draw my thoughts from the witness of the Apostle Paul and the Evangelists Mark, Luke, Matthew, and John.

Thesis I: Reconciliation must be understood in terms of overcoming the experience of alienation.

Thesis II: The primary effect of being reconciled to God is the experience of freedom.

Thesis III: Suffering must be so interpreted that its role in reconciliation emerges.

Thesis IV: Reconciliation through faith in Christ overcomes transcendent evil.

Thesis V: Reconciliation with the God of all humankind opens the Christian's life perspective to include all.

Thesis VI: Reconciliation is available to those who will accept the challenge of the Gospel and recognize their accountability before God in Christ.

Thesis VII: Reconciliation with God comes about through a costly discipleship that can withstand human rejection.

Thesis VIII: Ecumenical efforts must be based upon truth.

In the above theses I recognize issues and values to which many today can easily relate. They are intelligible to both believers and nonbelievers. I will now try to offer some reflections on the theses.

People today are quite interested in the issues of: alienation, freedom, suffering, transcendent evil, open mindedness, challenges, accountability, withstanding rejection, and truth. They are discussing these problems and issues in many areas of education. The values are human values, and if Christ's relevance is to be perceived it will have to somehow be perceived in these terms. We must never forget that salvation is being saved, and how we conceive it will depend upon how we conceptualize our problem. To a thirsty man salvation is a cup of cold water while to a desert shepherd it is surely green pastures! When people are feeling alienated from themselves, their families, and their society, they will have great difficulty seeing the relevance of a Christ who offers them a cup of cold water! We must have the radar to pick up the signal being sent by our contemporaries and then determine the significance reconciliation will have for them.

Often it has happened that key words are being used by religious educators in a quite different sense than they are being understood by those being educated. The word freedom is one such word. Freedom represents openness, receptivity, growth possibilities, and dynamism to contemporary young people. They think of freedom as a good thing. The word has just as frequently been understood as "libertine," "doing one's own thing," and selfishness to many churchpeople. They have preached and taught that we are "bound to Christ" and thereby sancti-fied. This is absolutely true, but a reconciliation that limits is not seen by our contemporaries as attractive but rather something to be escaped. Ironically, Christ the liberator seems to many to be Christ the incarcerator!

Human suffering is a universal human experience, but many of those being educated in the faith (the young) have not yet really suf-fered that much. They cannot personally identify with a great deal of pain and limit situations. Their youth invigorates them, and the need for a healer, especially for the personal wounds inflicted by life's hurts, is not apparent. The religious educator must probe his students for those areas where suffering and anguish have surfaced. Christ the healer can only be appreciated by those who suffer.

Reconciliation must be presented as the work of Christ that allows the believer to be a citizen of the world community and the human family. If he senses that faith in the work of Christ has made his view of human values myopic and limited, he cannot relate to it. The world has become so much smaller by means of the media and modern transportation. If the believer does not perceive he participates more fully in this world through faith, then he concludes faith is for those who cannot face the bigger world.

The reconciliation of Christ must be seen as having created a tre-mendously challenging situation in human history. The religious edu-cator must resist the temptation to accomodate the Gospel to his hear-ers. He must bring out the confronting aspect of Christ's work. Because a great reconciliation has been effected between our world and God, the believer must acknowledge this new state of affairs and measure up to God's standards rather than the world's standards. This will demand that the religious educator clearly points out that personal decision is involved in salvation and discipleship to Christ is not a cheap commodity. We cannot fit him into our lives but must build our lives around him! When we do this we must be prepared to be ostracized from the company of those who no longer walk with him.

Finally, I stress that reconciliation demands that as persons from one Christian denomination encounter persons from another denomination, that each takes the other's religious faith seriously. We can only work toward Christian unity, and we must not imagine that we can quickly overcome in a short period those obstacles that have developed over a long period. We must proceed carefully, always respecting the truth that we have been taught but allowing for others to have seen something that we have missed. Our ecumenical efforts must not compromise truth for a false sense of fellowship. Communion and fellowship not founded upon the bedrock will be like a house built upon sand. The storms will come and the house will fall and those who sought to dwell in that house will be more discouraged than ever.

Reconciliation between God and people and among people is the work of Christ's Spirit, but the religious educator must conceptualize and verbalize this in ways intelligible to those with whom he seeks to communicate.

Bibliography

Achtemeier, Paul J. *Invitation to Mark*. Image Books, 1978.

Karris, Robert J. *Invitation to Luke*. Image Books, 1978.

Karris, Robert J. *Invitation to Acts*. Image Books, 1978.

LaVerdiere, Eugene A. *Invitation to the New Testament Epistles II*. Image Books, 1980.

McRae, George. *Invitation to John*. Image Books, 1978.

Senior, Donald. *Invitation to Matthew*. Image Books, 1978.

Harrington, Wilfred J. *Mark (New Testament Message 4)*. Michael Glazier, Inc., 1979.

Meier, John P. *Matthew (New Testament Message 3)*. Michael Glazier, Inc., 1980.

Dupont, Jacques. *The Salvation of the Gentiles*. Paulist Press, 1979.

Brown, Raymond E. *The Community of the Beloved Disciple*. Paulist Press, 1979.

Montague, George T. *Mark, Good News for Hard Times*. Servant Books, 1981.

Reicke, Bo. *The Gospel of Luke.* John Knox Press, 1964.
Bruce, F. F. *Paul, Apostle of the Heart Set Free.* Eerdmans, 1977.
Martyn, J. Louis. *History & Theology in the Fourth Gospel.* Abingdon, 1979.
Barrett, C. K. *The Gospel of John and Judaism.* Fortress Press, 1975.

Profiles of Contributors

in the order of their contribution

JAMES MICHAEL LEE teaches at the University of Alabama in Birmingham. His doctorate is in the field of educational studies. Professor Lee's research specializations center around religious instruction theory and the teaching process in religious instruction. He has written and edited many books in the field including *The Shape of Religious Instruction*, *The Flow of Religious Instruction*, *The Content of Religious Instruction*, *Seminary Education in a Time of Change*, and *The Religious Education We Need*. He has written over fifty articles for professional magazines including *Religious Education*, *Living Light*, *Catholic Educational Review*, *Today's Catholic Teacher*, and *Modern Ministries*.

JOSEPH S. MARINO currently works in full-time ministry at the Cathedral of St. Paul in Birmingham, Alabama. The holder of a licentiate in Sacred Scripture, Father Marino's teaching and research speciality is the Old Testament.

DERMOT COX teaches in the Gregorian University. He holds the doctorate in Sacred Scripture. Professor Cox's research speciality centers around Old Testament exegesis with particular attention to Wisdom Literature. His books include *Triumph of Impotence: Job and the Tradition of the Absurd*, and *Proverbs*. Articles by Dr. Cox have appeared in many scholarly journals including *Liber Annuus*, *Studia Hierosolomytana*, *Antonianum*, *Studia Missionalia*, and *Proceedings of the Biblical Association*.

DAVID WHITTEN SMITH teaches at the College of Saint Thomas. He holds the licentiate in Sacred Scripture and the doctorate in theology. Dr. Smith's research specializations include New Testament Christology and miracle stories as related to charismatic healing. He has contributed two chapters to *Guidebook for Bible Study*.

UGO VANNI teaches in the Biblical Institute of the Gregorian University. He holds the doctorate in Sacred Scripture. Professor Vanni's research specialization centers around the New Testament with special attention to Paul, John, and the Book of Revelation. His books include *La struttura Letteraria dell'Apocalisse*, *L'Apocalisse*, and *Lettere ai Galati e ai Romani*. The many journals in which his scholarly articles appear include *Biblica*, *Revista Biblica*, *Gregorianum*, *Marianum*, and *Studia Missionalia*.

CARROLL STUHLMUELLER currently teaches in the Catholic Theological Union. He holds the doctorate in Sacred Scripture. Professor Stuhlmueller's research specialization centers around the Old Testament, with particular interest in Psalms, Prophets, and Mission. The many important books which he has authored include *Psalms* (2 volumes), *Biblical Mediatations for the Christian Year* (3 volumes), *Biblical Foundations for Mission*, *Thirsting for the Lord*, and *Creative Redemption in Deutero-Isaiah*. His articles have appeared in many journals including *Biblical Research*, *Catholic Biblical Quarterly*, *Chicago Studies*, *East Asian Pastoral Review*, and *The Bible Today*.

HORACIO SIMIAN-YOFRE teaches in the Biblical Institute of the Gregorian University. He holds the doctorate in theology. Professor Simian-Jofre's research specialization centers around the constellation of Prophecy, Isaiah, and Ezekiel. He has published the book *Die theologische Nachgeschichte der Prophetie Ezechiels*. Scholarly articles which he has written have appeared in *Biblica*, *Stromata*, *Mensaje*, and *Stimmen der Zeit*.

ALICE LAFFEY teaches at the College of the Holy Cross. She holds the doctorate in Sacred Scripture. Her research specialization lies in the field of Deuteronomic history. Articles in which Dr. Laffey's articles have appeared include *Bible Translator Technical Papers*, *Discover the Word*, and *Hospital Progress*.

ROBERT J. BARONE teaches at the University of Scranton. His doctorate is in theology. Dr. Barone's research specializations center around the II Temple Period Jerusalem and around the Pauline Heritage. His articles have appeared in *Theological Studies* and in *Catholic Light*.

Index of Names

Index of Subjects

OTHER IMPORTANT BOOKS FROM
RELIGIOUS EDUCATION PRESS

BIBLICAL INTERPRETATION IN RELIGIOUS EDUCATION
by *Mary C. Boys*
An illuminating examination of the way in which the bible and biblical interpretation have affected twentieth century religious education. The first part of this volume is a fine examination and critique of biblical revelation offered by twentieth century biblical scholars. The second part deals with how religious educators brought the bible into the field as salvation history. ISBN 0-89135-022-5

RELIGIOUS EDUCATION AND THEOLOGY
edited by *Norma H. Thompson*
This important book presents a wide variety of diverse and robust points of view on the dynamic relationship between religious education and theology. Original and seminal essays by the most important contemporary religious education scholars. A benchmark book in the sense that it provides the standard against which any future discussion of the relationship of religious education and theology will have to be measured. ISBN 0-89135-029-2

CHRIST THE PLACENTA
by *David A. Bickimer*
The major theme of this scintillating book is that religious education at every level and in every settirg must be education for transcendence. Written as a series of letters, this volume is dazzling in the way it integrates religion, poetry, art, modern physics, social science, contemporary theology, and everyday human experience into a spectacular vision of the means and ends of religious education. ISBN 0-89135-034-9

RELIGIOUS CONVERSION AND PERSONAL IDENTITY
by *V. Bailey Gillespie*
A sensitive treatment of religious conversion as a basic way of achieving personal identity and self-transcendence. This stimulating book integrates psychological findings with both the biblical perspective and theological insights. ISBN 0-89135-018-7

ABOVE OR WITHIN?: THE SUPERNATURAL IN RELIGIOUS EDUCATION
by Ian P. Knox
An illuminating survey of the basic theological issue permeating all religious education activity, namely: "How can the religious educator help learners of all ages meet God in their own lives?" A book centering on God's revelation in religious education. ISBN 0-89135-006-3

MODERN MASTERS OF RELIGIOUS EDUCATION
edited by Marlene Mayr
A seminal book providing a rare inside personal view of the major theories and forces which have shaped religious education in the second half of the twentieth century. The volume is a collection of revealing autobiographies of twelve persons who have decisively influenced the shape and direction of contemporary religious education. This remarkable book is especially helpful to those who wish to deeply understand the foundation of current religious education. ISBN 0-89135-033-0

THE SHAPE OF RELIGIOUS EDUCATION
by James Michael Lee
No one can discuss contemporary religious education meaningfully unless he or she has read this book. Widely acclaimed as a classic in the field. ISBN 0-89135-000-4

THE FLOW OF RELIGIOUS EDUCATION
by James Michael Lee
A serious in-depth look at the nature and structure of the religion teaching process. This volume provides that kind of solid and systematic framework so necessary for the effective *teaching* of religion. A major work. ISBN 0-89135-001-2

THE RELIGIOUS EDUCATION WE NEED
edited by James Michael Lee
A prophetic volume presenting Catholic and Protestant proposals on a viable future for religious education. Exciting chapters by Alfred McBride, Randolph Crump Miller, Carl F. H. Henry, John Westerhoff III, Gloria Durka, and James Michael Lee. This book has as its axis the renewal of Christian education. ISBN 0-89135-005-5

AN INVITATION TO RELIGIOUS EDUCATION
by *Harold William Burgess*
A careful examination of the most influential Protestant and Catholic theories of religious education proposed in our time. An essential book for understanding the foundational issues in religious education.
ISBN 0-89135-019-5

TRADITION AND TRANSFORMATION IN RELIGIOUS EDUCATION
edited by *Padraic O'Hare*
Four important religious education scholars reflect on the urgent but complex issue of how religious education can transform the world while at the same time faithfully hand on the Christian message.
ISBN 0-89135-016-0

CAN CHRISTIANS BE EDUCATED?
by *Morton Kelsey*
An examination from the standpoint of depth psychology some of the most critical concerns in contemporary religious education, including education for love, education for spiritual wholeness, and education for positive emotional values. This volume integrates religious education with growth in the religion teacher's own personal spirituality.
ISBN 0-89135-008-X

REGARDING RELIGIOUS EDUCATION
by *Mary K. Cove and Mary Louise Mueller*
A helpful volume for parish religious education directors striving to develop an effective program and to enhance the effectiveness of their teaching personnel. Topics include targeting instruction to here-and-now religious living, introducing accountability into all phases of the program, assessment of the learner's religious needs, and coordination of the religious education efforts of various parish and congregation groups.
ISBN 0-89135-011-X

PROCESS AND RELATIONSHIP
edited by *Iris V. Cully and Kendig Brubaker Cully*
A penetrating examination of how the interactive realities of process and relationship profoundly affect the structure of religious education, theology, and philosophy. Original essays by fourteen of North America's leading Protestant and Catholic thinkers. ISBN 0-89135-012-8

CLARITY IN RELIGIOUS EDUCATION
by *Robert Yorke O'Brien*
Clear and practical treatment of some of the most vexing areas in religious education today, such as teaching holiness, teaching biblical miracles, teaching the sacraments, and teaching the church.
ISBN 0-89135-013-6

WHO ARE WE?: THE QUEST FOR A RELIGIOUS EDUCATION
edited by *John H. Westerhoff III*
An exploration into the identity and special calling of the religious educator as seen by many of the most important religious education leaders of the twentieth century. Many of the most important issues facing religious education are treated in this book. ISBN 0-89135-014-4

IMPROVING CHURCH EDUCATION
by *H. W. Byrne*
A bible-centered approach to effective Christian education ministry. Written from an evangelical Protestant perspective, this comprehensive book explains practical and workable models for successful total church education, including models for grouping people for effective teaching and learning, models for improved instructional space, models for enriched teaching, and models for improved staffing. ISBN 0-89135-017-9

RESURGENCE OF RELIGIOUS INSTRUCTION
by *Didier-Jacques Piveteau and J. T. Dillon*
A well-developed theoretical foundation for the community and family model of religious education, together with concrete examples of ways in which family and community religious education programs have worked.
ISBN 0-89135-007-1

THE RELIGIOUS EDUCATION OF ADULTS
by *Leon McKenzie*
This superb and comprehensive book has taken its place as the standard treatment of adult religious education. Malcolm Knowles calls it "clearly the most important work to date on adult religious education and one of the most important books on adult education in general."
ISBN 0-89135-031-4

RELIGIOUS EDUCATION MINISTRY WITH YOUTH
edited by *D. Campbell Wyckoff and Don Richter*
An insightful in-depth exploration of present concerns and future directions of youth ministry. Informative chapters dealing with the available

research of youth ministry, the basic questions the Church needs to answer about youth ministry, the personal and social problems of youth, the ways in which youth can be bonded into a true community which is religious, and other chapters designed to help the religious educator empower youth for religious living and ecclesial service.
ISBN 0-89135-030-6

CELEBRATING THE SECOND YEAR OF LIFE: A PARENT'S GUIDE FOR A HAPPY CHILD
by Lucie W. Barber

A practical guide for religious parenting and educating. This book is organized around psychologically-proven ways in which parents and members of the helping professions can successfully develop five basic capacities in the child *and* in themselves: trust and faith; a positive self-image; self-confidence and independence; a joy for learning; the ability to associate with others happily. ISBN 0-89135-015-2

MORAL DEVELOPMENT, MORAL EDUCATION, AND KOHLBERG
edited by Brenda Munsey

A seminal volume on the interrelated topics of moral development, moral education, and religious education. An interdisciplinary treatment from the perspectives of religious education, philosophy, psychology, and general education. These original essays bring together some of the most important scholars in North America, Europe, and Israel.
ISBN 0-89135-020-9

THE BIG LITTLE SCHOOL, second edition revised and enlarged
by Robert W. Lynn and Elliott Wright

This classic history of the American Sunday School in a revised and updated form. A superb and delightful analysis of how the American Protestant Church perceived its educational mission throughout the years, and how it actually went about bringing religion to the hearts and minds of the taught as well as the teachers. ISBN 0-89135-021-7

DEVELOPMENTAL DISCIPLINE
by Kevin Walsh and Milly Cowles

This volume is the only current major book on discipline which views the discipline process primarily as a task of moral education. The axis of this fine book is that discipline is education in moral and religious discipleship. This volume provides the theoretical background and practical tools necessary for educational ministers to help children and youth to acquire positive discipline. ISBN 0-89135-32-2